STATE AND PEASANT SOCIETY
IN MEDIEVAL NORTH INDIA

State and Peasant Society in Medieval North India

*Essays on Changing Contours of Mewat,
Thirteenth to Eighteenth Century*

SURAJ BHAN BHARDWAJ

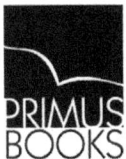

PRIMUS
BOOKS

PRIMUS BOOKS

An imprint of Ratna Sagar P. Ltd.
Virat Bhavan
Mukherjee Nagar Commercial Complex
Delhi 110 009

Offices at

CHENNAI LUCKNOW
AGRA AHMEDABAD BANGALORE COIMBATORE
DEHRADUN GUWAHATI HYDERABAD JAIPUR JALANDHAR
KANPUR KOCHI KOLKATA MADURAI MUMBAI
PATNA RANCHI VARANASI

First published 2019

ISBN: 978-93-86552-23-5 (hardback)
ISBN: 978-93-5290-886-8 (POD)

Published by Primus Books

Laser typeset in Adobe Garamond Pro
by Guru Typograph Technology
Crossings Republic, Ghaziabad 201 009

Contents

Acknowledgements

THIS BOOK HAS BEEN a product of my intellectual labour of several years during which several people have directly and indirectly helped in shaping and refining my ideas and arguments, as also their articulation. While they are too numerous to mention here, I would like to acknowledge, in particular, the debt I owe to a few who have been by my side through the years spent in the academia. I am ever grateful to Professors Dilbagh Singh and Harbans Mukhia, my teachers and mentors at the Centre for Historical Studies, Jawaharlal Nehru University, for offering their invaluable comments and suggestions on the drafts of the essays written over a long period of time. Professor R.P. Bahuguna of Jamia Millia Islamia has been a friend, advisor and teacher to me throughout the course of my academic career.

I am also grateful to the staff of Rajasthan State Archives, Bikaner, for unfailingly extending their help and hospitality to me in the course of my visits there for over two decades. Professor G.S.L. Devra of Vardhman Mahaveer Open University, Kota, has always taken interest in my research and shared his thoughts and insights. I thank the staff of Nehru Memorial Museum & Library, Jawaharlal Nehru University Library and Central Secretariat Library for helping me locate the much-needed references. I am indebted to Mayank Kumar, Iliyas Husain and Dipankar Das without whose help at different stages of the work it would not have been possible to put this book together. I acknowledge the strong emotional support I have always received from my family: my wife Sushila and my sons, Rahul and Madhulak. They have witnessed the long and arduous journey that I have made to prepare this book.

Motilal Nehru College
University of Delhi

SURAJ BHAN BHARDWAJ

Introduction

THE PROCESS OF state formation, the nature of state and the relationship between the state and the peasant society in precolonial India have attracted a good deal of scholarly attention. Ever since state came into being as a geographically delimited segment of society united by a common obedience to a sovereign political authority, attempts were made to understand and define the position and role of the political elite that embodied the state vis-à-vis its subjects. These attempts are arguably the most prominent in the discourse on the idea of kingship. Intellectual engagement with this idea can be found in texts of various genres and registers since ancient times, indicating how it has remained one of the major preoccupations of social and political thought through history.

Representative of this exercise of conceptualizing kingship are Brahmanical normative texts of early India, viz., *Dharmashastras* that contain precepts on social conduct from the Brahmanical perspective. These texts uphold the institution of monarchy as the unexceptionable political ideal and the king as its linchpin. They elaborate the components or elements of a monarchical system, the position and duties of a king and the constraints or checks on royal power. Recognizing treasury (*kosha*) as the base of a kingdom, they validate the extraction from subjects—peasants, artisans and traders—of a fixed share of their produce and/or labour as tax that is to be eventually deposited in the treasury. At the same time, they generally do not approve of arbitrariness in the imposition and collection of levies, i.e. they discountenance the extraction of taxes that are non-customary, barring exceptional circumstances. In doing so they place a moral limit on the ruler's right to the produce or labour of his subjects, and at the same time a moral obligation on the subjects to part with a stipulated share of their produce or labour for the king. They further enjoin the ruler to protect and take care of his subjects as his children and abide by the principle of justice and norms of customary conduct. Such prescriptions constitute the Brahmanical concept of *rajadharma* or the duty of a king (*raja*). The idea of *rajadharma* is further valorized in the epico-Puranic literature that contain stories praising mythical or semi-mythical kings who scrupulously discharged their *dharma*, upheld the ideal of justice and caused no pain or distress to their subjects. On the other hand, deviation from or violation of *rajadharma* is denounced, and accounts of murder or overthrow of oppressive, unjust, tyrannical rulers by their subjects are used to justify punishment for such deviations/violations. In the Brahmanical political thought, both ideal and counter-ideal of kingship rested on the concept of *rajadharma*, the adherence or non-adherence to it. Accounts of 'just' and 'unjust' rulers in the Sanskrit epico-Puranic literature underwent much mutation in bardic oral narratives in regional/local languages and dialects, and thereby became popular over a wide geographical area and among different rural communities.

With the establishment of Turkish rule and foundation of Delhi Sultanate in north India in the twelfth century, a fundamental change came about in the notion of kingship in the upper echelons of the ruling elite comprising royalty and nobility of non-Indian origin. The rulership in this new political formation derived its legitimacy, at least theoretically, from Islam, the religion of the new ruling elite. The formulators and advocates of a new Indo-Islamic idea of rulership—and the constituent norms of ruler's conduct and ruler's political morality—were the *ulema* or Islamic theologians patronized by the ruling elite, not the Brahmans. This new notion of political sovereignty was, therefore, based not on the shastric precepts but on interpretations of Islamic doctrines and laws. While at one level, there are parallels between Brahmanical and Islamic conceptions of rulership—for instance, in the idea of divine association of kingship or that of reciprocity between the ruler and the subjects—the Indo-Islamic idea marked, at another level, a departure from the past conceptions of ideal rulers popular among the people, especially in the rural society. The idea of kingship—particularly the constituent element of reciprocity—elaborated in the elite Brahmanical textual tradition and reinforced by epico-Puranic stories of 'good' and 'evil' kings had managed to percolate down to the masses by way of reiterative construction and narration of 'expropriated and modified' oral versions of such stories. In other words, this idea of 'Hindu' kingship had long been internalized by the medieval rural societies in ways that the Indo-Islamic construct of rulership could not be. The latter, unlike the former, lacked avenues or modes of building its popular appeal.

Like their ancient counterparts, the medieval states, whether ruled by Delhi Sultans or Mughal Emperors, aimed at appropriating a large share of the agricultural produce as land revenue for running the administrative machinery. While the sharing of produce between the state and the peasant was a perennial potential source of conflict, the possibilities of conflict were, to some extent, diffused by the peasant's belief in a reciprocal relation between the ruler and the subjects—a relation wherein the ruler and the subjects were morally bound by customary obligations, i.e. the duty of a ruler (*rajadharma*) to administer justice, afford protection and levy and collect customary taxes at customary rates; and the duty of a subject (*prajadharma*) to offer obedience and pay such taxes to the ruler. This ideal of reciprocity that was central to bardic tales of rulers may not always have been a historical reality for peasants, as such rulers or their stories would have been mythical or semi-mythical. Nevertheless, these stories and the perception of kingship therein played an important role in shaping the moral economy and worldview of the peasant communities. In doing so, these stories provided them the moral energy to challenge and resist the excesses of state or ruler particularly in the area of revenue administration. If the state exacted non-customary taxes, it—or rather its personification—the ruler, was seen as violating his *rajadharma* towards his *praja*, and protest and rebellion against the state was seen as a just remedy to the problem. The theoretical foundations of the medieval states ruled by a largely Muslim political elite lay in a notion of sovereignty wherein the royal power was not as much tempered by reciprocity, customary or moral constraints or obligations, as it was in the shastric, epico-Puranic and rural folk traditions. Nor was the ruler even notionally threatened by the possibility of rebellions, regicide or deposition in this theory of kingship, as he was in the earlier traditions and in the peasant's perception. Hence, in the medieval peasant's moral universe, there was a perceived imbalance between the ruler's duties towards his subjects and the peasant's expectations of justice and benevolence from him in situations where the ruler sought to appropriate more than his 'fair' share of the produce through non-customary levies and violated the customary norms of conduct. With the decline in the political authority and grievance-redressal mechanism of the Mughals and the rise of multiple claimants to land revenue through the practice of revenue-farming (ijara) in the late seventeenth and early eighteenth centuries, the ruthless exploitation of peasantry reached a crescendo and struck a fatal blow to its perception of ideal rulership. It was then that the relation between the state and peasant society underwent a major shift, and the chasm between the peasant's sociopolitical utopia and harsh reality widened. The stories of 'just' and 'evil' rulers that had been part of the longstanding oral tradition in the rural society gained a greater currency especially as a means of invigorating peasant protests against oppression and 'illegal' exactions. In this fraught relationship between the state and peasant society, the religion of the ruler was not as relevant as was the question whether or not he respected the customary norms of land revenue administration. It is these issues in the changing dynamics of relationship between the state and the peasant society that this book engages with.

The book charts the changing relationship between the state and the peasant society in Mewat from thirteenth to early eighteenth centuries. Denting the conventional image of peasant communities in medieval India as self-sufficient, changeless and autonomous entities, it takes up the case of Meo community of Mewat to argue that communities have regularly undergone profound socio-economic and cultural changes through a variety of engagements with the state, and such transformations have been an integral part of their histories. It begins with a discussion of the early political history of the region: the formation of Khanzada chiefdom, its failure to transform into a full-fledged state, and the establishment of Mughal imperial rule from the sixteenth century. Then it lays bare the process of community-formation among the Meos in the wake of their peasantization and Islamization. It also focuses on the emergence of a new class of zamindars, viz., the Rajputs and the Jats, at the cost of old zamindars, viz., the Khanzadas and the Meos—a phenomenon that generated agrarian turmoil in the rural society at large in the late seventeenth and early eighteenth centuries. It also addresses how such changes affected two crucial aspects of the peasant worldview: their self-consciousness as a class with distinctive economic interests and their conception of the state and their relation with it. The book, thus, offers a historically nuanced perspective of the evolution and changes in the identity of the Meo community of the region, as well as changes in its relation with the state.

The present study is largely based on Indo-Persian chronicles; various village- and pargana-level revenue records and reports preserved and catalogued in the Historical Section of Jaipur Records at the Rajasthan State Archives, Bikaner; and other works of local (Mewati) origin. All these sources provide rich information about the political, social and economic conditions prevailing during the late seventeenth and early eighteenth centuries in the Mewat region.

Given the dearth of information on the history of Mewat during the period of Delhi Sultans and early Mughal rulers, the Indo-Persian chronicles are helpful in understanding the nature of state formation under the Sultans and Mughals and the relationship of the Khanzada chiefs of Mewat with the Delhi Sultanate, the Mughal state and other regional potentiates. These chronicles, however, only record the political events involving the chiefs of Mewat in the form of narratives. Nevertheless, they foreground the strategic importance of Mewat for Delhi Sultanate, the Mughal state and other regional potentates.

As most of the parganas of Mewat were held by the rulers of Amber as jagir in their capacity as imperial mansabdars or ijaradars at various points of time during the period under study, various categories of surviving records illumine the revenue administration and agrarian conditions at the pargana and village levels, but they have not been extensively utilized so far. The information contained therein sheds light not only on the revenue administration and the mechanism of surplus extraction, but also on various aspects of the rural society and economy, such as the patterns of production and distribution of agricultural produce among the peasants and the various constituents of the ruling class; the relationship between production, prices and land revenue; and the nature of administrative control. Linkages between the nature of agrarian economy and the social relations and the impact thereof on the agrarian administration can also be discerned from these records.

These records, available from the second half of the seventeenth century, are *arsattas*, *arzdashts*, *chithis*, reports of the Amber *vakil*, *dastur-al-amals*, *yaddashtis*, Amber records, *dehai-ferhashtis*, *jamabandis*, *khatoot ahalkarans* and *dastur komwars*. As most of these records pertain to those parganas that were held by the Amber rulers as jagirs and on ijara, they do not provide any information about the parganas assigned as jagirs to other imperial mansabdars. Unfortunately, records pertaining to the latter have not survived. Nonetheless, the records left by the Amber rulers give us valuable insights into the conditions obtaining in the areas in the immediate vicinity of their own *tankhwah jagirs*.

The *arsattas* constitute the chief category of revenue records. They furnish a good deal of information on various aspects of the economy of Mewat, such as the total number of villages in each pargana; the number of villages assigned to the troopers and those held by the Amber Raja; the estimated income, arrears and revenue realized as well as the expenditure under various heads in each pargana; and the area under the cultivation of *zabti* and *batai-jinsi* crops for each pargana and also separately for each village within a pargana. By and large, it is the record of the amount of *mal* (tax on crop) and various other cesses contained in the *arsattas* that provides useful information on cropping patterns and revenue receipts of a pargana and thus has been extensively used in this study. Besides, information about expenditure in the parganas is useful for the purpose of analysing the claims of the holders of superior rights to income from land in the rural society.

Though the information provided by the *arsattas* is extremely valuable, this category of records has its own limitations. The *arsattas* do not cover the whole region and the period under study. For instance, one does not find *arsattas* for more than five years for parganas other than Khohri, Pahari, Gajika Thana, Jalalpur, Mojpur, Wazirpur, Atela Bhabra, Piragpur, Pindayan and Harsana. Further, the *arsattas* pertaining to a pargana are not available for successive years, there being long time gaps between two nearest dated *arsattas*.

Another category of records is the *arzdashts* written by the *amils*, *faujdars* and other officials of Amber, posted in various parganas. These *arzdashts* are addressed to the Amber Raja and each contains details of political, social and economic conditions prevailing in a particular pargana. Hence, they are of great importance in reconstructing the political, social and economic conditions of Mewat. They also contain the Amber Raja's directives to his officials, reflecting the attitudes of the jagirdars/ijaradars with regard to their territorial jurisdictions. As they are available for the entire period of the study, they are a more reliable source of information on the long-term trends in the social relations, political developments and economic conditions in the parganas of Mewat.

The *chithis* are letters written by the diwan of Amber to its officials, particularly *amils* and *faujdars*. Each *chithi* contains the substance of a complaint received by the diwan and his instructions for its redressal. These complaints, lodged by various aggrieved parties including peasants, throw considerable light on social conflicts and tensions as well as customary practices in the rural society. One could get a large number of *chithis* pertaining to the parganas of Mewat, but the majority are dated to the eighteenth century.

The reports addressed to the Amber Raja by his *vakil* posted at the Mughal court are in the form of *arzdashts*, written in Hindi but incorporating Rajasthani and Persian vocabulary. These reports contain details of political developments at the Mughal court that the Amber Raja was regularly informed about. As an imperial mansabdar, the Amber Raja had to depend on the goodwill of the emperor for various favours, i.e. the grant of mansabs, fixation of salary, assignment of jagirs, postings, promotions, etc. In view of the factional rivalries among the nobles at the imperial court, it was the duty of the *vakil* to keep a watchful eye on various developments at the court and inform his master regularly. In fact, the *vakil* was the official representative of the Amber Raja at the Mughal court and served as an intermediary between the Raja and the Mughal emperor. Being the representative of the Raja, he was directly responsible to him and, therefore, worked in consultation with him in all matters that affected his interests directly or indirectly. The reports of the *vakil* throw considerable light on the petty interests of the various groups of nobility at the Mughal court and their mutual conflicts, as also their attitude towards rebel zamindars like the Naruka Rajputs and the Jats.

The *dastur-al-amals* are schedules of revenue rates prepared by local revenue officials in conformity with the rules laid down by the central authority. One comes across many such *dastur-al-amals* for various parganas of Mewat. Each *dastur-al-amal* mentions the respective shares of the state and the cultivators in the produce of land, as also the differential rates of revenue applicable to various categories of cultivators. Some also state the amount of other cesses and *zabti* rates. The *dastur-al-amals* are extremely useful for computing the magnitude of revenue demand on the peasants.

The *yaddashti* is a kind of memorandum or a document of remembrance. The *yaddashtis* were written by village-level revenue officials like chaudharis, qanungos, patels and patwaris. They provide rich information about such aspects as arable and fallow land, livestock and bullocks owned by peasants of a village or a pargana. They also contain information about the availability of agricultural implements and other assets with the various categories of cultivators. However, the number of *yaddashtis* pertaining to Mewat is limited and as such they cannot be used extensively for the study of this region.

The Amber records contain letters written by the officials to the diwan of Amber. From these documents, one gets a good deal of information about the day-to-day functioning of the administration at the pargana level. The economic and political dimensions of the local administration are a recurrent theme of most of these letters. These documents are as important as the *arzdashts*. In fact, both these categories of documents provide ample scope for mutually corroborative evidence.

The *dehai-ferhashtis* are descriptive lists of villages in each pargana, prepared by village-level officials like patels and patwaris. They provide us village-wise information about the categories of land, i.e. arable and fallow, as also details of crops under the *zabti* and *batai-jinsi* systems of land revenue assessment. They mention whether a village was given on ijara or held as jagir or *khalisa*, as also reveal the names of ijaradars and jagirdars. Though only a few *dehai-ferhashtis* can be found pertaining to Khohri pargana in Mewat, they are an important source of information about various aspects of the village economy and society.

The *jamabandi* documents were prepared pargana-wise by the *amin*. They contain information about the methods of revenue assessment and the magnitude of land revenue demand. They provide details of land revenue for each village under *khalisa*, but do not include the revenue figures of villages held in ijara. Nevertheless, they are of immense value in measuring the magnitude of land revenue demand on those crops that were assessed under the *batai-jinsi* system.

The *khatoot ahalkarans* are written in the form of *arzdashts* and cover the period from 1633 to 1769. They provide useful information on various aspects of the internal administration of the jagirs in Mewat whose ijara was obtained by the Amber chiefs, as also the reaction of the peasantry against the non-customary taxes imposed by the Amber chiefs.

The non-archival records of the Alwar state, preserved at the Rajasthan State Archives of Bikaner, are useful for understanding the perceptions of people in the Mewat region, though some of this information is based on local folk traditions.

The other important works used in this study are: 'Hasan Khan Ki Katha', a historical ballad written by Narsingh Meo of Kajhota village in Mewat in the late sixteenth century, illumining the perceptions of Meos about the First Battle of Panipat (1526) and the Battle of Khanwa (1527); and *Arzang-i-Tijara* (1873) written by Sheikh Muhammad Makhdum, tehsildar of Tijara, narrating the history of the Khanzada chiefs of Mewat and their relation with Delhi Sultanate and the Mughal state. Being of local provenance, these sources are important for understanding the sociocultural history of the Meos and the Khanzadas during the medieval period. Besides, Abdul Shakur's *Tarikh Mev Chatri* (1919) in Urdu gives mythical genealogies (*vamshavalis*) of the Meos, connecting them with the Rajput clans. The work thus reveals the early-twentieth-century perceptions on the social origins of the Meos. Muhammad Habibur Rahman Khan's *Tazkirah-i-Sofiya-i-Mewat* betrays a clear Islamic orientation insofar as it seeks to chiefly argue that the Meos were the oldest community of the region to be converted to Islam, during the Sultanate period—a point belied by the Indo-Persian sources of the period itself. A useful compilation of scholarly articles on the Meo folklore can be found in G.D. Gulati's *Mewat: Folklore, Memory, History* (2013), though certain folk traditions, as discussed in this book, are in the want of corroboration by historical sources and can be seen as attempts to reinforce and legitimize certain self-perceptions of the Meos. However, several folktales, widely popular in parts of north and north-west India (e.g. eastern Rajasthan, Haryana, western Uttar Pradesh) and not exclusive to any community or caste group, have been utilized to explore certain common perceptions of peasantry about itself and its interaction with the state.

Mewat, the focus of this study, comprised parts of two important *subas* of the Mughal Empire, i.e. Delhi and Agra. A major part of Mewat was assigned as *tankhwah jagirs* to a number of imperial mansabdars including the Kachhwaha chiefs of Amber who also obtained the ijara of some parganas with greater frequency from the late seventeenth century onwards.

The first chapter surveys the political events in Mewat from the establishment of Turkish rule in India to the beginning of Akbar's reign, focusing on the process of state formation in the region and the oscillating relations of the Mewati chieftains, viz., the Khanzadas, with the Delhi Sultans and Mughals. The Meos had hostile relations with

Delhi Sultans who sought to contain their predatory activities. During Firozshah Tughlaq's reign in the late fourteenth century, Bahadur Nahar, a descendent of Jadon Rajputs who embraced Islam and was enrolled into Firozshah's nobility with the title 'Khanzad', established his chiefdom in Mewat. Periodic conflicts and conciliation characterized the relations of the Khanzada chiefs with the Tughlaq, Sayyid and Lodi rulers. The Khanzada chiefs inducted the former Firozi slaves in their ranks in order to utilize their administrative competencies, and induced the peasantization of Meos in order to strengthen the economic base of the evolving state. However, after the defeat of the Khanzadas in the battle of Khanwa at the hands of Babur, the annexation of Mewat, and the eventual establishment of direct Mughal rule over the region during Akbar's reign, the Khanzadas lost their political significance and autonomy. Though absorbed in the Mughal administration, they did not enjoy the same status as did the Rajputs, and survived as landlords (zamindars) in the rural society. Thus, the development of the Khanzada state in Mewat was undermined by the Mughal state which perceived it as a threat to its own consolidation.

The next chapter explains how the Meos gradually transformed themselves from a tribal to a sedentary peasant community. The Meos, originally settled in the hills, ravines and dense forests of the Aravalli range, belonged to various tribal groups (*pals*) and were engaged in cattle-lifting, raids and robberies, thus constituting a source of great trouble to the people of Delhi and its neighbourhood. However, from late fourteenth century they began to migrate to plains and settle down as peasants. This process of migration and peasantization that continued up to the late medieval period was induced by several factors: rigorous military campaigns, large-scale clearance of forests and construction of garrisoned forts by the Delhi Sultans to contain their depredations; growing Meo population pressure on the scarce resources of the hilly terrain; the pressure exerted by the Khanzada chiefs on the Meos for relocating to plains and taking up agriculture; and the administrative integration of Mewat into the Mughal Empire during Akbar's reign.

The process of the Islamization of Meos is discussed in the third chapter, a process that ran parallel to their peasantization, was initiated by the Khanzadas and further stimulated by the induction of the Meos in the Mughal administrative service as *dak* Meoras and *khidmatiyyas* (post-carriers, spies and palace guards). It also discusses the linkages of this process to political and socio-economic developments, and explores the issue of the formation and articulation of Meo-Islamic identity. However, this process remained incomplete and their religious identity remained ambiguous even as late as mid-nineteenth century, as they continued to worship Hindu village deities and observe several Hindu and Muslim festivals while adopting Muslim names.

The fourth chapter studies the working of ijara or the practice of revenue farming in Mewat during the late seventeenth and early eighteenth centuries and its far-reaching impact on the region's economy, polity and rural society. The practice entailed the transfer of revenue-collection rights over territories within the fiefs (jagirs) of mansabdars or officers of the Mughal Empire to various political entities in the region, notably the Amber chiefs and Jats. As the practice became widespread in the region due to the disturbed and unsettled conditions of the late Mughal period, there ensued a fierce contest among those seeking to control territories on ijara for various politico-economic reasons. While the recipients of ijara immensely profited from the practice, the ruthlessly exploited peasantry was provoked to protest against the abuses of the practice in various forms. Besides peasants and agriculture, other economic activities and sections of society, such as trade and traders, were also adversely affected by the excesses of ijara-holders and the resultant social unrest. At the same time, competition over acquiring ijara among the contestants for political ascendancy in the region led to increased militarization and channelization of resources to this end. Exploring these varied impacts of the practice, the chapter stresses that at the heart of the practice lay not an efficient method of revenue collection, but an intense conflict over agrarian surplus between its various claimants and increased alienation of the oppressed primary producers, i.e. the peasants from the state. It is this feature that rendered the practice not only immensely detrimental to the region's economy and social relations, but also unviable as a mechanism of resource-appropriation for the emergent polity in the region.

The fifth chapter addresses an important issue not adequately addressed so far in the studies on peasantry in medieval India, particularly peasant protests in the late Mughal period: the issue of class consciousness in peasantry or that of class character of peasant protests against the state. It offers the argument that the peasantry in late medieval north India did develop a degree of self-consciousness as a class and that its conflict with the state did betray a certain class character. The folksongs and folktales popular among the peasantry since the medieval times have all the ingredients with which to construct a definite peasant class ideology that included conceptions of economic interest, social ethics and relation with the ruling class. The chapter details the various ways in which the state intervened in the peasants' sociocultural and economic lives and the ways in which the peasants responded to these interventions. It also shows how the peasants' class consciousness conditioned their engagement with the state in specific areas, whether grievance redressal, conflict-resolution or agricultural production and surplus-distribution. Further, it discusses how caste consciousness in a stratified peasant society impinged on its class consciousness. However, there remained certain limits to the fuller development of this class consciousness, which ultimately constrained the fuller realization of the potential of peasants' class struggle against the state. The chapter locates these limits in the peasants' periodic negotiations with the state and their belief in the ideal of a non-conflictual, harmonious relation with the state.

The final chapter explores a hitherto unstudied dimension of an issue that has otherwise received a good deal of attention from scholars for a long time—the idea of kingship in precolonial India. Modern scholarly literature on the conception of kingship or sovereignty has been heavily based on textual sources of ancient and medieval periods, such as Brahmanical normative texts in Sanskrit or Indo-Persian court chronicles produced by members of the intellectual and social elite, and providing a largely classist and statist perspective on kingship. This chapter seeks to trace alternative perceptions of kingship in certain select and widely popular folk songs and folktales of precolonial rural society in late medieval north and north-western India (more precisely, eastern Rajasthan, parts of Haryana, and western Uttar Pradesh) that in the extant form were recorded by colonial ethnographers in the late nineteenth century and/or fashioned into musical performative narratives (*sang*) by rural bards in the late nineteenth and early twentieth centuries. This chapter also demonstrates that the perceptions of kingship in these stories, while converging and diverging with those in literary sources on several points, constitute a unique discourse on ideal kingship prevalent in the politically disempowered and socio-economically under- or non-privileged class/es. This discourse can be construed as a subaltern perspective on kingship, among other things, and a counterpoint to the dominant precolonial discourse on kingship represented by the texts and textual traditions. For the peasant communities grappling with various forms of inequity, injustice and oppression arising out of the state and society through the ages, constructing and engaging in this discourse and thereby valorizing a simple ethical ideal of kingship was not only a way of envisioning an alternative socio-political utopia, but also that of enduring and even resisting heightened oppression by the political elite, particularly in times of acute distress such as during the disturbed political conditions following the decline of Mughal imperial authority in the late seventeenth and early eighteenth centuries.

The book explores the changing dynamics of historical interaction between the state or the ruling elite and the peasant society, and the peasant concept of moral economy that underlay this interaction. The moral economy encapsulated in the oral traditions of the peasant society was shaped by the lived experiences of the peasantry engaging with a stratified ruling elite at multiple levels and, in turn, shaped its shifting responses to the conduct of the ruling elite. The peasants' responses included complex ways of complying with, negotiating with and resisting, covertly and overtly, the state's fiscal demands at specific historical junctures, but they were all underpinned by the peasant's conception of an ideal ruler and his ideal relation with the state, imbued with principles of mutuality, fairness and justice. Through the study of state records and rural oral traditions, this book makes a case for a nuanced approach to the complex, layered relationship between the state and peasant, departing from the simplistic oppressor-oppressed binaries that have been used to characterize this relationship.

1

State Formation in Mewat

Rise and Demise of Khanzada Chiefdom in the Politics of North India

A POPULAR PERCEPTION prevails among the Meos that they were allotted lands by the Mughal Emperor Akbar. This perception seems to be grounded in historical reality, as Abul-Fazl observes in the *Ain-i-Akbari* that for the first time the Mewat region was brought under direct Mughal administration during Akbar's reign. The whole of Mewat was divided into four *sarkars* comprised within the two Mughal *subas* (provinces) of Agra and Delhi.[1] These sarkars were further divided into 67 parganas,[2] and the Meos established their zamindari rights over 12, 14 and 4 parganas of Alwar, Tijara and Sahar sarkars, respectively.[3] The preponderance of Meo zamindaris in the region and their recognition by the Mughal administration under Akbar gradually gave birth to the myth that land was allotted to each Meo *pal* (lineage group) by Akbar.[4] By the end of the sixteenth century, the Meos had not only been transformed into a landed peasantry but had also established their zamindari rights in the Mewat region. However, other cultivating classes such as Jats, Gujjars, Ahirs, Rajputs, Brahmins and Malis also lived—and continue to live—in the region.[5]

Mewat is situated approximately 64 km. south-west of Delhi, roughly corresponding to modern Alwar and Bharatpur districts of present-day Rajasthan, and Nuh district of present-day Haryana. Presently, it comprises of nine tehsils: Tijara, Kishangarh, Alwar and Lachhmangarh in Alwar district; Deeg, Nagar and Kama in Bharatpur district; and Nuh and Firozpur Jhirka in Nuh district.

Mewat is the popular name for the region inhabited by the Meos or Mevs. The Meos believe that the term 'Mewat' is derived from 'Mev', and 'Meo' or 'Mev' from 'Mewas' which means a hiding place for the robbers. Therefore, in the Indo-Persian court chronicles and colonial records, the term 'Mev' became synonymous with robber, ruffian or rogue.[6] The topography of Mewat is varied due to a combination of Aravalli hill ranges, plains and dense forests. The Aravalli Hills have served as a habitat for wild animals like tigers, panthers, wolves, hyenas, foxes, jackals and deer. Sultan Firozshah Tughlaq (r. 1351–88) had a keen interest in hunting wild beasts; therefore, he constructed a fortress near a lake at Kotla in the Kala Pahad (Black Mountain) ridge for the purpose of undertaking royal hunts.[7] The Kala Pahad ridge is at the centre of Mewat and demarcates Haryana from Rajasthan. It rises abruptly to more than 300 metres at some places and is remarkable for its uninterrupted stretch. In the words of O.H.K. Spate, 'All the hills are dissected by generally dry but at times torrent-field nullahs, and surrounded by pediment fans.'[8] According to F.C. Channing, parts of the plains were rendered waste because the torrents at the foothills of Kala Pahad formed deep gorges and caused erosion.[9] In the medieval times, Mewat was dotted with lakes, seasonal streams, springs and dams which played an important role as a source of irrigation for agricultural production.[10] The principal lakes were Kotla, Chandeni, Siliserh and Deoti. Some channels were cut from these lakes when the waterbed was full, in order to support the cultivation of food and cash crops.[11] Later, when these lakes dried up, their fertile beds served for growing superior crops, such as cotton, wheat and sugarcane. Abul-Fazl mentions that Meo peasants cultivated not only food crops but also indigo, cotton, sugarcane, mustard and pulses.[12] The Kala Pahad and other hills of the Aravalli Range have been a source of food, water, shelter and protection to a number of tribal communities since the pre-Sultanate period. There is a popular saying about the Kala Pahad which also describes the geographical setting of Mewat:

इत दिल्ली उत आगरा, इत मथुरा और बैराठ
मेरो कालो पहाड़ सुहावणों, जाके बीच बसे मेवात ।[13]

[The geographical setting of Mewat is such that one of its sides is bordered by Delhi and others by Mathura, Agra and Bairat. The stretches of Kala Pahad pass through the centre of Mewat whose beautiful ranges and ravines enhance the beauty of Mewat.]

This popular saying is significant, since both sides of the Kala Pahad have densely populated villages and agriculturally fertile tracts. There has also been an old popular perception that Kala Pahad is a blessing for the Mewat region, as from time immemorial it has provided food, shelter, water and immense benefits to various tribal communities and wild animals.

According to Minhaj Siraj's *Tabakat-i-Nasiri*, the attitude of the Meos of Mewat towards the Delhi Sultanate had been one of hostility.[14] They also had conflict with the Mughal state that continued intermittently till the downfall of the empire, though its intensity varied over time. The nature of the Mughal-Meo conflicts—and their impact on the fortunes of the people of Mewat—forms a key subject of the study of political history of medieval north India. Here, a preliminary examination of the nature of political and administrative structures of the region would be relevant in assessing its impact on the society and economy of the region.

I

The most conspicuous phenomenon in the polity of early medieval India was the rise of independent and semi-independent principalities, one of which was Mewat. The topographical features of Mewat influenced the course of its political history. The hilly region offered not only considerable protection against external attacks but was a veritable stronghold too. Although Mewat was often prone to invasions due to its proximity to Delhi and Agra, a striking fact is that up to the beginning of sixteenth century, the chieftains of Mewat could not be brought under total subjugation for any considerable length of time.[15]

A brief survey of the political events in Mewat from the establishment of the Turkish rule in India to the beginning of the reign of Akbar is necessary in order to understand the nature of state formation in the region, as well as the relationship between the Khanzada chiefs (the ruling class of Mewat from late fourteenth to early sixteenth century), the Delhi Sultans, other regional potentates and the imperial Mughal authority. The earliest references to the Meos can be traced in the Indo-Persian chronicles of the Sultanate period. Both Minhaj Siraj and Ziauddin Barani describe the Meos as lawless, plunderers, raiders, robbers and assaulters who had become a serious threat for the Sultans of Delhi.[16] Minhaj Siraj writes:

Balban (Ulugh Khan) and other nobles, with the royal troops and their own followers suddenly resolved upon a campaign in the hills and made the first march in advance on Monday, 4th Safar 658H (Jan. 20, AD 1260). They retreated to the summits of the mountains, the defiles, to deep gorges and narrow valley, but they were all taken and put to the swords. For twenty days, the troops traversed the hills in all directions. The villages and the habitations of the mountaineers were on the summit of the loftiest hills and rocks and were of great strength, but they were all taken and ravaged by the order of Ulugh Khan, and the inhabitants who were thieves, robbers and highwaymen were all slain.[17]

One hundred years later, Ziauddin Barani expresses similar views about the Meos in *Tarikh-i-Firozshahi*:

The daring of the Mewatis in the neighborhood of Delhi was carried to such an extent that the Western gates of the city were at afternoon prayer, and no one dared to go out of the city in that direction after that hour, whether he travelled as a pilgrim or with the display of a sovereign. At afternoon prayer, the Mewati would often come to the girls who were fetching water; they would strip them and carry off their clothes. These daring acts of the Mewatis had caused a great ferment in Delhi.[18]

The aforementioned Indo-Persian writings project the Meos as robbers, plunderers and dacoits who disrupted the trade and travel and became a great source of trouble to the people of Delhi and its neighbourhood. However, on the basis of their lifestyle and occupational pursuits, it appears that the Meos had to struggle a lot to eke out their living. On the other hand, their geographical and social isolation enabled them to lead a life of relative sociopolitical freedom. Nevertheless, being in the vicinity of Delhi and Agra, Mewat remained within the reach of the Sultans of Delhi who undertook military campaigns to control the lawlessness and marauding activities of the Meos. For instance, in January 1260, Balban marched from Delhi to Mewat with a huge force to punish the Mewati rebels who used to conduct organized plunder in the villages of Haryana, Siwalik and Bayana regions. They used to rob the property of the Muslims and harass the common people. Three years before, the Meos had so much courage that under the leadership of Malka, they took away the camels from the royal camp of Balban near Hansi and distributed these camels among the Chauhan Rajputs of Ranthambore.[19] Balban personally led a campaign against the Meos and for 20 days, the royal army remained in the Mewat region.[20]

It appears from the above descriptions of Minhaj and Barani that along with the Meos, the Rajputs were also involved in committing dacoities in the Mewat region. The Meo-Rajput nexus of looting and robbery has also been pointed out by A.B.M. Habibullah. He writes that the frequent mention of Ranthambore in connection with the operations of the Meos in Mewat may imply a link between the Mewati rebels and the Chauhan Rajputs of Ranthambore.[21] This is corroborated by the instance of Qutlugh Khan, a rebel noble of Sultan Nasiruddin Mahmud Shah, seeking refuge in Santur, Rana Ran Pal's capital situated in the Aravalli Hills of Mewat. Rana Ran Pal, the descendent of Jadon Rajputs of Karauli, had carved out a principality at Santur in the Aravalli Hills during the early Sultanate period and must have accepted the overlordship of Balban. As the chief of Mewat, he enjoyed a high reputation among the Meos. Ulugh Khan reached Santur with a big military contingent and destroyed the fortress of Santur, thereby forcing Qutlugh Khan to leave Mewat.[22]

In 1266 again, Sultan Balban took severe action against the Meos. He devoted a whole year to suppressing the Meos and clearing the forests around Delhi; he constructed a fort to guard the south-western side of Delhi against the incursions of the Mewatis. Subsequently, Mewat was brought under the direct administrative control of the Sultan and 3,000 Afghan soldiers were posted in the neighbourhood of Delhi to closely watch the activities of the Mewatis. A number of military posts (*thanas*) were established in Mewat, manned by the Afghan soldiers.[23] These postings helped the Afghans considerably in establishing and consolidating their base in the region. In order to terrorize the Meos, Balban ordered the reward of one silver *tanka* for a head, and two for every living prisoner. Minhaj even states that the Afghan section of the imperial army was particularly active and each of them brought at least 100 prisoners. The rebel chief Malka was arrested along with his entire family and 250 other leading men of the Meo tribes. They were brought to Delhi and cruelly put to death near Hauz Rani in front of the Badaun Gate of the city. Besides, 142 horses were captured and 60 cotton bags containing 30,000 *tankas* of loot seized by the army.[24] It was during these campaigns that Ulugh Khan captured Santur, the capital city of Mewat. Alexander Cunningham identified Santur as Indore, which was situated 6 mi. to the north of Kotla Lake and about 70 mi. to the south of Delhi. The foundation of the fort is attributed to the Nikumbha Rajputs, although no historical records exist about them. It seems that the fort was actually founded by the Jadon Rajputs, a branch of Yaduvanshi Rajputs who ruled over Karauli-Bayana regions.[25]

Amir Khusrau informs that when Sultan Alauddin Khalji launched his military expedition against Ranthambore, he went through the Mewat region. However, it may be noted that he does not mention the lawlessness and predatory activities of the Meos, though he remarks that the Mewat region was surrounded by high Aravalli Hills and infested with wild animals.[26] Alauddin Khalji continued Balban's policy of suppressing the turbulent chiefs in the vicinity of Delhi. He made the trade route between Delhi and Gujarat reasonably secure after thorough subjugation of the Meos. Therefore, it may be assumed that Alauddin Khalji had full administrative control over Mewat.

According to the oral tradition of the Khanzadas, Adhanpal—a Jadon Rajput descended from Tahanpal who was the Jadon chief of Bayana—had carved out his settlement in Sarheta near Tijara hills. It is possible that the Jadon Rajputs may have shifted their principality from Sarheta to Santur (Indore) during the reign of Nasiruddin Mahmud Shah. The point that needs to be highlighted is that there, indeed, existed a Meo-Rajput nexus in plundering, otherwise it was not possible for the Meo tribes to possess huge amounts of currency and horses captured at Santur by Balban's army during his campaign against the Meos. Therefore, the complex relationship between the Meos and the central authority may be understood in the light of a combined Meo-Rajput struggle for their survival in the thick forests and Aravalli Hills of the Mewat region till the reign of Firozshah Tughlaq.

However, during the Tughlaq period, the Mewatis went back to their old habit of plundering, as reflected in the contemporary writings. Firozshah Tughlaq posted a force at Firozpur Jhirka for controlling the depredations of the Mewatis,[27] and constructed a fortress at Indore in the Aravalli Hills for the purpose of hunting as well as military expeditions.[28] It appears that during the reign of Firozshah Tughlaq, the Meos and a section of the Jadon Rajputs actively indulged in plundering activities. The Urdu work *Arzang-i-Tijara* informs us that a branch of Jadon Rajputs and the Meos were notorious for loot and plunder, arson and lawlessness in the Mewat region, and had created a serious law and order problem for the Sultan of Delhi.[29]

According to *Tarikh-i-Mubarakshahi*, in 1379–80, Firozshah Tughlaq invaded Mewat and reached Santur and forced the Rai of Mewat to pay regular tributes.[30] The name of the Rai is not mentioned, but it appears that Bahadur Nahar may have been the Rai of Santur at that time. It appears from Firozshah Tughlaq's *Futuhat-i-Firozshahi* that he had paid much attention to Mewat as he writes:

In the village of Malúh [Malab],[31] there is a tank which they [the Hindus] call *kund* (tank). Here they had built idol-temples, and on certain days the Hindus were accustomed to proceed thither on horseback, and wearing arms. Their women and children also went out in palankíns and carts. There, they assembled in thousands and performed idol worship. This abuse had been so overlooked that the *bázár* people took out there all sorts of provisions, and set up stalls and sold their goods. Some graceless Musulmáns, thinking only of their own gratification took part in these meetings. When intelligence of this came to my ears my religious feelings prompted me at once to put a stop to this scandal and offence to the religion of Islám. On the day of the assembling I went there in person . . . [and] I destroyed their idol temples, and instead thereof raised mosques. I founded two flourishing towns (*kasba*) one called Tughlikpúr, the other Sálárpúr. Where infidels and idolaters worshiped idols, Musulmáns now, by God's mercy, perform their devotions to the true God. Praise of God and the summons to prayer are now heard there, and that place which was formerly the home of infidels has become the habitation of the faithful, who there repeat their creed and offer up their praises to God'.[32]

Further, he adds, 'Information was brought to me that some Hindús had erected a new idol-temple in the village of Sálihpúr, and were performing worship to their idol. I sent some persons there to destroy the idol temple, and to put a stop to their pernicious incitements to error.'[33]

From the late fourteenth century onwards, i.e. towards the end of Firozshah's reign, the region witnessed the formation of a chiefdom of the Khanzadas which would significantly change the region's political trajectory and relations with a host of well established states, including Delhi Sultanate, other regional states and, later, the Mughal imperial state. The history of the Khanzadas of Mewat begins with Bahadur Nahar, who embraced Islam during the reign of Firozshah Tughlaq. His ancestors were Jadon Rajputs, who had ruled over Bayana and Thangir before the invasions of Muhammad Ghori. During the fourteenth century, Lakhanpal, a Jadon Rajput, was the chief of a small tract of Mewat around Tijara. Lakhanpal had two sons, Sambharpal and Somparpal. The former took the name of Bahadur Nahar and gained control over Sarheta situated 4 mi. to the east of Tijara, while the latter took the name of Chhaju Khan and got possession of Jhirka. The two brothers embraced Islam in order to save their estates from annexation by Firozshah Tughlaq. The name of the town was also changed from Jhirka to Firozpur Jhirka.[34] The author of *Arzang-i-Tijara* has given the two reasons for the conversion of Bahadur Nahar: the first was his deep faith in the Sufi saint Hazrat Nasiruddin Chirag-Delhvi; and second was his and his brother's arrest and imprisonment in Delhi by Firozshah's troops for his predatory activities in the neighbourhood of Delhi that posed a serious law and order problem for the sultanate of Delhi.[35]

Historical evidence shows that after embracing Islam, Bahadur Nahar was enrolled into nobility and given the title of Khanazad by Firozshah. The title 'Khanazad' or 'Khanazadun' was also given to those Firozi slaves who happened to be very close and loyal to the Sultan.[36] Many of the Firozi slaves were appointed to high positions in the military and administrative departments of the government by the Sultan. Afif mentions 36 *karkhanas* under Firozshah run by these slaves in different capacities.[37]

As a succession struggle broke out in Delhi after Firozshah's death (1388), Bahadur Nahar became a staunch supporter of Abu Bakr Shah, son of Fateh Khan, grandson of Firozshah and the leader of one of the factions of Firozi slaves. But Muhammad Shah became the Sultan of Delhi with the help of another faction of Firozi slaves. Abu Bakr fled to Kotla, Bahadur Nahar's fortress in Mewat.[38] The Firozi slaves supporting Abu Bakr were ordered to vacate their official positions in the government and asked to leave Delhi within a short period as their loyalty to the new Sultan was suspected. One of the first acts of Sultan Muhammad was to seize the royal elephants from the Firozi slaves and hand them over to their old keepers. It is said that many innocent persons were killed at the order of the new Sultan. He ordered that everyone who could correctly pronounce 'Khara Khari Kara Jana' would be considered a free man. In course of this test, many Firozi slaves of local origin were disgraced and put to the sword. This story was supposedly well known throughout Hind and Sind and is recounted in *Tarikh-i-Mubarakshahi*.[39] Sirhindi narrates in detail the blood war that subsequently took place between the Firozi slaves and Sultan Muhammad Shah. Many Firozi slaves whose loyalty to the new Sultan was suspect, were killed while many others fled with their families to Kotla, seeking refuge with Bahadur Nahar.[40] On 31 August 1390, a decisive battle was fought at Kotla, in which Abu Bakr Shah and Firozi slaves were defeated. Abu Bakr Shah and Bahadur Nahar came out of the Kotla fortress and asked for amnesty. Muhammad Shah's son, Humayun Khan gave a robe to Bahadur Nahar and sent him back to Mewat, but imprisoned Abu Bakr and sent him to Meerut where he later died.[41] However, after the death of Muhammad Shah in January 1394, Bahadur Nahar managed to re-enter the arena of court politics, taking advantage of the civil war that now ensued among Muhammad Shah's successors. His friend Mukarrab Khan, who was a leader of one of the rival groups, called him from Kotla and put him in charge of the fortress of old Delhi.[42] In the wake of the general confusion that followed Timur's occupation of Delhi at the close of 1398, Bahadur Nahar withdrew to Kotla from where he watched the subsequent developments.[43]

Bahadur Nahar's position vis-à-vis the Delhi Sultanate further suffered a setback with the Sayyid rulers coming to power. When the Sayyids claimed the throne of Delhi, they were opposed by Bahadur Nahar. Sultan Mubarak Shah, the founder of the Sayyid dynasty, led military campaigns against the Mewati chiefs in 1421, 1422 and 1425–6, but could not achieve much success due to the natural defence provided by the Aravalli Hills and the thick forests of Mewat.[44]

Bahadur Nahar's successors, Kadar Khan (Khadu) and Jalal Khan (Jallu), were equally hostile to the Sayyids and refused to pay tribute to the Sayyid rulers. Mubarak Shah personally led his army into Mewat in order to subdue the Mewati chiefs.[45] Malik Kadar Khan was captured and executed on the charge of exchanging presents and envoys with the Sharqi ruler of Jaunpur who were the arch-rivals of the Sayyids. Sarwar Malik was sent with a big force to suppress the Mewatis, and he destroyed many *qasbas* and villages of Mewat. Realizing the gravity of the situation, Jalal Khan and other Mewati nobles assembled at the fortress of Indore and decided not to offend the Sultan any further. They also agreed to pay the tribute.[46] Mubarak Sayyid's suppression of the Mewati chiefs Kadar Khan and Ahmad Khan on account of the latter's relations with the Sharqi rulers of Jaunpur points to a brief alliance between the chiefs of Mewat and the Sharqis during the sultanate period.

When Bahlul Lodi became the sultan of Delhi, the whole of India was divided into provinces governed by petty rulers. The Meo chief Ahmad Khan Mewati ruled the area extending from Mehrauli to Lado Sarai,[47] near the city of Delhi. As Bahlul consolidated his position, he sought to expand his authority. He forced Ahmad Khan Mewati to submit to his rule and deprived him of seven parganas including Tijara, but allowed him to retain the rest of Mewat and rule as a tributary chief. These parganas were bestowed upon Tartar Khan Lodi who retained them till the reign of Sikandar Lodi. This was an important event in the history of Mewat insofar as the Mewati chief was dispossessed of the core parganas of his chiefdom and his political autonomy stood compromised. Thereafter, the Mewati chiefs had to shift their capital from Tijara to Alwar. Ahmad Khan appointed his uncle Mubarak Khan to be perpetually in attendance at the court in Delhi. He soon won the confidence of the Sultan which he and his descendants continued to enjoy till the end of the Lodi rule. His son Alwal Khan and grandson Hasan Khan governed their ancestral state during the reigns of Sikandar Lodi and Ibrahim Lodi, respectively. It appears that they had to pay only a nominal sum of money as annual tribute to the Lodi Sultans.[48] Ahmad Khan Mewati figures in the list of 34 nobles of Bahlul Lodi, provided in *Tabaqat-i-Akbari*.[49] During the reign of Sikandar Lodi, Alam Khan Mewati held an important position at the Delhi court.[50] This cordial relationship between the Lodis and the Mewati chiefs continued till the end of the reign of Ibrahim Lodi. Hasan Khan Mewati, a powerful Mewati chieftain, fought for Ibrahim Lodi in the first battle of Panipat,[51] but later joined hands with Rana Sanga against Babur and fell in the battle of Khanwa.[52]

II

As discussed in the previous section, a large number of Firozi slaves, along with their families, had fled from Delhi to Kotla in Mewat, to save their lives from Sultan Muhammad Shah. Bahadur Nahar, in all probability, inducted the former Firozi slaves into his aristocracy by giving them important positions. Subsequently, the former Firozi slaves merged with the local elite of Mewat, i.e. the military-cum-land-proprietors. This can be inferred from the fact that they were also called Khanazads,[53] and later commonly spoken of as Khanzadas. On account of their military skills and past administrative experience, the former Firozi slaves were able to carve out a place for themselves in the Khanzada state of Mewat.

The social organization of the Khanzadas as the political elite of their evolving state in Mewat was rather loose and fluid, and they absorbed new groups like Firozi slaves within their ranks. Once the former Firozi slaves joined the state, their social identity became one with that of the ruling Khanzada class. The state assigned them villages in lieu of remuneration, but eventually they claimed hereditary rights over these villages. This can be inferred from *Ain-i-Akbari* which states that by the end of the sixteenth century, the Khanzadas had acquired zamindari rights over 18 parganas out of a total of 61 parganas in the Alwar and Tijara sarkars.[54]

Since many of the former Firozi slaves inducted into the Khanzada state had acquired administrative knowledge and experience of the *iqta* system[55] during the reign of Firozshah Tughlaq, they directed much of their attention towards the expansion of agricultural production in order to increase the state's financial resources. They militarily coerced the Meo and other tribal communities living in the Aravalli Hills (Kala Pahad) to practice agriculture. This is borne from a Meo folk tale that five Meo pals, viz., Chhiraklot, Duhlot, Pundlot, Daimrot and Nai (Jadon Vamshi), living in the Kala Pahad used to harass people, but when the traders and citizens lodged several complaints against them with the king, the state pressurized them to give up their old predatory habits and they settled down in the plains. The Jagga records[56] also reveal that by the end of the fifteenth century these five Meo pals settled down in the plains of Nuh-Firozpur-Jhirka, Ramgarh and Lachhmangarh regions in the vicinity of Kala Pahad. Another folk tale about Ahmad Khan Mewati's reign tells that the Khanzadas exercised considerable pressure on the Meos to leave their old occupations and shift to agriculture in order to strengthen the economic base of the state. The Meos of Sonkh village, situated between Nuh and Palwal, were arrested by Ahmad Khan Mewati's army on account of the non-payment of land revenue to the state. They were imprisoned and deployed as labourers in the construction of the fortress at Indore. Ladh Begam, the daughter of Ahmad Khan Mewati, lost her heart to a young and handsome Meo boy named Santhal who also worked as labourer. Finally, Ahmad Khan Mewati had to submit to his daughter's wishes and marry her to Santhal. After the marriage, they were assigned an *iqta* where they found a village and named it Ladhpuri after the name of Ladh Begam.[57] The folk tale also conveys that matrimonial relations with the Meos was essential for Ahmad Khan Mewati to expand the social base of the Khanzadas among the Meos.

It appears that the Khanzadas of Mewat adopted a very pragmatic approach towards the Meos because the Meos formed the majority of peasants in the Mewat region. Whatever little information is available about the relationship between the Khanzadas and the Meos suggests that the Khanzada chiefs enjoyed the support of the Meos. An early-sixteenth-century ballad, 'Hasan Khan Ki Katha', by Narsingh Meo of Kajhota village of Mewat reveals that not only did the Meos constitute the majority of peasants, but the army of Hasan Khan Mewati also had a large number of Meo soldiers. Moreover, he enjoyed the full support and cooperation of all the twelve chiefs of the Meo pals in the battle of Khanwa.[58] The Khanzada chiefs established their matrimonial relations not only with the Meos but also with the Meenas. 'Hasan Khan Ki Katha' tells us that he lost his life in the battle of Khanwa along with his two sons who were born to his wife from the Meena caste.[59] A large number of Meena peasants inhabited the Alwar sarkar where the Khanzada chiefs had shifted their capital from Tijara during the reign of Bahlul Lodi, as mentioned before. This explains Hasan Khan's efforts to establish matrimonial alliance with the Meenas in order to extend his social base.

The foregoing discussion shows that many new villages and qasbas were founded and settled particularly in the periphery of Tijara by the Khanzadas in the wake of the assignment of land grants to the former Firozi slaves who were absorbed into the ranks of Khanzadas. Following this, the second stage of expansion of the Khanzada state set in during the Lodi period with the shift of its capital to Alwar in eastern Rajasthan.[60]

The expansion of the Khanzada state was partially guided by their expansionist policy, but the cession of important parganas to Bahlul Lodi, as mentioned before, mainly forced the Khanzadas to move towards eastern Rajasthan. The land in eastern Rajasthan was more fertile than their heavily forested and hilly ancestral land of

Mewat. Thus, more land was brought under plough leading to further peasantization of the Meos and the Meenas. The folk tradition of the Khanzadas has it that they controlled 1,484 *kheras* (settlements) of Mewat.[61]

In his memoir, Babur has also described the political conditions of Mewat under the rule of Hasan Khan Mewati:

The country of Mewât lies not far from Delhi and yields a revenue of three or four *krors*. Hassan Khan Mewâti had inherited the government of that country from his ancestors, who had governed it, in uninterrupted succession for nearly two hundred years. They had yielded an imperfect kind of submission to the Sultan of Delhi. The Sultan of Hind, whether from the extent of their territories, from want of opportunity, or from the obstacles posed by the mountainous nature of the country, had never subdued Mewât. They had never been able to reduce it to order, and were content to receive such a degree of obedience as was tendered to them.[62]

Condemning Hasan Khan for his hostility to Babur, Zain Khan, his secretary, writes:

Mewat, one of the most fortified towns in Indian land, was under Hasan Khan Mewāti, who had put it in a strong defensive position. He was the prime mover of all the insurrections, and had become the chief of the agitators and leaders of the many pagans and infidels. Having thrown down the banner of faith (of Islam) at his feet, he had associated himself with, joined and submitted to the refractory wicked people and thus he supported their hostile cause.[63]

Accounts of both Zain Khan and Shaikh Rizqullah Mustaqi record that after the death of Ibrahim Lodi in first battle of Panipat, Hasan Khan Mewati, who had fought for Ibrahim Lodi, invited Rana Sanga of Chittor, Rai Silahdi and the Khan of Nagore and persuaded them to make Mahmud, the son of Sikandar Lodi, the Sultan of Delhi and fight against Babur in Khanwa.[64] Hasan Khan's alliances with these rulers against Babur for the battle of Khanwa points to his ability to influence the neighbouring chiefs.

Offering a regional perspective on these events, the sixteenth-century Mewati ballad 'Hasan Khan Ki Katha' criticizes the role of Hasan Khan in the battles of Panipat and Khanwa, arguing that there was no reason for him to fight against Babur. In the beginning of the ballad, the author, Narsingh Meo, pays his respect to Gods (Narayana and Paigambar [the Prophet]), and assures the audience that whatever he has written in the ballad, is absolutely based on 'facts and hearsay'. He states that in the ancient times there were many kings and kingdoms, but only a handful of them are remembered for their right judgements and thoughts about the masses. He then goes on to cite instances of supposedly 'good' and 'bad' mythical and historical rulers. Ravana, the king of Lanka, possessed a great kingdom, but his irrational thinking and excess pride brought ruination to his kingdom at the hands of Rama and his army of monkeys. King Vikramaditya, on the other hand, was known for his just treatment of the masses. Ibrahim Lodi, the king of Hindustan, remained in his palace all the time and used to play *chaupar*. He was neither bothered about the masses nor about his state. On the other hand, Babur came to India, fully prepared for the battle of Panipat. It was a known fact to every man of Babur that Rana Sanga, the king of Chittor, also wanted to destroy the kingdom of Ibrahim Lodi.[65] Lodi fought against Babur in Panipat until afternoon, but thereafter never came back alive from the battlefield. The war was over, and the battlefield was full of dead soldiers and horses. The traders (*banias* and *baqqals*) were making profits, while the other artisans like tailors (*darjis*) and goldsmiths (*sunars*) were being harassed and looted. The Turks, Kolis and Malis were completely decimated in the battlefield of Panipat.[66] After his defeat at the battle of Panipat, Mahmud Lodi, the son of Sikandar Lodi, came to Hasan Khan Mewati at Alwar seeking refuge and help against Babur. Hasan Khan, the son of Alawal Khan Mewati, was a great warrior and a man of his word. He summoned Karam Chand Khatri, the commander-in-chief of his army, to discuss the strategy for the imminent battle of Khanwa. He brought Sher Khan Nagori to his side and invited all the chiefs of the Meo pals to his palace to discuss the war strategy. Among them, the Duhlot and Singhal Meo pals held the front position in Hasan Khan's army.[67] Hasan Khan sent two messengers, Harna Meo and Sukhna Meo, with a letter to Rana Sanga at Chittor asking for his support in the war. In the letter, he promised that if they won the battle of Khanwa, the entire middle region (Madhya desh) of Ibrahim Lodi's regime would be part of Rana's dominions. In his response, proud Rana declared that he would push back Babur from the battlefield of Khanwa to Kabul.[68] Both rulers gave assurances to each other that they would stick to this alliance. Hasan Khan ordered Karam Chand Khatri to proceed with the army towards the battlefield of Khanwa. Eventually, in the ensuing war, Hasan Khan and his two sons lost their lives and his kingdom was ruined by Babur. In the ballad, the author accuses Hasan Khan for bringing about the destruction of his kingdom. He twice invited unnecessary trouble for himself: first, by joining forces with Ibrahim Lodi in the First Battle of Panipat against Babur, and then, by inviting Rana Sanga for the battle of Khanwa against Babur for the cause of Sikander Lodi's son even when Babur had shown clemency by releasing his son, Nahar Khan, from captivity.[69] According to the author, Rana Sanga was untrustworthy and thoroughly dishonest; he had committed the heinous crime of killing some Brahmins in his own state and thereby incurred a great curse. Nevertheless, the author held Hasan Khan responsible for his own and his kingdom's tragic end since he sided with the sinner and dishonest.[70] While criticizing Hasan Khan's role in the two battles, the author of the ballad, perhaps, implicitly projects the perceptions of some sections of the Meo community about these battles.

Ahmad Yadgar, in his *Tarikh-i-Salatin-i Afghana*, an account of Lodi and Afghan dynasties, describes the aforementioned events in the following words:

Hasan Khan Mewati was a man of royal descent from several generations and his family had possessed regal power until the reign of Fíroz Sháh. Ráná Sánká, who was at that time a powerful chief, sent a message to Hasan Khán saying, 'The Mughals have entered Hindustan, have slain Sultán Ibráhím and taken possession of the country; it is evident that they will likewise send an army against both of us; if you will side with me, we will be allies, and not suffer them to take possession.' Hasan Khán, carried away by the vanity which the possession of so large a force produced, and by the Ráná's message, did not send the presents which he had prepared for the Sultán, and the King's *vakíl* returned home without accomplishing his purpose. These things came to the King's hearing in Ágra, and Mírzá Hindál and Muhammad Mahdí Khwája, the king's son-in-law, were sent with an immense army, which was shortly afterwards followed by Bábar himself. When Hasan Khán was informed of the approach of the victorious army, he send to tell Ráná Sánká of it. Upon this the Ráná left his home, and assembled an army of Hindús with the intention of making war. He marched and joined Hasan Khán and prepared for action in the plains near Fírozpúr Jharka. Ráná Sánká placed Hasan Khán on right, and took up his own post on the left. As he was secretly displeased with Hasan Khán, he determined to ensnare and ruin him. He, therefore, privately sent a *vakíl* to Mírzá Hindál and Khwája Mahdí, to say that he was the slave and obedient servant of the King, and that he consented to the reading of the *khutba* and the coining of money in His Majesty's name; that Hasan Khán had compelled him to go to war, but that he would not fight the royal troops, but retire early; and that they should make arrangements so that Hasan might be either captured or slain, as in the event of his death they would obtain country of Mewát.[71]

III

The consequences of the battle of Khanwa affected the fortunes of a number of Indian chiefs, though in varying degrees, but the Khanzadas of Mewat were the worst hit. The territory of Mewat which yielded revenue amounting to three to four crore *dam*s was annexed by Babur and this shifted the control of Mewat from the Khanzadas who had enjoyed it for over 175 years to the Mughals. Babur assigned only a few parganas of Mewat to Nahar Khan.[72] A jagir worth 50 lakh *dam*s, including Tijara, was assigned to Chin Timur Sultan, one of Babur's nobles. Amir Tardika, who in the battle with Rana Sanga had commanded *tulughma* (or flanking division) on the right, was given the charge of Alwar fort, along with a jagir worth 15 lakh *dam*s. The treasure of the fort was given to Humayun.[73] Thus, the Khanzadas remained no longer a regional political entity of any great significance, though the Mughal emperors tried to cultivate them by either forging matrimonial relations or co-opting them into the mansab system. For instance, when Humayun regained his lost power in 1555, he tried to consolidate his position vis-à-vis the Khanzadas by marrying the elder daughter of Jamal Khan Mewati, nephew of Hasan Khan; his powerful Turkish noble Bairam Khan married the younger one.[74] In fact, Jamal Khan presented himself before Humayun at Delhi and offered his daughters in marriage.[75] According to *Arzang-i-Tijara*, Akbar married the daughter of Hasan Khan's brother,[76] however, this event is not recorded in the Persian chronicles. However, Akbar did marry Bairam Khan's widow, daughter of Jamal Khan and mother of Abdur Rahim Khan-i-Khana.[77] The mother of Aman-ullah 'Khan Zaman', son and heir of Mahabat Khan Zaman Beg and a noble of Shah Jahan, belonged to the Khanzadas of Mewat.[78]

It appears that Akbar must have paid some attention to Mewat, since a revenue document of his reign dated *rabi-ul-awal*, AH 970 (CE 1592) contains an imperial order for the village-level revenue officials, viz., chaudharis, qanungos and muqaddams of Alwar sarkar to assist certain Khanzadas of the Indore family who had been commissioned to put down an insurrection in that sarkar.[79] Further, the conduct of the Khanzadas must have satisfied Akbar during his military campaigns. Nonetheless, the Khanzada's relations with Akbar can be broadly understood a part of his policy towards nobility, which was aimed at maintaining a balance of power among the different groups of nobles.[80] Abul-Fazl specifically mentions in the *Akbarnama* that Akbar cultivated the Khanzadas of Mewat on account of their military background.[81] Powlett, too, cites an account of Akbar's visit to Alwar on his way to Fatehpur Sikri.[82]

During the reign of Akbar, there were Rajput converts to Islam settled in Mungana, a few miles to the south of Alwar city, and known for their plundering activities. Akbar gave orders to punish them. In the ensuing punitive campaign, many of them were killed and captured, the entire fortress town of Mungana was destroyed, and a new qasba named Akbarpur was founded on the site of the destroyed town.[83] This is corroborated by the non-archival records of the Alwar state, according to which this incident took place in 1578. Akbar received reports that the notorious Meos of Mungana and Binak villages had not paid their land revenue for past several years to the Mughal state, but no official had the courage to go to these villages and forcibly collect revenue. Therefore, Akbar personally led a military campaign against these Meos who fled out of fear to the Aravalli Hills. With the help of a local Brahmin, the Mughal forces found them out, and captured and punished all of them. The two villages were completely destroyed and a new village, Akbarpur, was founded on the site.[84] The Khanzada nobles must have played a supportive role in the Mughal campaign. Whatever may have been Akbar's reasons for their inclusion in the Mughal nobility, but the fact is that one comes across many references to the Khanzadas posted in different capacities by successive Mughal emperors, from Akbar to Muhammad Shah. *Arzang-i-Tijara* tells that Akbar deployed the best talent from the Khanzadas in the service of the empire, and they, too, proved loyal to the emperors.[85]

IV

During Akbar's reign, Mewat became an integral part of the Mughal Empire. It was brought under direct imperial administration and divided into five sarkars—Alwar, Tijara, Sahar, Rewari and Narnol—within the two *subas* of Agra and Delhi.[86] The strategic location of Mewat had manifold advantages for the Mughal state. Firstly, from the economic point of view, its suitability for the cultivation of rich cash crops like indigo and cotton made it an extremely viable source of revenue. Secondly, its proximity to Agra and Delhi facilitated the transport of agricultural commodities to support the urban population. Thirdly, through the region passed a vital trade route that linked western India to Agra and Delhi. That Mewat was a crucial link between the ports of Gujarat and its upcountry hinterland has also been stressed upon by scholars.[87] Hence, any political disturbance in the region would perhaps be reflected in the disruption of trade between Gujarat and Gangetic Doab. Finally, control over Mewat was crucial for the Mughal state, since a hostile power based in Mewat could threaten the safety of Delhi and Agra, the seats of imperial power. These considerations were, to a great extent, responsible for shaping the Mughal policy towards the chiefs of Mewat.

With the absorption of Mewat by the Mughal Empire, the Mewati chiefs lost their political autonomy, as is evident from the fact that no Mughal chronicles made any reference to them. Nevertheless, they continued to hold on to dominant positions in the rural society as zamindars of varying statures. On the other hand, the Meos were accommodated in the lower rungs of the administration as Meoras and *khidmatiyyas* (post-carriers, spies and palace guards). Akbar employed about 1000 Meos as post carriers (*dak* Meoras).[88] The Amber rulers, too, appointed many Meos as messengers or post carriers because of their reputation as good runners.[89] The disintegration of the Mughal Empire in the eighteenth century led to many political changes in the Mewat region. Many parganas of Mewat were taken by the Kachhwaha state of Amber (later known as Jaipur), while all the parganas of Sahar, Alwar and Tijara sarkars were occupied by the emergent Jat state of Bharatpur and Naruka Rajput state of Alwar, respectively.

Here, the question arises is: why the Khanzada chieftains were not cultivated by the Mughals, as the Rajput chieftains were? Akbar had a specific policy towards the Rajput chiefs. Their principalities were not only protected as *watan jagir*, but the chiefs were given autonomy to manage their home affairs. Thus, the Rajput states survived even the decline of Mughal Empire. The Khanzadas, on the other hand, lost their political importance after the battle of Khanwa. Most of Mewat was annexed by Babur and parcelled out among his nobles. Nahar Khan (son of Hasan Khan Mewati) was given a few parganas for the maintenance of his own family, according to the author of 'Hasan Khan Ki Katha'. During the rule of Sher Shah Suri, Mewat remained an administrative unit of the Sur Empire. On the accession of Islam Shah (1545), the parganas of Tijara sarkar were assigned as a jagir to Khawas Khan, Sher Shah's slave and general who established his headquarters at Firozpur Jhirka.[90] During the reign of Islam Shah Sur, a water tank was constructed in Alwar by Chand Qazi, the in-charge of Alwar fort.[91] It appears that at the time of Sur Empire, the position of the Khanzada chiefs of Mewat had become insignificant. However, when Humayun returned to India in 1555, he decided to develop his political relations with the regional chiefs through matrimonial alliances. To quote Abul-Fazl:

When Humayun was at Delhi, he, in order to soothe the minds of the zamindars, entered into matrimonial relations with them. Among these, Jamal Khan, the cousin of Hasan Khan of Mewat, who was one of the great zamindars of India, came and paid homage. He had two beautiful daughters. Humayun himself married the elder sister, and gave the younger in marriage to Bairam Khan. At the time the standards of the Shahinshah [emperor] were directed towards the suppression of Hemu.[92]

According to *Ain-i-Akbari*, Jamal Khan Mewati came from the Khanzada family of Mewat and happened to be a 'great zamindar of Hindustan', by which Abul-Fazl meant the image of Hasan Khan Mewati who had fought against Babur. Therefore, Abul-Fazl states that though the political position of Jamal Khan Mewati may not have been very significant during the reign of Humayun, he belonged to a family that had acquired a great importance in the past.[93] However, it was very clear to Akbar that the Khanzada chiefs of Mewat had lost their erstwhile political power and, if absorbed into his nobility, might not be able to play as important a role as the Rajputs or the Sheikhzadas would. Further, as mentioned before, Mewat, lying on the trade route between Agra and Delhi, was close to these two centres of Mughal power and, therefore, formation of a Khanzada state there could have become a serious threat to the consolidation of the Mughal state. In 1560, when Akbar sacked Bairam Khan from his position, the latter revolted from Mewat; It was the Khanzadas who not only provided him protection, but were sympathetic to his cause.[94] This might have caused Akbar's annoyance at the Khanzadas. Finally, the state formation required a strong material base which the Khanzadas of Mewat lacked. All the aforementioned factors, if present, may have contributed to the formation of the Khanzada state of Mewat.

After the decline of the Mughal Empire, the socio-economic and political position of the Khanzadas also declined drastically. The author of *Arzang-i-Tijara* says that due to fear of the Meos, many Khanzada families migrated eastward and took to trade in the Gangetic cities, while some joined the military service of the Rajput Narukas of Alwar and the British.[95] But the Khanzadas who had been living in the villages of Mewat as *khudkashta* peasants and zamindars were oppressed by the Meos.[96] The Non-archival Records of Alwar State highlight that many Khanzada villages were forcibly evacuated by the Meos. These villages were Gadhola, Alawalpur, Amli Sahabad, Babuhera, Khizarpur, Muradbas, Bharkol, Hasanpur Bara, Dhoj, Shalahera, Kaliabad, Palaria, Hadia, Mohammadabas, Ghatawasan, Kherli Kalan, Ghata, Shamshabad, Pinangwan, Shahebpur, Fakharpur Khohri, Bazidpur, Bagada Pahari, Naharpur, Fatehpur and Bahadurpur, etc.[97] Most of these were occupied by the Dahangal and Baghoria Meo pals.[98] The main reasons for the Meo occupation of the Khanzada-owned lands were high soil fertility and availability of sweet ground water for irrigation. Commenting on the decline in the Khanzadas' power and wealth and speculating on their fate, Fraser writes:

The Khanzadas, some centuries ago, did, beyond doubt, possess extensive property in this district [Gurgaon] and the ruins and tombs in the vicinity of Sohna (also in other places) forcefully attest their past importance. The power of Khanzadas is popularly stated to have waned about three centuries ago, when they were supplanted by the Meos. What has become of them? Have they gradually merged into the conquering class? Have they been destroyed in the struggle for property occurring under weak government.[99]

Powlett, however, reveals their reduced social status in the late nineteenth century: 'There are twenty-six Khanzada villages in the state [Alwar], in most of which the proprietors themselves work in the fields and follow the plough.'[100] Another settlement officer, F.C. Channing, too, mentions:

In Alwar . . . the Khanzadas have fallen from their ancient rank, and now possess but few settlements. I have a suspicion that they are more intimately connected than they acknowledge with the Meos whom they seem to me to resemble in personal appearance. They do not ordinarily intermarry with Meos, but the Meo inhabitants of Ghatwásan, Poul, Nasírbas, Kherli Khurd and Muhammadabas in the Firozpur Tahsíl profess to have been formerly Khanzádas, and to have become Meos by intermarriage.[101]

Thus, as per Channing's testimony, the Khanzadas of these villages apparently merged their social identity with the Meos.[102]

Thus, the Khanzadas who had been absorbed in the land revenue administration and nobility by the Mughal state suffered a sharp decline in their socio-economic status after the decline of the Mughal state. And the Meos, who asserted their social identity more aggressively in the Mewat region, occupied the more fertile lands and the villages of the Khanzadas.

Notes

1. Abul-Fazl, *The Ain-i-Akbari*, vol. 2, tr. H.S. Jarrett, corr. and ann. Sir Jadunath Sarkar, 3rd edn., Calcutta: Royal Asiatic Society of Bengal, 1978, pp. 202–6; these sarkars were Alwar (43 parganas), Tijara (18 parganas), Sahar (7 parganas) and Rewari (2 parganas).
2. Ibid.
3. Ibid.
4. Pratap C. Aggarwal, *Caste, Religion and Power: An Indian Case Study*, New Delhi: SRC, 1971, pp. 24–5. The territory of Mewat has been subdivided into 13 geographical units. Twelve of these are referred to as pals and one as *palkra*. However, in practice, all of them are equal in status. There is no record of when and why Mewat was divided. According to a legend, however, the various pals were demarcated in Akbar's time. The different clans of the Meos often fought with each other over territory. Because of these feuds, it was realized that their collective strength against external adversary was severely affected, and an assembly was convened in which leaders of all the clans participated. After a good deal of deliberation, Mewat was divided into these units.
5. Abul-Fazl, *The Ain-i-Akbari*, vol. 2, pp. 202–6.
6. Sita Ram Lalus, ed., *Rajasthani-Hindi Sangshipt Shabdakosh*, vol. 2, Jodhpur: Rajasthan Oriental Research Institute, 1988, p. 415.
7. Siraj Afif, 'Tarikh-i-Firozshahi', in *History of India as Told by Its Own*

Historians, ed. H.M. Elliot and John Dowson, vol. 3, Delhi: Low Price Publications, 2001, p. 354.

8. O.H.K. Spate, *India and Pakistan: A General and Regional Geography*, London: Metheun, 1957, p. 572.

9. F.C. Channing, *Land Revenue Settlement of the Gurgaon District*, Lahore: Central Jail Press, 1882, pp. 2–5.

10. Ibid., pp. 4–5; Major P.W. Powlett, *Gazetteer of Ulwur*, London: Trübner and Co., 1878, pp. 28–9.

11. Abul-Fazl, *The Ain-i-Akbari*, vol. 2, pp. 76–8.

12. Ibid.

13. Bhagwan Das Morwal, 'Mewati Lok Sahitya Mein Jeevan Darshan', in *Shrijan*, ed. Changa Ram Mina, Alwar: Babu Shobharam Arts Government College, 2005–6, pp. 99–102.

14. Minhaj Siraj, *Tabakat-i-Nasiri*, tr. H.G. Raverty, 1881; repr., New Delhi: Oriental Books Reprint Corp., 1970, p. 864.

15. Babur, referring to the Mewat rulers, admitted, 'the Sultans of Hind, whether from the extent of their territories, from want of opportunity, or from obstacles posed by the mountainous nature of the country, had never subdued Mewat. They had never been able to reduce it to order and obedience as was tendered to them'; see Babur, *Baburnama*, vol. 2, tr. A.S. Beveridge, 1921; repr., Delhi: Low Price Publications, 1995, pp. 368–9.

16. Minhaj Siraj, 'Tabakat-i-Nasiri', in *The History of India as Told by Its Own Historians*, ed. H.M. Elliot and John Dowson, vol. 2, Delhi: Low Price Publications, 1990, pp. 380–3; Ziauddin Barani, 'Tarikh-i-Firoz Shahi', in *The History of India as Told by Its Own Historians*, ed. H.M. Elliot and John Dowson, vol. 3, Delhi: Low Price Publications, 1990, pp. 104–5.

17. Siraj, 'Tabakat-i-Nasiri', ed. Elliot and Dowson, pp. 380–3.

18. Barani, 'Tarikh-i-Firoz Shahi', pp. 104–5.

19. Ibid., p. 380.

20. Ibid., p. 383.

21. A.B.M. Habibullah, *The Foundation of Muslim Rule in India*, Allahabad: Central Book Depot, 1961, pp. 153–4.

22. Siraj, 'Tabakat-i-Nasiri', ed. Elliot and Dowson, pp. 375–6.

23. Barani, 'Tarikh-i-Firozshahi', pp. 104–5.

24. Siraj, *Tabakat-i-Nasiri*, vol. 2, pp. 381–2.

25. Alexander Cunningham, *Report of a Tour in Eastern Rajputana in 1882–83*, vol. XX, Archaeological Survey of India Reports, 1885; repr., Varanasi: Indological Book House, 1969, p. 13.

26. Amir Khusrau, 'Khazaina-i-Futuh and the Kiranu-i-Sadain (The Poem of Amir Khusrau)', in *The History of India as Told by Its Own Historians*,

ed. H.M. Elliot and John Dowson, vol. 3, Delhi: Low Price Publications, 2001, p. 540.

27. Cunningham, *Report of a Tour in Eastern Rajputana*, p. 14.
28. Afif, 'Tarikh-i-Firozshahi', p. 354.
29. Sheikh Muhammad Makhdum, *Arzang-i-Tijara* (in Urdu), Agra: Agra Akhbar, AH 1290/CE 1873, translated to Hindi by Anil Joshi, Alwar, 1989, pp. 3–4.
30. Yahya Bin Ahmad Bin 'Abdullah' Sirhindi, *The Tarikh-i-Mubarakshahi*, tr. H. Beveridge, Delhi: Low Price Publications, 1990, p. 141.
31. The village Malab is situated on the main road between Nuh and Firozpur Jhirka. The water pond and old structure of the mosque is still there.
32. Firozshah Tughlaq, 'Futuhat-i-Firozshahi', in *The History of India as Told by Its Own Historians*, ed. H.M. Elliot and John Dowson, vol. 3, Delhi: Low Price Publications, 2001, pp. 380–1.
33. Ibid., p. 381
34. Cunningham, *Report of a Tour in Eastern Rajputana*, pp. 15–16.
35. Makhdum, *Arzang-i-Tijara*, pp. 15–16.
36. A.M. Husain, *Tughluq Dynasty*, Calcutta: Thacker, Spink & Co., 1963, p. 336. After being given the title of Khanazadar Khanazadun by Firozshah, Bahadur Nahar became a powerful and respectable chief of Mewat. Later, the word 'Khanazad' changed to 'Khanzada'; see Makhdum, *Arzang-i-Tijara*, p. 3.
37. Afif, 'Tarikh-i-Firozshahi', pp. 444–5. Some of the slaves were appointed to high positions by Firozshah. One such slave was Bashir-i-Sultani who was awarded the title of Imad-ul-Mulk. He was appointed the *mufti* of Rapri and, later, the commander-in-chief of the army (*sar-lashkar*). Another slave was made the superintendent of hunting; yet another one was appointed the auditor (*mustaufi*) of Gujarat with the title of Iffikhark-i-Mulk. A slave by the name of Malik Shamsuddin Abu Rija was so favoured by Firozshah that he was able to grab the positions of *wazir*, *naib wazir* and the controller of accounts; see Afif, 'Tarikh-i-Firozshahi', pp. 444–5.
38. Sirhindi, *The Tarikh-i-Mubarakshahi*, pp. 153–4.
39. Ibid., pp. 158–9. Firozshah took interest in buying both foreign and Indian slaves. Among the former, his favourites were those who hailed from Hazara (present-day Pakistan); Afif describes them as mounted on Arab and Turkish horses and bearing standards and axes. It appears that the Firozi slaves of Indian origin called Hindustanis may have created trouble for Muhammad Shah during his struggle with Abu Bakr. Upon becoming the Sultan, Muhammad Shah thus sought to eliminate the dissident Hindustani slaves. The test was thus meant to distinguish them by having them pronounce

the phrase 'Khara Khari Kara Jana'. See Athar Ali, 'Ethnic Character of the Army during the Delhi Sultanate (13th–14th Centuries)', in *Medieval India 2: Essays in Medieval Indian History and Culture*, ed. Shahbuddin Iraqi, Delhi: Manohar, 2008, pp. 165–72.

40. Sirhindi, *The Tarikh-i-Mubarakshahi*, p. 159.
41. Ibid., pp. 159–60.
42. Ibid., p. 168.
43. Timur, 'Malfuzat-i-Timuri', in *The History of India as Told by Its Own Historians*, ed. H.M. Elliot and John Dowson, vol. 3, Delhi: Low Price Publications, 2001, p. 449. When Timur occupied Delhi, he came to know that Bahadur Nahar Khanzada had been held an important position in the court of Delhi. Timur sent two messengers—Alauddin and Naib Karkari—to Bahadur Nahar at Kotla. Nahar courteously replied,
    I am one of the most insignificant servants of the great Amir, and will proceed to his court to wait upon him'. Nahar sent two white parrots to Timur, which could talk well and pleasantly. These two parrots had belonged to Sultan Tughlaq Shah, and they had lived at the courts of the Sultans ever since. Timur writes that the sight of these parrots and the sound of their voices gave him great satisfaction. Bahadur Nahar and his son came to Timur to pay their respects. As Timur writes, 'they brought rare and suitable presents from Hindustan, but I looked upon the two parrots as the best of their gifts. After I had ascertained their sincerity from their words and actions, I honoured them with my royal favour and bounty, and having raised their dignity, I removed all doubt and apprehension from their minds.
44. Sirhindi, *The Tarikh-i-Mubarakshahi*, p. 29.
45. Ibid., p. 19.
46. Ibid., p. 221.
47. The village Lado Sarai was/is situated to the north-east of Mehrauli.
48. Naimutulla, 'Tarikh-i-Khan-Jahan Lodi', in *The History of India as Told by Its Own Historians*, ed. H.M. Elliot and John Dowson, vol. 5, Delhi: Low Price Publications, 1990, pp. 74, 79.
49. Sirhindi, *The Tarikh-i-Mubarakshahi*, p. 251.
50. Naimutulla, 'Tarikh-i-Khan-Jahan Lodi', p. 97.
51. Ibid.; Babur, *Baburnama*, pp. 273–4.
52. Babur, 'Tuzuk-i-Baburi', in *The History of India as Told by Its Own Historians*, ed. H.M. Elliot and John Dowson, vol. 4, Allahabad: Kitab Mahal, 1975, p. 273.
53. Makhdum, *Arzang-i-Tijara*, p. 3.
54. Abul-Fazl, *The Ain-i-Akbari*, vol. 2, pp. 202–6.
55. A tract, varying from a village to an entire province, assigned in the Delhi Sultanate to a noble in lieu of his cash salary was known as his *iqta'*. Under

the *iqta'* system, land itself was not granted but only the revenue from land was assigned in lieu of salaries.

56. Jagga Records, *pothi* no. 1, in the personal possession of Jagdish, son of Shri Ghasi Ram Jagga, village Kuteta Kalan, tehsil Ramgarh, district Alwar, Rajasthan. The Jagga caste maintained the genealogical records of the Meos and Khanzadas since the colonization of the villages by them. These records are divided on the basis of the *gotras* and pals of the Meos.

57. Non-archival Records of Alwar State, Rajasthan State Archives, Bikaner, *Bandhak* no. 4, *granthank* no. 83.

58. Narsingh Meo, 'Hasan Khan ki Katha', *Shodh Patrika*, vol. 4, October–December 1970, pp. 53–62, couplet no. 86.

59. Ibid., couplet no. 114.

60. Makhdum, *Arzang-i-Tijara*, p. 26. A popular local legend attributes the defeat of the Nikumbha Rajputs of Alwar at the hands of the Khanzadas to the practice of human sacrifice by the former. They used to offer men and women of lower castes to Durga Devi, their patron goddess. When a young boy was sacrificed, his mother, a widow *domani* (i.e. a woman of the *dom* caste) sought revenge. She went to Alawal Khan, the Khanzada chief of Kotla, and disclosed to him the way to defeat the Nikumbha Rajputs. She told the Khanzadas that the Rajputs could be attacked suddenly at a time when they worshipped the goddess and had laid down their arms. Accordingly, the Khanzadas attacked the disarmed Nikumbha Rajputs and slayed them. The story, whether true or not, suggests the maltreatment of the lower castes by the Nikumbha Rajputs and their decline as a consequence of provoking their hostility. More importantly, it also suggests that the Khanzadas sought to legitimize their military prowess and rule in Alwar by their 'heroic' act of overthrowing Rajputs who were otherwise noted for their chivalry in the oral traditions and written records. For the legend, see Powlett, *Gazetteer of Ulwur*, p. 155.

61. Powlett, *Gazetteer of Ulwur*, p. 7.

62. Babur, 'Tuzuk-i-Baburi', p. 273.

63. Zain Khan, *Tabaqat-i-Baburi*, tr. S. Hasan Askari, New Delhi: Idarah-i Adabiyat-i Delli, 1982, p. 138.

64. Shaikh Rizqullah Mustaqi, *Waqiat-e-Mustaqi*, tr. and ed. I.H. Siddiqui, Delhi: Northern Book Centre, 1993, p. 116; Khan, *Tabaqat-i-Baburi*, p. 138.

65. Meo, 'Hasan Khan Ki Katha', couplet nos. 15–22.

66. Ibid., couplet nos. 49–50.

67. Ibid., couplet no. 86.

68. Ibid., couplet no. 72.

69. This is also corroborated by Babur who writes, 'I advanced four marches,

and after the fifth encamped six kos from the fort of Alwâr, which was the seat of the government, on the bank of river Manisni. . . . A person named Kermchand, one of Hassan Khan's head men, who had come to visit Hassan Khan's son while he was a prisoner in Agra, now arrived from the son, commissioned to ask a pardon. I sent him back, accompanied by Abdal-i-rahîm Shaghâwel, with letters to quiet his apprehensions, and promising him personal safety; and they returned along with Nâhar Khan, Hassan Khan's son. I again received him into favour, and bestowed on him a Perganna [pargana] of several laks for his support'; see Babur, 'Tuzuk-i-Baburi', pp. 273–4.

70. Meo, 'Hasan Khan Ki Katha', couplet nos. 115–17.

71. Ahmad Yadgar, 'Tarikh-i-Salatin-i-Afghana', in *The History of India as Told by Its Own Historians*, ed. H.M. Elliot and John Dowson, vol. 5, Delhi: Low Price Publications, 1990, p. 36.

72. Babur, 'Tuzuk-i-Baburi', p. 274.

73. Ibid.

74. Abul-Fazl, *The Ain-i-Akbari*, vol. 1, tr. H. Blochmann, 3rd edn., Calcutta: Royal Asiatic Society, 1977, p. 354; Abul-Fazl, *The Akbarnama*, vol. 2, tr. H. Beveridge, repr., New Delhi: Low Price Publications, 1993, p. 76. Jamal Khan Khanzada was a famous zamindar of Mewat; see H. Beveridge, tr., *The Maathir-ul-Umara*, vol. 1, revised, annotated and compiled by Baini Prasad, Patna: Janaki Prakashan, 1979, p. 50.

75. Abul-Fazl, *The Akbarnama*, vol. 2, p. 76.

76. Makhdum, *Arzang-i-Tijara*, p. 13.

77. Beveridge, *The Maathir-ul-Umara*, p. 50.

78. Ibid., p. 212.

79. Powlett, *Gazetteer of Ulwur*, p. 135.

80. Iqtidar Alam Khan, 'The Nobility under Akbar and the Development of His Religious Policy, 1560–1580', *Journal of the Royal Asiatic Society of Great Britain and Ireland*, no. 1/2, 1968, pp. 29–36.

81. Abul-Fazl, *The Akbarnama*, vol. 2, p. 76.

82. Powlett, *Gazetteer of Ulwur*, p. 10.

83. In 1579, Akbar visited Alwar on his way to Fatehpur Sikri. Ibid., p. 11.

84. *Bandhak* no. 13, *granthank* no. 1.

85. Makhdum, *Arzang-i-Tijara*, p. 13. The Khanzadas of Indore were appointed chaudharis in Alwar sarkar. Mohabat Khan and Daulat Khan Khanzadas of Guwalla village were appointed as imperial mansabdars. Khalil Ulugh Khan, Vaki Khan, Wajehdi Khan, Sukrala Khan and Nusaratyar Khan Khanzadas were appointed as fauzdars of Mewat, following each other in succession; see Suraj Bhan Bharadwaj, 'Socio-economic Conditions in the Mewat Region, c. 1650-1750', unpublished PhD thesis, Centre for Historical Studies,

Jawaharlal Nehru University, 1990, p. 199. Firoz Khan Mewati, who was very close to Dara Shukoh, sided with him in the war of succession during the reign of Shahjahan, but was later appointed by Aurangzeb as an imperial mansabdar; see Khafi Khan, 'Muntakhab-ul-Lubab', in *The History of India as Told by Its Own Historians*, ed. H.M. Elliot and John Dowson, vol. 7, Delhi: Low Price Publications, 1999, p. 240. Purdil Khan, son of Firoz Khan Mewati, was also an imperial mansabdar during the reign of Aurangzeb and was sent with other mansabdars to crush the Satnami revolt at Narnaul; see Saqi Mustad Khan, *Maasir-i-Alamgiri*, tr. Jadunath Sarkar, New Delhi: Munshiram Manoharlal, 2nd edn., 1986, pp. 71–2. Khan-i-Zaman Mewati was a learned man and received many titles, such as Kartabah Khan, Ali Askar Khan and Khan Zaman Bahadur, during the reign of Bahadurshah. His father, Sheikh Gulam Mustafi Kartalab Khan, was the bodyguard of Bahadurshah; see Beveridge, *The Maathir-ul-Umara*, vol. 1, p. 808.

86. Abul-Fazl, *The Ain-i-Akbari*, vol. 2, pp. 202–6. The sarkars of Tijara and Narnaul were transferred from the province of Agra to Delhi just before the end of Shahjahan's reign; see Irfan Habib, *The Agrarian System of Mughal India, 1556-1707*, Bombay: Asia Publishing House, 1963, p. 8.

87. Ashin Das Gupta, 'Trade and Politics in 18th Century India', in *Islam and the Trade of Asia: A Colloquium*, ed. D.S. Richards, Pennsylvania: University of Pennsylvania Press, 1970.

88. Abul-Fazl, *The Ain-i-Akbari*, vol. 1, p. 262.

89. *Arzdasht, Chait Sudi* 1, vs 1740/CE 1683, Historical Section, Jaipur Records, Rajasthan State Archives, Bikaner.

90. Khawas Khan revolted against Islam Shah on account of his treachery against his brother Adil Khan, but was defeated in a battle near Agra. Thereafter, he fled to Firozpur Jhirka in Mewat, but Islam Shah sent a powerful force in pursuit of Khawas Khan. A battle was fought between the army of Islam Shah and Khawas Khan at Firozpur Jhirka in which Khawas Khan found it difficult to continue the war and fled to the outskirts of Kumaon hills; see Abdullah, 'Tarikh-i-Daudi', in *The History of India as Told by Its Own Historians*, ed. H.M. Elliot and John Dowson, vol. 4, Allahabad: Kitab Mahal, 1975, pp. 482–4.

91. An inscription on a tank in the Alwar fort states that it was constructed by Chand Kazi (Hakim Killa) at the order of Islam Shah; the construction was completed in AH 958/CE 1550 (*bandhak* no. 6, *granthank* no. 71).

92. Abul-Fazl, *The Akbarnama*, tr. H. Beveridge, vol. 3, repr., New Delhi: Low Price Publications, 1993, p. 76.

93. Abul-Fazl, *The Ain-i-Akbari*, vol. 1, p. 426. Their military fame completely overshadowed the renown of the Sayyids of Amroha of Manikpur, the Khanzadas of Mewat.

94. Ibid., p. 349. When Bairam Khan incurred the displeasure of Emperor Akbar, he left Agra and proceeded towards Alwar. Khan Jahan brought Bairam Khan's insignia from Mewat to Akbar and as he was a near relation of the rebel Bairam Khan, he was detained and left under the charge of Asaf Khan, the commander of Delhi.

95. Makhdum, *Arzang-i-Tijara*, p. 5.

96. *Khudkashta* peasants were those who belonged to upper castes, i.e. Brahmins, Rajputs, and mahajans and other members of the rural aristocracy (patels, patwaris, qanungos and chaudharis). They possessed their own ploughs, bullocks, seeds and other agricultural implements.

97. *Bandhak* no. 3, *granthank* no. 81; *bandhak* no. 4, *granthank* no. 43; *bandhak* no. 5, *granthank* no. 89; *bandhak* no. 12, *granthank* nos. 10, 89; *bandhak* no. 66, *granthank* nos. 3, 7; *bandhak* no. 67, *granthank* nos. 4, 6; *bandhak* no. 68, *granthank* nos. 4, 5; *bandhak* no. 71, *granthank* nos. 6, 7, 12.

98. *Bandhak* no. 3, *granthank* no. 81; Makhdum, *Arzang-i-Tijara*, pp. 22–5.

99. A. Fraser, *Statistical Report of Zillah Gurgaon*, Lahore: n.p., 1846, p. 14.

100. Powlett, *Gazetteer of Ulwur*, p. 40.

101. Channing, *Land Revenue Settlement*, p. 30.

102. For a discussion of intermarriages between Khanzadas and Meos and implications for their sociocultural identities, see Chapter 3 of this volume.

2

Socio-economic Transformation in Mewat

Migration, De-tribalization and Peasantization

INDO-PERSIAN CHRONICLES and Meo oral traditions inform that before the peasantization of the Meos, they settled in the Kala Pahad and other hills of the Aravalli Range, ravines and dense forests in the Mewat region, belonged to various tribal groups and engaged in cattle-lifting, raids and robberies on traders and travellers, thereby becoming a great source of trouble to the people of Delhi and its neighbourhood. On account of their depredatory activities, they were commonly spoken of as 'Meo', the word being derived from 'Mewas' which means a hiding place for the robbers. The Aravalli Hills were thus a home to a number of tribal communities who had to struggle a lot to eke out their living. At the same time, their relative geographical and social isolation enabled them to lead a life of relatively greater degree of social and political freedom. However, from the late fourteenth century, this predatory lifestyle was ruptured by the emergence of the Khanzada chiefdom, which—in order to strengthen its economic base—induced and coerced the Meo tribes to settle down on plains and adopt agriculture as the chief means of subsistence. This process of migration and peasantization effected profound changes in their sociocultural life.

I

Abdul Aziz has identified twelve rural sites on the high hills which were claimed by the Meo *pals* (lineage groups) as the sites of their original settlements. Though all these Meo-claimed sites now stand deserted and ruined,[1] what is more remarkable is a trend of continuity of settlements between the old and the new sites and the current existence of all the twelve settlements in the plains. The abandonment of the original sites in the hills and the subsequent occupation of new sites in the plains by the Meo pals indicate a massive migration of the Meo population from hills to plains. This is attested by the Jagga Records and some Meo oral traditions.

The Jagga Records[2] inform that the ancestors of the Deharwal Meos lived in the Kala Pahad and were known as 'Naths' or snake charmers. Owing to this perceived common ancestry, they considered (and still consider) the Naths as their kin. The ancestral villages of the Deharwal Meos were at Meoli (near Nuh) colonized by Mewa Singh, the head of fifty-two *khorei* (settlements) in the Kala Pahad. The name 'Dehrawal' was derived from Dehar which comprised the low-lying area near the Kotla Lake in the Nuh region. Another Meo group hailing from Shahbad (Tijara *sarkar*) had Sapen (snake charmer) as its *gotra*, identical to that of the Naths.

The folk tradition of the Landawat Meos—also known as Baghoria Meos after Baghore, the ancestral village of their pal—explains the circumstances in which they migrated from the Kala Pahad to the plains near Ramgarh tehsil in Alwar district. In course of their peasantization, they had to face a lot of difficulties in making the plains arable because the whole area was covered by thorny bushes and thick forests.

The Jagga Records also locate the ancestral settlements of five *Jadon-vamshi* Meo pals, viz., Chhiraklot, Pundlot, Daimrot, Duhlot and Nai, in the Kala Pahad region. Their main occupations were cattle-rearing, cattle-lifting, raids and robberies. Folklore also considers these five Meo pals to be brethren or a fraternity (even today these pals prohibit intermarriage on account of their supposed kinship). According to a popular story of the origin of these pals, a local king (possibly a Khanzada chief) upon receiving numerous complaints against the robberies committed by these pals, sent his army to capture the leaders of these five 'rogue' groups. However, all the five escaped from the clutches of the army, in the guise of a juggler, a snake charmer, a drummer, a basket-weaver and a grass-cutter. Subsequently, they settled in the plains and took to farming. The juggler settled in the Lachhmangarh region of Alwar and found a village called Kajhota which later came to be known as the ancestral village of the Daimrot pal. The snake charmer took to agriculture in the vicinity of Alwar and found a village called Neemli which became the ancestral village of the Pundlot pal. The third Meo leader settled near Firozpur Jhirka and established the Chhiraklot pal. The fourth settled in the Ramgarh region of Alwar and became the founder of the Nai pal. The fifth one settled in the region between Nagar (Bharatpur) and Firozpur Jhirka and became the founder of the Duhlot pal.

The Jagga Records indicate the peasantization of Meos between late fourteenth and early sixteenth centuries when the region was ruled by the Khanzadas.[3] During this period, many new Meo villages were established in the plains between Nuh-Firozpur Jhirka and Tijara regions, and were in the vicinity of Kala Pahad. Geographically, the Meo villages fall into three divisions: (a) the area adjoining Kala Pahad comprising of Nuh, Ferozpur Jhirka, Taoru, Punahana, Tijara and Ramgarh; (b) Kishangarh, Lachhmangarh and Rajgarh; and (c) Alwar, Kama, Deeg and Pahari.

That their migration from hills to plains within Mewat continued up to late medieval period is evinced by the dispersal of members of the same pal in different areas. For instance, the Daimrot pal consists of 160 villages, divided into three clusters. Of these, the biggest cluster, consisting of 108 villages, was settled in Lachhmangarh tehsil (Alwar district); the second cluster of 40 villages, in the area between Firozpur Jhirka and Kama (Bharatpur district); and the third cluster of 12 villages, in the area near Punahana (Firozpur Jhirka tehsil of Gurgaon district). All these clusters had their own *chaudharis* (chiefs). The Nai pal, too, underwent a similar process of dispersal. Originally settled between Ramgarh and Alwar, the pal split up into two clusters. The biggest one, consisting of 50 villages, settled to the west of Ramgarh town, while the second cluster of 10 villages settled near Kama town (Bharatpur district). Though belonging to the same pal, they were separated by a distance of about 50 km. and had their own chaudharis. This phenomenon of villages of the same Meo pal settling down in different areas indicates that as the cultivable land might have become insufficient to support the rising population of a pal, some families of that pal migrated to plains in Mewat where they could find land sufficient for settlement and suitable for cultivation. All Meo pals underwent the concurrent processes of emigration, relocation and peasantization. This is also implicit in a major shift in the way the Meos were described in the

Indo-Persian court chronicles. The accounts of Meo raids and robberies in the Indo-Persian chroniclers of the early Sultanate period, such as those of Minhaj Siraj and Barani, are not found in the works of this genre from the late Sultanate period. After the fifteenth century, the Indo-Persian court chronicles, however, mention the non-payment of *kharaj* (land revenue) by the Meos, indicating that they had already become a settled agrarian peasant community by then. Their conflicts with the state on the issue of land revenue further intensified during the Mughal period.

Now the question arises: under what circumstances the Meos were forced to migrate from the Aravalli Hills to the plains, and when and how did they transform themselves from a tribal to peasant community? Going by the early Indo-Persian court chronicles, they might as well have posed a serious law and order problem in the early days of the Delhi Sultanate, threatening the smooth conduct of trade and flow of commercial traffic through the Mewat region. However, a combination of several factors contributed to their peasantization, especially in the post-Tughlaq period. First, the rigorous military campaigns by the Sultans of Delhi against them must have forced them to give up their 'lawless' activities. Second, the increasing Meo population in the Aravalli Hills must have caused a scarcity of resources. The massive clearing of forests in Mewat carried out by Balban must be viewed in terms of the political expediency of the Delhi Sultans to curb the predatory activities of the Meos. Barani reports that immediately after ascending the throne of Delhi, Balban tried to contain the Mewati menace. He 'employed himself in harrying the jungles and routing out the Mewatis'; he 'built a fort at Gopal-gir, and established several posts in the vicinity of the city, which he placed in the charge of Afghans, with assignments of land [for their maintenance]'.[4] Large-scale deforestation drive, construction of forts, appointment of Afghan soldiers and introduction of a system of land assignments for their maintenance—all were accompanied by the attempts to create conditions conducive for the introduction of agriculture in Mewat. The first major initiative in this regard was the conversion of forest land into agricultural land.

However, more than the aforementioned factors, it was the formation of the state of Khanzadas (1390–1527), who had carved out a small principality at Kotla in the vicinity of Tijara in Mewat—a development that socio-economically transformed the Meo population.[5]

The Khanzadas, who were Jadon Rajputs prior to their conversion to Islam, exercised considerable pressure on the Meos to abandon their predatory activities and take up cultivation in order to strengthen the economic base of the state through an assured means of state income from land revenue. The Khanzadas had the plains of Mewat brought under cultivation and seem to have pressurized the tribal communities living in the Aravalli Hills to take up agriculture. Not only is this borne out by the aforementioned folktale of the five pals who were forced to relocate to the plains and take up cultivation, but the Jagga Records, too, reveal that in the early fifteenth century, five pal villages were founded in the parganas of Nuh, Firozpur-Jhirka, Ramgarh (Khilohra) and Lachhmangarh.[6] Significantly, the Tijara region where these five pals had settled was the epicentre of the Khanzada state in its early days. Being under tremendous state pressure to abandon their previous plundering activities, the Meos were hardly left with any alternative except shifting to agriculture. This is evident from one instance of Khanzada ruler Ahmad Khan Mewati sending his soldiers to arrest the Meos of Sonkh village on account of their non-payment of land revenue.[7] The early-sixteenth-century historical ballad 'Hasan Khan ki Katha' mentions 12 Meo pals serving in the army of Hasan Khan Mewati,[8] who had fought against Babur in the battle of Khanwa. This shows that by this time the Meos had not only become peasants but also turned into soldiers.

In the *Ain-i-Akbari*, Abul-Fazl mentions the zamindari rights of the Meos over many parganas of Mewat during Akbar's reign. In Tijara sarkar, out of a total of 18 parganas, the Meos exclusively held zamindari rights over 14 parganas and shared their zamindari rights over another four parganas with other castes like Khanzadas and Thathars.[9] In Alwar sarkar, out of a total of 43 parganas, they exclusively controlled five parganas and shared zamindari rights over another seven parganas with other castes like Khanzadas, Jats and Gujjars. The *Ain-i-Akbari*, however, does not mention the existence of any Meo zamindari in the rest 31 parganas of Alwar sarkar.[10] In Sahar sarkar, they did not have any pargana exclusively under their zamindari, but shared their zamindari rights over four out of seven parganas with other castes like Jats, Thathars and Gujjars.[11] That in the rest three parganas they did not have any zamindari rights at all, shows that the process of peasantization of the Pahat Meos settled there remained slow during Akbar's reign. In Rewari sarkar, the two parganas, namely Taoru and Sohana, were part of Mewat, but had no Meo zamindari during Akbar's reign.[12] Therefore, it may be inferred that the peasantization of Meos in these parganas was not widespread enough to give rise to Meo zamindaris.

From the statistics of Meo zamindaris in Mewat, it may be concluded that the administrative integration of Mewat into the Mughal Empire during Akbar's reign contributed significantly to the process of Meo peasantization. This process continued in the centuries following Akbar's reign and by the second half of the nineteenth century, one comes across a large number of Meo peasant households in the Alwar region. According to the census of 1872, out of the total 1,80,225 households in the Alwar state, the population of Meo peasant households was 94,546, accounting for more than half the population of the region,[13] a stark contrast to the situation during Akbar's reign wherein the Meos did not have zamindaris in 31 out of 43 parganas of Alwar sarkar. Therefore, it may be assumed that the process of Meo peasantization in this sarkar intensified during the period between Akbar's death and mid-nineteenth century. This process was characterized by a prolonged struggle with nature whereby the Meos cleared the dense forests to render land arable and adopted plough technology for cultivation. Similarly, the Pahat Meos had come to occupy larger number of villages than any other caste in the parganas of Pahari, Kama, Nagar and Kho-mujahid of Sahar sarkar by the second half of the nineteenth century.[14] A report of 1840s shows that the Meos held 47 out of 55 villages in pargana Taoru; and 47 out of 169 villages in pargana Sohana.[15] This indicates that the process of Meo peasantization in these parganas had gathered momentum in the period after Akbar's death. The following observation of the report's author and the first British Collector of Gurgaon district, A. Fraser, testifies to the growing reputation of the Meos as a peasant community:

The Meos have been considered to be remarkable for their lawless and thieving propensities; but in these respects they are now less conspicuous than either Rangurs or Goojurs. I have not seen more beautiful cultivation in India than I have observed in Firozepoor, a purgunah exclusively Meo; and their attachment to the soil, a feeling beyond all others strong in India is in this race stronger than in most.[16]

Thus, the first phase of the process of Meo peasantization was more marked in Tijara sarkar, the core area of the Khanzada chiefdom. Later, the Meos settled in Alwar, Sahar and Rewari sarkars. Thus, gradually the Meos were transformed from a tribal to a peasant community, organized through the pal system and other institutions of settled agrarian society. The Jagga caste played an important role in restructuring the Meo identity on the basis of Hindu gotra system which brought about significant changes in their social life. The names of the founders of Meo villages and the years of their establishment are mentioned in the Jagga records. These records indicate that the process of peasantization among the Meos was facilitated by the pre-existing pal system, since tribes belonging to a particular pal tended to occupy particular areas and establish villages there. For example, the ancestral villages, Kajhota and Doha, of the Daimrot and Duhlot pals were founded in 1423. Similarly, Neekach and Neemli, the ancestral villages of the Nai, Chhiraklot and Pundlot pals, were established in 1428 and 1458, respectively. According to the Jagga Records, their gotras[17] were derived from the names of their chiefs who had founded their ancestral villages. For example, the name 'Chhiraklot' of a Meo pal and gotra is derived from that of its chief Chhirakan. Similarly, the Duhlot pal traces its name from that of its chief. Several gotra names, too, originated from the names of various chiefs, such as Duhal from Duhlot, Mangria from Mangraj, Besar from Besar Singh, Matiavat from Matia Singh and Sugdhavat from Sughadh Singh. In Sahar sarkar, the gotra name of the Meos of Sakatpur, Khangavali, Baghola and Meerpur villages is Bahmanavat. According to the Jagga Records, the Meos of these villages were previously Brahmins, who—due to social insecurity—joined the Pahat pal and became part of the Meo community. It is significant that each Meo family has some gotra name or the other, but many of them were not originally part of the pal system. This suggests that the Meo social structure also extended beyond the confines of the pal system.

II

The territory of Mewat has been subdivided into 13 Meo pals: 12 of these are referred to as pals, and one, viz., the Pahat Meo pal, as *palakra*. The word 'palakra' has the same meaning as pal, except that it signifies smallness of size and inferior status. Nevertheless, in practice, all of them are equal in status. When and why the Pahat Meo pal came to be called palakra is not known. There is a popular traditional perception among the Meos that during Akbar's reign when all the Meo pals had distributed land among themselves amicably, the representatives of the Pahat clan arrived late and were therefore contemptuously called palakra, not pal. But it seems that the name owes to certain historical circumstances. The Pahat Meos, located in the Kama-Pahari and Deeg parganas of Mathura-Bharatpur which was part of the Braj region, were culturally different from the other Meo pals. This is indicated by the stories of 'Dariya Khan Meo and Shashi Badani Meeni' and 'Panch Pahad ki Ladai', popular among them. The love story of 'Dariya Khan Meo and Shashi Badani Meeni' centres on the conflict between the Pahat Meos and the Meenas that ensued over Dariya Khan Meo's refusal to eat meat at his Meena bride's house, indicating the differences in the food habits between the two communities.[18] The story 'Panch Pahad ki Ladai' narrates the conflict between the Pahat Meos and Mughal state: it was essentially an agrarian revolt of the Pahat Meos of Kama-Pahari and Deeg parganas and the Jats of the Braj region against the Mughal state during the reign of Shah Jahan (1650). The emperor entrusted Amber Raja and his son Kirat Singh with the responsibility to crush the rebels. Upon their success, both were rewarded by the emperor with a rise in their mansabs. Both Persian and Rajasthani sources reveal that the agrarian revolt of the Pahat Meos was not different in nature from that of the Jats of Braj later during Aurangzeb's reign, while the Rajasthani sources highlight the solidarity between the Pahat Meos and the Jats during these revolts.[19] Therefore, culturally, the Pahat Meos found themselves closer to the Jats than to other Meo pals, and their cultural differences from the other Meos probably led them to forge a distinct social identity that is also confirmed by the Rajasthani sources.[20] Therefore, the Pahat Meos came to be addressed as *palakra* rather than pal by other Meo pals despite the fact that the former possessed a large area under cultivation and enjoyed a favourable socio-economic position in the Mewat region. In this context, it should also be noted that the Pahat Meos have always refuted the allegation that their representatives were late-comers to the Meo pal assembly during Akbar's reign and have maintained that the question of their late appearance at the assembly did not arise because Akbar had given them a respectable position. This is reflected in a popular folk saying:

पचंपहाडकीराजाहिऔरपूरोतेरादल।
आधेअखबरबादशाह, आधेपहाट्टोडरमल॥

'In the kingdom of the five hills, with its force complete, one half belongs to emperor Akbar and the other half to Todar Mal.'[21]

This statement was supposedly made before Akbar by Todar Mal, the zamindar of Pahat Meos, when the former once sent for Todar Mal and demanded to know why he considered himself equal to the Mughal emperor. By this statement, Todar Mal conveyed to Akbar that just as the latter was the emperor of the Mughal state, so was he (Todar Mal) the king (zamindar) of his region; and hence one half of the produce belonged to him and the other half to the emperor. The folklore further has it that Akbar was so pleased with his reply that he gave Todar Mal a jagir with the rank of mansabdar.[22] The folklore perhaps sought to convey the message to other Meo pals that the Pahat Meos were in no way inferior to them and also legitimize the Pahat Meo chief's claim over half of the area's produce in the face of the Mughal attempt to bring the area under their land revenue system. Therefore, it is not likely that the Pahat Meos were called palakra on account of their late arrival for the allotment of land among the Meo pals by the emperor. Rather, their separate cultural identity allowed little interaction with other Meo pals which provoked the latter to coin the disparaging name palakra for them. It may be pointed out that the popular folk tradition of the Pahat Meos arriving late for receiving land from the emperor appears to be the invention of *mirasis* (bards) during the late eighteenth and early nineteenth centuries. It was at this time that the pal polity of the Meos assumed a concrete shape, and the chaudhari or chief of each pal began to glorify his own pal and demonstrate his socio-economic and political power through songs and legends composed by his own bards.[23] It also became the moral duty of the bards to sing songs or narrate legends in praise of their respective pals and chaudharis. It seems that the chaudharis of the Meo pals adopted the Rajput practice of patronizing bardic oral histories of their clans. It may be noted that this tradition of bardic legends and songs started first in the domain of the Pahat Meos due to the influence of the Jats of Bharatpur. This is evident from the fact that the terms used by the bards of the Pahat Meo pal to address their chaudharis, such as *rao*, *raja*, *mal*, *sardar* and *thakur*, were the same as those used to address the eighteenth- and nineteenth-century Jat chiefs of Bharatpur such as Rao Churaman, Rao Badan Singh, Thakur Badan Singh, Raja Mohkam Singh, Raja Surajmal, etc. Thus, folktales of the Pahat Meos, such as 'Panch Pahad ki Ladai'and 'Dariya Khan Meo and Shashi Badani Meeni', are apparently bardic compositions of late eighteenth or early nineteenth centuries. Significantly, the early-sixteenth-century ballad 'Hasan Khan Ki Katha' omits the Pahat Meos from the list of twelve Meo pals whose chaudharis were invited by the Khanzada chief Hasan Khan Mewati to his court before the battle of Khanwa against Babur.[24] This further supports the possibility that the Pahat Meos became part of the pan-Meo community only after the eighteenth century.

The thirteen Meo pals into which most Meos were divided were clustered into four groups, each of which claimed descent from a Rajput clan or caste group and carried its name. The Rajput clans, in turn, belonged to two chief *Puranic* lineages (*vamshas*), viz., *chandravamsha* and *suryavamsha*. One group of five pals, viz., Chhiraklot, Duhlot, Daimrot, Nai and Pundlot, was linked with the Jadon Rajputs, while another group of five, viz., Balot, Dairwal, Kalesa, Landawat and Rajawat, was linked with the Tanwar Rajputs; both the Jadons and the Tanwars were regarded as *chandravamshis*. A third group of two pals—Dingal and Singal—was linked with the Kachhwaha Rajputs and the fourth group, consisting only of the Pahat Meos, with the Chauhan Rajputs; both the Kachhwahas and the Chauhans were regarded as *suryavamshis*.[25] It seems that the Meos forged this new social identity based on their claim to descent from Rajput clans only after their peasantization. Their peasantization, however, did not occur simultaneously but in different periods of time during which they were divided into various groups. In the initial stages, pals were tribal social units each of which had its independent identity, its head being regarded as the chaudhari of the pal. The Jaggas aided in the transformation of their tribal identity into a new prestigious identity by preparing their genealogical records. The state, too, might have contributed to this process. Each pal was located in a fixed territory and the pal system enabled them to develop strong social bonds because they considered their kinsmen as the progeny of a common ancestor.

However, the Meos were not an exception in this regard, as the identity of the Meenas was also transformed through their association with the Rajputs. Eastern Rajasthan, controlled by the Rajputs, was a fertile agricultural zone, large parts of which were cultivated by the Meos and the Meenas. During the pre-Sultanate period, the Badgujars and the Jadon Rajputs (Surasenas) ruled this region which, after the reign of Firozshah Tughlaq and until the reign of Akbar, came under the rule of the Khanzadas. With the Khanzadas being originally Jadon Rajputs, converted to Islam, it is also possible that the Jaggas linked the five Meo pals with the Jadon Rajputs with help of the Khanzada political elite in order to provide legitimacy to or strengthen the social base of the new Khanzada state. This region became part of the *tankhwah jagirs* of the Kachhwahas and other imperial mansabdars in the heyday of the Mughal rule, and witnessed, in the late eighteenth century, the emergence of the state of Alwar under Naruka (Kachhwaha) Rajputs with a substantial Meo population. Again, the Rajputization of the Meos and Meenas, i.e. accounts of their mythical origin from the Rajputs, served to buttress the expansion of the Rajput state.

The myth of Rajput origin and adoption of Hindu gotras helped the Meos construct a new and more prestigious social identity in the Mughal period. This new identity was not restricted to adopting Hindu gotras alone, but also encompassed the observance of Hindu festivals, traditions and rituals, and giving Brahmins an important role in their social and cultural life, particularly in marriage and birth ceremonies. It is to be noted that in pre-colonial times, like the Meos, several tribes in other parts of India which had undergone the process of peasantization, tried to exploit myths of Rajput origin, and embrace Hindu customs and traditions in order to forge new social identities. Among these, some tribes were even able to assume the status of Rajputs by developing state systems though many others failed to do so.[26] It may be observed here that the unsuccessful claims of the Meos to Rajput status was the outcome of their inability to ultimately carve out a state for themselves. Similar is the case of the Meenas who made a transition from tribalism to agriculture but failed to create a state.[27]

It is necessary here to interrogate some significant points raised about the Meo pal system by Shail Mayaram. She argues that the Meo pal polity was traditionally autonomous and hostile to monopolistic sovereignty; favoured decentralization of power; and retained its pristine character without undergoing any change over a long period of time. In her words, 'Contrasted with the imperial [Mughal] system is the Meo Pal, which is the territorial unit of the relatively autonomous self-governing community.' Thus, given this inherently autonomous nature of the Meo palpolity, confrontation with powerful Mughal and Rajput states was inevitable.[28] It would be interesting to examine Mayaram's assumptions in the light of historical developments. Pal can be defined as a social unit characterized by a strong feeling of brotherhood on account of all its members claiming descent from a common ancestor; even though it literally means that only a group of tribes originated from a common ancestor. Like the Meos, the Meenas and Bhils are also divided into pals. In a tribal society, the position of the pal chaudhari was like that of a tribal chief who would consult the important members (*thama*) of his pal before delivering judgments or taking decisions. His main duty was to organize raids with the help of other members of the tribe and protect the tribe from external aggression. The pal system of the Meos underwent unprecedented changes in the wake of their peasantization. As the Meo tribes got transformed into a cultivating class, the power of the pal chaudhari diminished and the nature of his authority changed. Now, the chaudhari could no longer rely on raids to support his family and clan, but rather had to depend on the rains and the loans from moneylenders for raising desirable crops. In the event of non-payment of revenue, the helpless chaudhari could neither protect the defaulting peasants from the lashes of revenue authorities nor himself pay their share of revenue. This diminution in the position and role of the chaudhari also meant a prolonged struggle for survival for the individual peasant. In the event of crop failure or famine, it was no longer possible for the peasant to conduct raids as before; he was forced to abandon his village and take up agricultural work elsewhere as a *pahi*. The Mughal administrative control was relatively stronger in Mewat due to its strategic location between the two centres of Mughal power, Delhi and Agra, and probably acted as a check on Meo depredations. The Persian and Rajasthani records of the Mughal times, too, no longer refer to the Meos as raiders or robbers, indicating that they had, by and large, abandoned their earlier predatory activities. (The description of Meos as 'raiders' or robbers' is found in the earlier writings of Minhaj Siraj and Barani during the Sultanate period, or in the later colonial British records that, in turn, drew upon Siraj and Barani's writings.) However, the Rajasthani sources do describe them as *mufsid* (rebel), a term largely used for the Rajputs (Narukas and Chauhans), frequently for the Jats and the Meos, and generally for all those peasants and zamindars who defaulted in revenue payment or defied state orders. With their transformation into a settled peasant community, not only did their subsistence base and the character of their clan leadership undergo a major change, but their socialcultural life also witnessed a certain degree of 'Hinduization', as discussed before. Nevertheless, they emerged as a dominant community in the region.

Now, in the context of this change in the role of the pal chaudharis with the peasantization of Meos and the integration of Mewat with the Mughal administration, it is pertinent to examine the extent of the role of chaudharis in the pal system in resolving the disputes of Meo peasants during the Mughal period. Did these chaudharis exercise independent decisions like a sovereign in the settlement of mutual conflicts of Meo peasants as has been suggested by Mayaram? The *hasil farohi* (tax on crime) column of the *arsattas* mentions the details of different kinds of disputes and criminal cases over land, crops and women involving the cultivators, including the names, the native villages and the caste status of the accused, as also the penalties in form of fines (in rupees and *takas*) imposed by the *amil* or the *faujdar* in accordance with the nature of offence. For instance, Manna Meo of village Pahari in pargana Pindayan lodged a complaint at the sarkar (*darbar* of the amil) against the misconduct of Tara Meora who had fixed his daughter's engagement with the son of Manna Meo, but married her off to another boy. The case was investigated by the *patel* of the village, and Tara Meora was found guilty and penalized. This kind of problem was considered a serious matter in the Meo society, and communitarian pressure was exerted on the person who broke off an engagement. But the pal chaudhari is not found to have played any role in the settlement of this matter.[29] In another case, Penna Meo of village Nainapur in pargana Harsana lodged a complaint at the office of amil against Govinda Meo, who had ran off with his *lugai* (wife). The probe found Govinda guilty, and the amil imposed upon him a fine of Rs.11. Such cases happened to be common in the Meo community, but, again, one may observe that the chaudhari did not play any role in the conflict resolution.[30] Cases of fights among the Meos and punishments meted out therein, too, have been reported in the *arsattas*. For instance, about twenty-eight cases of clash among the Meos of *pargana* Khohri are reported to have taken place, wherein the amil imposed fine of Rs.28 on the guilty for unlawful activities. No involvement of the pal chaudharis, however, is noticed in these cases.[31]

Stealing of crop, grain or cattle was also a common crime amongst the Meos. If caught or proven guilty, the thief was definitely punished by the state. Such was the case of Jenna Meo of village Mirhu in pargana Pahari who was caught red-handed while stealing grain from the house of a fellow Meo peasant of his own village. An enquiry led to his conviction, and he was arrested and imprisoned by the amil. When the personnel of the amil searched Jenna's house, nothing was found because he had already sold the stolen grain. Therefore, the personnel took away two bullocks found in his house and sold them at the rate of Rs.12.[32] Similarly, Kuka Meo of village Khedali Nai in pargana Mandawar had stolen the share (gram) of his Meena partner. Having proved his crime, the state imposed a penalty of Rs.5 on him.[33] In another case, a Meo peasant of Khoh village in pargana Pahari, had occupied the fields of another peasant adjacent to his own. With the help of the qanungo, the amil got the fields of the land-grabber measured by the patwari, and the seized land was returned to the complainant.[34]

Mayaram's argument that the pal chaudhari played the role of a sovereign chief in settling internal disputes among the Meos of his pal may also be questioned in the light of the flexibility in the marriage norms of the Meos over which the chaudhari had little control during the Mughal period. According to the *gharecha* or *gharijna* custom, a Meo man could marry a woman of any caste, and children born of her would enjoy equal rights to property inheritance. The Shah Chokha cult, popular in Mewat, facilitated this practice. Meo men who desired to marry would gather in the fair of Shah Chokha; and a woman brought home by a Meo as his wife would be taken to the shrine of Shah Chokha for his blessings. The *gharecha* column in the *arsattas* informs us of cases wherein Meo men married women of other castes and paid *hasil gharecha* (tax on re-marriage) to the state. For instance, Bhajru Meo of qasba Jalalpur married Cheta Gujjar's wife and paid *hasil gharecha*.[35] So did Nooro Meo of pargana Mojpur who married Uda Meena's wife,[36] and Dalo Meo of village Bhadpura in pargana Mandawar who married Dayaram Meena's wife.[37] Further, by the same custom, a Meo man, in the event of his younger or elder brother's death, could treat the widow of the deceased as his wife. In Mughal India, the custom was not exclusive to the Meos, but prevalent among some middle castes, such as Jats, Ahirs, Gujjars and Malis, as well. The *arsattas* also refer to the frequent sale and purchase of married women. Several instances can be noticed of women married twice, i.e. a married woman sold off by her husband to another. This shows that in medieval peasant society women were treated as a chattel, their chief function being bearing children and sharing the burden of farming.

On the grounds of similarities in the tribal identity of the Meos and Meenas, the British administrators-cum-ethnographers considered them as belonging to the same 'race'. As a further evidence for this, they cited the folk love story of 'Dariya Khan Meo and Shashi Badani Meeni' to argue that marriage relationships once existed between the two communities but later broke off. According to the story, set in Akbar's reign, Todar Mal Pahat, the zamindar of Ajangarh, and Rao Bada Meena, respectively the fathers of Dariya Khan Meo and Shashi Badani, were close friends and arranged the marriage of their children. However, during the marriage, a clash between the Meos and Meenas took place at the bride's house when the Meenas tried to compel the vegetarian Meos to eat non-vegetarian food. The ensuing estrangement of relationship thus led to a prohibition of intermarriage.[38] But Rajasthani records contain several instances of intermarriage between the Meos and Meenas and thus do not corroborate the inference from this story that marriage relations between the two came to an end following this friction. Therefore, the story proves neither of the two arguments, that the Meos and Meenas once belonged to one 'race' and thus had matrimonial relations, and that these relations were terminated after a single decisive conflict. Apparently, this story was popularized by the region's bards (*mirasis*) because it was associated with two important zamindars and involved a large number of Meos and Meenas. That the Meos and the Meenas did not belong to the same 'racial' stock is also evident from several seventeenth- and eighteenth-century documentary references to *hasil gharecha* paid by the Meos for entering into marriage ties with not only the Meenas but also other castes, such as Jats, Ahirs, Gujjars, Telis and Bhats.

From the foregoing discussion of the Meo peasant society, one can safely argue that the pal chaudharis did not play any significant role in the resolution of disputes pertaining to engagements, marriages and thefts of grain and cattle, at least during the Mughal period. Rather, these conflicts were resolved by the amils on behalf of the state. In other words, in order to solve their disputes and problems, the Meo peasants approached the state instead of their pal chaudharis. At the same time, it is feasible that Akbar obtained the services of the pal chaudharis by accommodating them in the Mughal revenue administration. Therefore, the position of the chaudharis turned out to be more like zamindars, their main responsibility being collection of revenue from the cultivators. After the fall of the Mughal Empire, large parts of

Mewat were absorbed into the Alwar state, while the territory of the Pahat Meos was incorporated into the Bharatpur state of the Jats. In both these states, the burden of land revenue on the Meos was increased to the point of driving them to rebellion. The pal chaudharis reaped the benefits of this contentious situation because after the decline of Mughal state they had not been incorporated into the state structure by the rulers of states in which their territories had been absorbed. Hence, the pal chaudharis began to organize their own pal communities and, possibly, might have attained the sovereign position in the post-eighteenth-century period.

Yet another important and related argument of Mayaram is that the Meos were perpetually and uncompromisingly against the state, whether Mughal or Rajput. This argument ignores multiple forms of negotiations and interactions between the Meo peasants and the state. Resistance, defiance and rebellion constituted only one of these forms, the other important form being supplication before the dominant power to get concessions and relief. Petitioning was thus an important 'weapon of the weak' in the hands of the Meo peasants.[39] This will be discussed in detail in Chapters 4 and 5 of this volume.

As observed before, the Meo pal polity and Meo autonomy were non-existent during the Mughal period. This is because the land revenue and jagirdari systems of the Mughals transformed each village of Mewat into an administrative-cum-revenue-paying unit and placed all of them under larger units, viz., parganas. In tying the peasant society with such units, the Mughal state hardly conceded any space for their autonomy. Further, even after the decline of the Mughals, the Meos could not establish their independent state because in a large portion of Mewat (Alwar sarkar with 43 parganas), the Naruka Rajputs had established their zamindaris leading to the foundation of the Alwar state (1784). The Jats, too, set up their zamindaris in the parganas Kama Pahari and Khohri, this leading to the formation of the Bharatpur state. Therefore, in such circumstances, the Meos got sandwiched in the power struggle among various competing groups of Rajputs and Jats and could not establish their own state.

III

The terms *raiyati* or *asami* were synonymous and covered all categories of cultivators paying land revenue to the state.[40] There have been major studies on various regions of medieval India;[41] of these, a few are on agrarian economy and rural society of medieval eastern Rajasthan,[42] of which Mewat was a part. The medieval records indicate that the peasantry of Mewat was economically differentiated and socially stratified.[43] The position of a peasant was determined by his economic strength (size of landholding and income), social status (rank in rural caste hierarchy) and official position in the land revenue administration. The peasants belonging to upper castes, i.e. Brahmins, Rajputs, mahajans and other members of the rural aristocracy (patels, patwaris, qanungos and chaudharis), were designated as *khudkashta* peasants.[44] In Mewat, the *khudkashta* peasants were also called *gharuhallas*, i.e. those who possessed their own ploughs, bullocks, seeds and other agricultural implements;[45] and *riyayatis*, i.e. peasants who had their personal holdings assessed on concessional rates. They had to pay land revenue to the Mughal state at the rate of 25–33 per cent of their gross produce.[46]

The size of the landholdings of a *khudkashta* determined whether he required hired labour or not.[47] Those *khudkashtas* who held one plough or two bullocks used to cultivate their fields with the help of family labour, supplemented by hired labour at the time of harvesting or sowing.[48] But the owners of large family holdings depended on regular hired labour. They also leased out their livestock and equipment that yielded substantial additional income. For example, in pargana Chalkaliyana, Begraj and Narwar of Kakrauli Mota village and Lakhman of Phogat Dhani village held 21½, 8½ and 4 ploughs in their possession, respectively.[49] This implies that they possessed landholdings that could not be cultivated with the help of family labour alone. On the other hand, 10 Brahmin *asamis* of Dhareru village in same pargana held two ploughs each, and used to cultivate their fields with the help of family labour, resorting to hired labour at the time of harvesting and sowing.[50] Similarly, 12 Bania *asamis* of Sanwar village and 10 Brahmin *asamis* of Kadma village in pargana Chalkaliyana held one plough each, and always used family labour in cultivation.[51] However, regardless of whether the labour was familial or hired, an essential aspect of the region's agriculture was that the responsibility of providing agricultural implements rested with the *khudkashta* peasants.

The *khudkashta* peasants were expected by the state to improve and extend cultivation in view of their superior land rights and relatively better economic conditions. The position of a *khudkashta* in the rural society was determined by his official status in the rural administration and the number of ploughs at his disposal. If he had an official status of patwari, qanungo and chaudhari, he always enjoyed an advantageous position in terms of the payment of land revenue and other cesses, in comparison to the other *khudkashta* peasants belonging to higher castes.[52] He had to pay nominal land revenue on his personal holdings and was exempted from the payment of *malba* (common financial pool of the village) and other cesses.[53] Other *khudkashtas* who merely had a high-caste status had to pay their land revenue and other cesses at customary rates.[54] Thus, land could be held by different kinds of *khudkashtas* on different terms and conditions. However, both the *riyayati* and non-*riyayati* sections of the *khudkashta* peasantry were characterized by: (a) the ownership of land that they cultivated; and (b) the use of personal ploughs, bullocks, seeds and other implements. In normal conditions, the *khudkashta* peasants could not expand their landholding at the cost of *raiyati* peasants. For instance, in 1716 Jat Chaudhary had cultivated the common land of qasba Pahari. The matter was taken up by the amil who took control of the standing crop on that land and had it harvested by the hired labourers, thereby producing 60 maunds of grain.[55] However, in times of drought, there were many incidents of the lands of *palti* peasants being occupied by the *khudkashtas*. For instance, the Meo peasants of six villages in pargana Khohri complained to the diwan of Amber that during drought they had left their villages in search of livelihood, but upon their return found their lands occupied by the high-caste Rajputs.[56] This suggests that the state was not able to prevent the *khudkashta* peasants from expanding their landholdings at the cost of small peasants. In fact, whenever some peasants abandoned their fields and villages due to the high-handedness of the jagirdars or ijaradars, the *khudkashtas* tended to convert the abandoned land into their *gharujot* (personal holding). Nevertheless, the amils used to issue injunctions from time to time to the *khudkashtas* against occupying the lands of those *palti* peasants who had abandoned them.[57] Such restrictions on the expansion of the *khudkashta* landholdings seem to have been motivated by the fear that it would result in the loss of revenue.

The second category of peasants was known as *gaveti* or *palti* who formed the single largest stratum, as also the majority, of the peasantry and bore almost the entire burden of revenue. Irrespective of their residential status and ownership of land, they were not termed as *khudkashta*. Most of them belonged to the intermediate or middle castes, viz., Jats, Meos, Gujjars, Ahirs, Meenas and Malis.[58] They were non-privileged members of the peasant community and were inferior in social status to the *khudkashta/riyayati* peasants.[59] They had to pay land revenue at the rate of 40–50 per cent of their gross produce— much higher than that charged from the *khudkashtas*—as well as several other cesses.[60] Majority of the *paltis* had to depend on *taqavi* (agricultural loan) advanced by the mahajans and zamindars. In many Rajasthani documents, they are found borrowing money from the mahajans to purchase seeds, ploughs, bullocks, etc.[61] In 1729, peasants belonging to an unspecified village of pargana Pahari took loan from the *mahajans*, but, as they could not return the amount on time, the entire agricultural produce of the village was seized by the amil to recover the loaned amount.[62] At the same time, in 1730, the peasants belonging to 18 villages of pargana Mandawar returned the loan amount well before time.[63] The mahajans used to extend loans to the *paltis* at high rates of interest.[64] For instance, the peasants belonging to a village of pargana Pahari borrowed money of Rs.1,221 from the mahajan to purchase seeds and bullocks. At the harvest time, they returned the principal with interest amounting to Rs.235.12*an.*[65] The mahajans used to extend loan to the needy *paltis* only when either the amil or the zamindar of the village submitted his undertaking promising repayment by the *paltis*. There are some instances of Meo peasants belonging to the villages of pargana Khohri being denied loan by the mahajans due to the absence of any undertaking in their favour from the amil.[66] In the years of drought or famine, the economic conditions of the *paltis* became more miserable, and sometimes, unable to bear the situation, they had to leave their villages and migrate elsewhere. It is borne out by the evidence that a large number of *paltis* became extremely impoverished due to the cumulative effect of natural and man-made calamities.

The third category of peasants was known as pahi. These were mainly depressed peasants who wandered from village to village and pargana to pargana in search of better livelihood opportunities. They usually cultivated the arable wastelands or the lands abandoned by the *paltis* in the neighbouring villages without becoming the residents of these villages or the proprietors of lands they cultivated. They tilled such lands as tenants and had no right to sell or mortgage them. They could keep the lands under their tillage as long as they wished, on the condition of paying land revenue regularly. In normal conditions, such pahis were required to pay land revenue at customary rates.[67] It is evident from the *dastur-ul-amals* that in depopulated or newly settled villages, the pahis paid their land revenue at lower rates than did the *paltis*.[68] The pahis were granted *patta* (lease agreement) for the cultivation of *banjar* (virgin land); the *patta* fixed the land revenue demand at a concessional rate of 33 per cent of the gross produce, this concession being extended for 2–3 years.[69] Those pahis who had their own ploughs and bullocks could bargain with the amil or other land revenue officials and get favourable terms and conditions for cultivation.[70] Those who came from other parganas and far-off villages were known as pahi *gaharla pargana*.[71] Such pahis were essentially migratory cultivators who were permitted to settle with their families and construct their *chhappars* (hutments) in the village.[72] They had their own ploughs and bullocks.[73] As a rule, they were offered attractive terms and conditions on the consideration that they had to leave their native villages. In due course of time, such pahis became the permanent residents of the villages they had settled in, and acquired the status of *palti*, thereby becoming an integral part of the village community.[74] For instance, three pahis named Masto, Shauma and Harkishan who had come from pargana Narnol and settled in Sanwar village of pargana Chalkaliyana acquired the status of *palti*.[75] Similarly, Ram Singh of Biran village, Bhimo Jat of Pali village, Talo of Bhatol village, and Dala and Shivebla of Basaiyra village of the parganas Tosham, Kanore, Hansi and Damra, respectively, had elevated their status from pahi to *palti* in Sanwar village.[76] Six pahi peasants who had come from different parganas acquired the status of *palti* in Dhareru village of pargana Chalkaliyana. Manbhar and Prama from Saamar village of pargana Rohtak also raised their status from pahi to *palti* in Ramsingh pura of pargana Chalkaliyana.[77] Twelve Jat peasants who had come from Shekhawati in pargana Churu (Rajasthan) acquired the status of *palti* in Mithathal village of pargana Chalkaliyana.[78] It appears from the Rajasthani documents that the percentage of pahis in the rural community varied across villages and parganas. For instance, in pargana Pindayan, the pahi peasants constituted 19.7 per cent of the peasant community.[79] In Uchhari village of pargana Pindayan, out of a total of 29 ploughs, 11 belonged to the pahis, whereas in Gharatwari, Kapaho, Toda Khurd and Jai Singhpura villages of the same pargana, the presence of pahi is not attested.[80]

In Mewat, the percentage of pahis increased from late seventeenth to early eighteenth centuries, a period during which massive agrarian disturbances were taking place. This is evident from an *arzdasht* wherein the amil of the Amber state wrote to his *raja* (chief) that only 14 out of 204 villages in pargana Pahari were settled before the pargana was included in Amber's *tankhwah jagir*, but now 100 more villages were colonized with the help of Ahir pahis.[81] Similar conditions prevailed in pargana Khohri where attempts were made to resettle a large number of villages deserted in the wake of agrarian disturbances caused by the Jats and Meos. The amil's concern for the rehabilitation of such deserted villages is borne out by the Rajasthani documents wherein he repeatedly mentions his efforts to rehabilitate deserted villages with the help of pahi peasants. For instance, in 1664, 32 deserted villages of pargana Khohri were rehabilitated by the pahi caste peasants.[82]

Finally, at the bottom of the hierarchy were the *kamins* or low-caste landless agricultural workers who sold their labour for wages. This vast body of landless rural poor fulfilled the labour requirements of the entire landowning peasantry. Their labour was not much in demand throughout the year, but increased hugely at the time of sowing and harvesting. They were prevented from acquiring any land for full-time cultivation by the dominant landholding castes who needed their labour round the year, particularly in the peak season. This was perhaps the basic reason for not allowing them to own land even when favourable conditions of land-man ratio existed. Here, it is significant to note that the Mughal state aimed 'to generate larger revenues from the village and lower the wage cost in the cities',[83] without disturbing the pre-existing caste inequities.

Nevertheless, the *kamins* were indispensable for agricultural production and even for normal functioning of the rural society, as they provided perennial cheap labour to the privileged section of the rural society, i.e. *khudkashtas/gharuhallas*, as also part-time or seasonal labour to others at the crucial time of sowing and harvesting.[84] In return, they received a fixed share of the produce in accordance with the customary practices. Thus, low-caste *chamars* (leather-workers) and *dhanuks* (weavers), while pursuing their traditional hereditary occupations, also worked as *halis* (ploughmen) on the lands owned by the high-caste peasants. In many cases, the *chamars*, along with the other artisanal castes, even had ploughs and bullocks. For instance, four *chamar asamis* had one plough each in Bamla, Kadma and Bijana villages of pargana Chalkaliyana, respectively.[85] In Bhahu, Golari and Mohammadpur villages of the same pargana, *chamars* possessed half-a-plough each.[86] Though the *chamars* appeared as cultivators in a few cases, in majority of cases they were landless labourers working for the *khudkashta* peasants.

The unequal distribution of resources among these different categories of peasants, the ability of the socio-economically dominant sections to accumulate reserve capital and the pattern of its investment had a far-reaching impact on the degree of peasant stratification. The pre-existing inequalities in the rural society became aggravated with the passage of time, tilting the balance of social and economic power in favour of the richer sections despite the abundance of land.

Notes

1. Abdul Aziz, 'Measurement of Agricultural Productivity, A Case Study of Mewat', unpublished PhD thesis, North-Eastern Hill University, Shillong, 1981, pp. 10–34.

2. Jagga Records, *pothi* no. 1, in personal possession of Jagdish, son of Shri Ghasi Ram Jagga, village Khuteta Kalan, tehsil Ramgarh, district Alwar, Rajasthan.

3. Ibid.

4. Ziauddin Barani, 'Tarikh-i-Firoz Shahi', in *The History of India as Told by Its Own Historians*, ed. H.M. Elliot and John Dowson, vol. 3, New Delhi: Low Price Publications, 2001, pp. 103–4.

5. See Chapter 1 in this volume.

6. This region was situated in the vicinity of Kala Pahad.

7. *Bandhak* no. 12, *granthak* no.13, Non-archival Records of Alwar State, Rajasthan State Archives, Bikaner.

8. Narsingh Meo, 'Hasan Khan Ki Katha', *Shodh Patrika*, vol. 4, October–December 1970, pp. 53–62.

9. Abul-Fazl, *The Ain-i-Akbari*, vol. 2, tr. H. Blochmann, corr. and ann. Sir Jadunath Sarkar, 3rd edn., Calcutta: Royal Asiatic Society, 1978, pp. 203–4.

10. Ibid., pp. 202–3.

11. Ibid., p. 206.

12. Ibid., p. 298.

13. P.W. Powlett, *Gazetteer of Ulwur*, London: Trübner and Co., 1878, p. 37.

14. Alexander Cunningham, *Report of a Tour in Eastern Rajputana in 1882–83*, vol. XX, Archaeological Survey of India Reports, 1885; repr., Varanasi: Indological Book House, 1969, p. 24.

15. A. Fraser, *Statistical Report of Zillah Gurgaon*, Lahore: n.p., 1846, Appendix-C, p. xxi; Appendix-P, p. cxxi.

16. Ibid., p. 15.

17. According to the Jagga Records, the Meos are divided into about 80 gotras, while the British settlement reports mention 52 gotras; see Fraser, *Statistical Report*, pp. 29–30; and Powlett, *Gazetteer of Ulwur*, pp.37–8.

18. Cunningham, *Report of a Tour in Eastern Rajputana in 1882–83*, pp. 3–4.

19. S. Nurul Hasan, 'Further Light on Zamindars under the Mughals: A Case Study of (Mirza) Raja Jai Singh under Shahjahan', *Proceedings of the Indian History Congress*, 39th session, Hyderabad, 1978, pp. 497–502; A.R. Fuller, tr., *The Shah Jahan Nama of 'Inayat Khan*, edited and compiled by W.E. Begley and Z.A. Desai, New Delhi: Oxford University Press, 1990, pp. 448–9; H. Beveridge, tr., *The Maathir-ul-Umara*, vol. 1, revised, annotated and compiled by Baini Prasad, Patna: Janaki Prakashan, 1979, p. 813; *Arzdasht, Sawan Sudi* 6, vs 1750/CE 1693; *Asad Vadi* 15, vs 1766/CE 1709; *Kartik Vadi* 4, vs 1766/CE 1709; *Chithi* to the amil, pargana Pahari, vs 1784/CE 1727; vs 1781/CE 1724; *Arsatta, pargana* Pahari, vs 1788/CE 1731; Suraj Bhan Bhardwaj, 'Socio-economic Conditions in the Mewat Region, AD 1650–1750', unpublished PhD thesis, Centre for Historical Studies, Jawaharlal Nehru University, Delhi, 1990, pp. 245–54.

20. *Arzdasht, Mah Vadi* 9, vs 1774/CE 1717; *Chithi* to the amil, pargana Pahari, vs 1784/CE 1727.

21. This Todar Mal was the chief of the Pahat Meos and should not be confused with Raja Todar Mal, Akbar's revenue minister; see Cunningham, *Report of a Tour in Eastern Rajputana in 1882–83*, p. 26.

22. Ibid., pp. 25–6.

23. Each pal had its own group of bards whose task was to prepare the oral history of the pal in the form of legends. Most of these legends happen to glorify and attribute several acts of valour to one or the other pal. A bard's success depended on how evocatively he managed to sing or narrate the legends and how large an audience he managed to move; he, in turn, received gifts from the pal chaudharis. For example, in 1882, when Mirab Khan (chaudhari of the Garwal Meos) died at Reoli village near Firozpur-Jhirka, the bard was rewarded with one camel and one gold *mohur*, besides clothing and other items, by the sons of the late chaudhari for his narration of the legend at the funeral feast on the 40th day after the chaudhari's death.

24. Meo, 'Hasan Khan Ki Katha'.

25. A large number of Meos were not associated with any pal, they were/are just called *nepalia* (without pal); see Cunnningham, *Report of a Tour in Eastern Rajputana in 1882–83*, pp. 23–4.

26. Surajit Sinha, 'State Formation and Rajput Myth in Tribal Central India', *Man in India*, vol. 42, no. 1, 1962, pp. 35–80.

27. S.H.M. Rizvi, *Mina: The Ruling Tribe of Rajasthan: Socio-Biological Appraisal*, New Delhi: B.R. Publishing Corporation, 1987; Saraswat Rawat, *Mina Ithihas* (Hindi), Jaipur: Jhunthlal Nandala, vs 2025; Nandini Sinha, 'Reconstructing Identity and Situating Themselves in History: A Preliminary Note on the Meenas of Jaipur Locality', *Indian Historical Review*, vol. 27, no. 1, 2000, pp. 29–43.

28. Shail Mayaram, *Against History, Against State: Counterperspectives from the Margins*, New Delhi: Permanent Black, 2004, p. 120.

29. *Arsatta*, pargana Pindayan, vs 1777/CE 1720.

30. *Arsatta*, pargana Harsana, vs 1787/CE 1730.

31. *Arsatta*, pargana Khohri, vs 1773/CE 1716.

32. *Arsatta*, pargana Pahari, vs1788/CE 1731.

33. *Arsatta*, pargana Mundawar, vs 1787/CE 1730.

34. *Arsatta*, pargana Pahari, vs 1807/CE 1747.

35. *Arsatta*, pargana Jalalpur, vs 1784/CE 1732.

36. *Arsatta*, pargana Mojpur, vs 1789/CE 1732.

37. *Arsatta*, pargana Mundawar, vs 1781/CE 1724.

38. Powlett, *Gazetteer of Ulwur*, p. 38; Channing, *Land Revenue Settlement of the Gurgaon District*, p. 29; D. Ibbetson, *Panjab Castes: Being a Reprint of the Chapter on 'The Races, Castes and Tribes of the People' in the Report on the Census of the Panjab Published in 1883*, Lahore: Superintendent, Government Printing, 1916, p. 179; Cunningham, *Report of a Tour in Eastern Rajputana in 1882–83*, p. 27.

39. James C. Scott, *Weapons of the Weak: Everyday Forms of Peasant Resistance*, New Delhi: Oxford University Press, 1990.

40. *Yaddashati Hal Bail*, pargana Chalkaliyana, vs 1722/CE 1665; pargana Kotla, vs 1723/CE 1666; pargana Pindayan, vs 1783/CE 1726; *Arsatta*, pargana Atela Bhabra, vs 1785/CE 1728; *Dastur-al-amal*, pargana Khohri, vs 1723/CE 1666.

41. A.R. Kulkarni, 'The Indian Village with Special Reference to Medieval Deccan (Maratha Country): General Presidential Address', *Proceedings of the Indian History Congress*, 52nd session, New Delhi, 1992, pp. 1–62; Indu Banga, *Agrarian System of the Sikhs: Late Eighteenth and Early Nineteenth Century*, New Delhi: Manohar, 1978; H. Fukuzawa, *The Medieval Deccan: Peasants, Social Systems and States, Sixteenth to Eighteenth Centuries*, New Delhi: Oxford University Press, 1991; Chetan Singh, *Region and Empire: Panjab in the Seventeenth Century*, New Delhi: Oxford University Press, 1991.

42. Satish Chandra, *Medieval India: Society, the Jagirdari Crisis and the Village*, New Delhi: Macmillan, 1982; S.P. Gupta, *The Agrarian System of Eastern*

Rajasthan (c.1650–1750), New Delhi: Manohar, 1986; Dilbagh Singh, *The State, Landlords and Peasants: Rajasthan in the 18th Century*, New Delhi: Manohar, 1990.

43. *Dastur-al-amal*, pargana Khohri, vs 1723/ce 1666; *Arsatta*, pargana Piragpur, vs 1789/ce 1732; pargana Mojpur, vs 1771/ce 1714.

44. *Arsatta*, pargana Mojpur, vs 1771/ce 1714; pargana Piragpur, vs 1789/ce 1732.

45. *Yaddashti Hal Bail*, pargana Kotla, vs 1723/ce 1766; pargana Pindayan, vs 1783/ce 1726; pargana Chalkaliyana, vs 1722/ce 1665.

46. *Dastur-al-amal*, pargana Atela Bhabra, vs 1767/ce 1710; pargana Mojpur, vs 1770/ce 1713; pargana Khohri, vs 1723/ce 1666.

47. *Yaddashti Hal Bail*, pargana Chalkaliyana, vs 1722/ce 1665.

48. Ibid.

49. Ibid.

50. Ibid.

51. Ibid.

52. *Dastur-al-amal*, pargana Piragpur, vs 1789/ce 1732; pargana Mojpur, vs 1770/ce 1713; pargana Khohri, vs 1723/ce 1666.

53. *Chithi* to the amil, pargana Piragpur, *Bhadva Sudi* 2, vs 1800/ce 1743.

54. *Dastur-al-amal*, pargana Khohri, vs 1723/ce 1666; pargana Mojpur, vs 1770/ce 1713.

55. *Arsatta*, pargana Pahari, vs 1773/ce 1716.

56. *Chithi* to the amil, pargana Khohri, vs 1784/ce 1727.

57. *Chithi* to the amil, pargana Pahari, *Fagun Vadi* 10, vs 1784/ce 1727; pargana Piragpur, *Posh Vadi* 1, vs 1791/ce 1734; *Kartik Vadi* 4, vs 1782/ce 1725; *Chait Sudi* 6, vs 1793/ce 1736.

58. See *hasil farohi* section in the *arsattas*.

59. *Dastur-al-amal*, pargana Piragpur, vs 1789/ce 1732; pargana Mojpur, vs 1770/ce 1713.

60. *Dastur-al-amal*, pargana Khohri, ah 1049/ce 1642–3; pargana Mojpur, vs 1770/ce 1713; pargana Shonkhar-Shonkhari, vs 1773/ce 1716.

61. *Arsatta*, pargana Pahari, vs 1788/ce 1731; *Arzdasht*, *Bhadva Sudi* 6, vs 1741/ce 1684.

62. *Arsatta*, pargana Pahari, vs 1786/ce 1729.

63. *Arsatta*, pargana Mandawar, vs 1787/ce 1730.

64. *Arsatta*, pargana Pahari, vs 1786/ce 1729; pargana Khohri, vs 1773/ce 1716.

65. *Arsatta*, pargana Pahari, vs 1786/ce 1729.

66. *Chithi* to the amil, pargana Khohri, *Mah Vadi* 5, vs 1784/ce 1727.

67. Dilbagh Singh, 'Caste and Structure of Village Society in Eastern Rajasthan during the Eighteenth Century', *Indian History Review*, vol. 2, 1976, pp. 299–311.

68. *Chithi* to the amil, pargana Khohri, *Asad Vadi* 9, vs 1781/CE 1724; *Asad Vadi* 11, vs 1781/CE 1724.

69. Singh, 'Caste and Structure of the Village Society'.

70. *Arzdasht*, pargana Pahari, *Bhadva Sudi* 6, vs 1741/CE 1684. On account of their possession of ploughs and bullocks, the Ahir *pahi* peasants were given concessions in the payment of land revenue on the lands they cultivated in pargana Pahari.

71. *Dastur-al-amal*, pargana Khohri, vs 1723/CE 1666.

72. *Arsatta*, pargana Pahari, vs 1791/CE 1734; *Arzdasht*, pargana Pahari, *Bhadva Sudi* 6, vs 1741/CE 1684.

73. *Yaddashti Hal Bail*, pargana Chalkaliyana, vs 1722/CE 1665; pargana Pindayan, vs 1783/CE 1726.

74. *Arsatta*, pargana Pahari, vs 1790/CE 1733; *Yaddashti Hal Bail*, pargana Chalkaliyana, vs 1722/CE 1665.

75. *Yaddashti Hal Bail*, pargana Chalkaliyana, vs 1722/CE 1665.

76. Ibid.

77. Ibid.

78. Ibid.

79. *Yaddashti Hal bail*, pargana Pindayan, vs 1783/CE 1726.

80. Ibid.

81. *Arzdasht, Fagun Sudi* 12, vs 1746/CE 1689.

82. *Arshatta*, pargana Khohri, vs 1721/CE 1664.

83. Irfan Habib, 'Caste System in Indian History', in *Essays in Indian History: Towards a Marxist Perception*, London: Anthem Press, 2002, pp. 172–3.

84. Irfan Habib, *The Agrarian System of Mughal India, 1550–1707*, 2nd revd edn., New Delhi: Oxford University Press, 1999, pp. 123–60.

85. *Yaddashti Hal Bail*, pargana Chalkaliyana, vs 1722/CE 1665.

86. Ibid.

3

Islamization in Mewat

A Case of Acculturation and Syncretism

THE SPREAD OF Islam in India has been a contentious site of history-writing and politico-ideological polemics. Historians have grappled with the question of how and why Islam came to be accepted by vast sections of people during the precolonial period, offering explanations ranging from the coercive role and political patronage of state to the influence of Sufism and the appeal of egalitarianism in Islam. The question has also been linked to broader issues such as the nature of medieval state, the so-called 'religious policy' of rulers, the political alliances and conflicts between states, and processes such as agrarianization, peasantization and acculturation. Furthermore, the question has been complicated by debates on the varying degrees of fixity and fluidity of precolonial religious identities among various social strata and communities in different regions and periods. Clearly, scholarly studies, notwithstanding disagreements, have shown that the phenomenon was anything but monocausal and uniform throughout the subcontinent. On the other hand, the complexity of the issue in the public discourse has often been reduced to simplistic, decontextualized and generalized explanations for the spread of Islam such as mass conversions driven by inherent proselytizing zeal of Islam and effected by physical force, threats or material inducements. Such explanations forwarded and popularized from time to time by organizations, groups or persons, whether motivated by divisive political agendas or majoritarian biases or both, have had serious and adverse implications for inter-communal relations and political culture in a multireligious nation-state founded on the constitutional principle of secularism. These reductive explanations for Islamization, often projecting Islam as a 'religion of the sword' and medieval period as one of 'Muslim tyranny', have achieved a certain currency in recent times and thus have posed a renewed and serious challenge to historians and their academic approach to the issue.

In the backdrop of this fraught debate on the spread of Islam in academic and public discourse, the chapter discusses the process of Islamization in medieval Mewat and its linkages to political and socio-economic developments, and explores the issue of the formation and articulation of Meo Islamic identity. It demonstrates that not only was the process gradual and phased, but also that it involved far more acculturation than formal conversion, and that the religio-cultural identity thus created was far from being fixed and monolithic. Rather, when articulated it presents a case of syncretism of non-Islamic and Islamic beliefs and practices. Further, the agents of this process were both the ruling elite and common people, and several factors generally cited for the spread of Islam such as coercion, political patronage and liberal, egalitarian spirit of Islam do not seem to have played a major role in this region.

I

Richard M. Eaton, in his seminal study on Islamization in West Punjab (present-day Pakistan) and East Bengal (present-day Bangladesh),[1] considers Islamic conversion a subject of serious research. According to him, the debate on conversion among historians is generally based on three theories that focus on Islam as a religion of sword, of political patronage and of social liberation. The first theory is the ground for communal history-writing and political propaganda; the argument based on it is that medieval Muslim rulers, driven by religious fanaticism and proselytizing zeal, forced Hindus to convert to Islam through the use or threat of force. Conversion by coercion thus made Islam a religion of sword. Underlying this theory are a set of historically untenable assumptions about precolonial India. Some of these are: 'Islamic' state was a well established entity and an agent of conversion in all areas where Islamization occurred; most, if not all, medieval Muslim rulers were uniformly zealous Muslims bent on proselytizing non-Muslim subjects as a matter of policy; and the 'converts' had a uniformly monolithic self-conscious Hindu identity in contradistinction to a monolithic self-conscious Muslim identity. While none of these assumptions is supported by historical evidence, historians who dispassionately study the issue of Islamization and reject the theory of conversion by sword incur the risk of being accused—indeed have been accused—of sympathy for Muslim rulers and bias against their 'Hindu' subject population.

As far as the case of Islamization of Meos is concerned, evidence for the proselytizing role of state is virtually absent. Some colonial ethnographers such as F.C. Channing and Alexander Cunningham argued that the Meos adopted Islam due to the cruelties inflicted by Sultan Balban.[2] However, during Balban's reign, the Meos had neither become peasants nor formed a distinct community. Moreover, even Indo-Persian chroniclers of the time such as Barani and Minhaj Siraj do not state that Balban forcibly converted Meos to Islam. Others argued that the Islamization of Meos took place exactly during the period when Akbar carried out the territorial division of Meo *pals* (lineage groups). However, this view, too, lacks credibility because Akbar's religious policy was not discriminatory but inclusive. Yet others pointed out that the conversion of Meos to Islam occurred during the reign of Aurangzeb as a result of his bigoted religious policy that was prejudiced against non-Muslims.[3] There is no historical evidence to support this view either. Mewat was close to Delhi and Agra, and its resident Meo community historically had a conflictual relation with the Delhi Sultans and, to some extent, the Mughal emperors. Therefore, it may be argued that it would have been possible, even easy, for the Sultans and Mughal emperors to convert them by force while suppressing them. However, a *khatoot ahalkaran* of CE 1684 records a complaint made by the Meo peasants against the levy of *jizyah* and other non-customary taxes at the Mughal court. This suggests that even as late as Aurangzeb's reign the Muslim identity of Meos had not taken shape. Further, the *hasil farohi* columns of *arsattas* maintained by the amil's office in Alwar state contain detailed records of those who had been convicted of various crimes, including their names, as well as their castes, names of their native villages and the nature of their crimes and punishment, but telltale Islamic names cannot be found among the names of Meos.

The second theory of Islamization is that Muslim rulers extended political patronage to 'Hindu' officials by way of promises of material rewards or higher positions in order to induce them to accept Islam either individually or with their families. Political patronage by Muslim rulers could have facilitated the conversion of an individual, family or a group, as it indeed did for some families in Delhi and Agra. Even then, it did not play a significant role in religious conversion and upward socio-political mobility as evinced by the presence of a sizeable proportion of non-Muslim sections in the ruling elite of states under Muslim rulers. Further, the theory does not explain the mass conversion or Islamization as in the case of West Punjab and East Bengal. Even in the case of Meos who were inducted in the lower echelons of the imperial Mughal administration from Akbar's reign and gradually adopted Islamic customs, political patronage was not a direct operative factor in their Islamization, as will be discussed in section III of this chapter.

According to the third theory, Hinduism sanctions a rigid, hierarchical, Brahmanical social organization, viz., the caste system, while Islam is based—at least in principle—on the ideas of social equality and fraternity, and hence attracted the Hindu lower castes, discriminated against and oppressed by upper castes, especially the Brahmins. As a 'religion of social liberation', Islam, thus, offered the lower castes respite from caste inequities and served the cause of conversion. However, historical evidence shows that Islamization occurred in areas where Brahmanical caste system was rather weak such as West Punjab and East Bengal, pointing, again, to the limitations of this theory. This theory also does not explain the Islamization of Meos for various reasons. First, Meos were dominant in the rural society of Mewat and far from being oppressed by the Brahmanical caste system. Meos were socially organized into pals or tribal lineages of more or less equal status, each headed by a *chaudhari* (chief), though later they, like the caste Hindus, also came to be divided into *gotras*. They observed several Hindu cultural practices and had Brahmins officiating at almost all their rituals, including wedding, digging of a *pucca* well, birth of a son, etc. By the early twentieth century, they were found to be celebrating Hindu festivals such as Holi, Diwali and Dussehra, though at the same time they had acquired an Islamic social identity. An instance of this interesting paradox is a practice recorded in 1920.[4] In a Meo village near Khuteta Kalan in Alwar district, on the occasion of Diwali a Meo *lambardar* would put a silver coin in a basket, sit on a *mora* outside his home and had it announced by the beating of *munadi* (drum) in his and neighbouring villages that any Hindu who wished to have a *darshan* (glimpse) of a silver coin but did not have one could come to him (having a glimpse of and worshipping with a silver coin on Diwali was—and is—considered auspicious by Hindus in north India, since the act was thought to make Lakshmi, the goddess of wealth, reside in the house and increase its wealth and prosperity). As long as the *lambardar* lived, he continued the practice year after year, welcoming people from many villages to see the coin (silver coin was a mark of great wealth possessed by a few in the rural society). This instance shows that Meos, even while being perceived as Muslim in the early twentieth century, observed Hindu practices and were far from being victims of caste oppression. Thus, neither the might of Islam as a 'religion of sword', nor its appeal as a source of political patronage, nor a force of social liberation can adequately explain the diffusion of Islamic culture in Mewat.

II

The Khanzadas were the first Muslim ruling group to play an important role in the social, cultural and economic history of the region. The social history of the Khanzadas begins during the later part of the reign of Firozshah Tughlaq (r. 1351–88). After the death of the Firozshah Tughlaq, the Khanzadas formed their chiefdom in the vicinity of Tijara and emerged as a ruling class in the region. In the early days of their rule, Indori, Kotla and Tijara used to be their capitals; later, they extended their territory up to the Alwar town which became their capital. The local tradition of the Khanzadas testifies to their claim over a vast territory in the Mewat region, i.e. 1,484 *kheras* (towns and villages) under their jurisdiction in the early sixteenth century.[5]

There are disparate and late accounts of their origin, all pointing to their non-Islamic ancestry. Alexander Cunningham's late-nineteenth-century report on his tours in eastern Rajasthan offers an account of their descent from Jadon Rajputs who ruled over Bayana and Thangir before the invasions of Muhammad Ghori. In the fourteenth century, Lakhanpal, a Jadon Rajput, was the chief of a small tract of Mewat around Tijara. Lakhanpal's two sons, Sambharpal and Somparpal, embraced Islam in order to save their domains from annexation by Sultan Firozshah Tughlaq. The former took the name of Bahadur Nahar and gained control over Sarehta situated four miles to the east of Tijara, while the latter took the name of Chhaju Khan, and got possession of Jhirka and renamed it Firozpur Jhirka.[6] An early-eighteenth-century

Urdu work, *Arzang-i-Tijara* gives two reasons for the conversion of Bahadur Nahar: the first was his deep faith in the Sufi saint Hazrat Nasiruddin Chirag-Delhvi; and the second was his and his brother's arrest and imprisonment in Delhi by Firozshah's troops for his predatory activities in the neighbourhood of Delhi that posed a serious law and order problem for the sultanate of Delhi.[7] A. Fraser in his mid-nineteenth-century report on Gurgaon district recounts stories tracing the ancestry of the Khanzadas differently: '[One account] represent[s] them as being descended from the Jadoon [Jadon] Rajputs . . . [another] account . . . represents the Khanzadas as descended from a Dhanuk (low caste) named Beejbul converted to Mahomedanism as before with the title of Khan, and hence Khanzadas'.[8] The *Arzang-i-Tijara* adds that during marriages they paid their respect to and worshipped Bejal, their ancestor.[9] It appears that one Bejal or Bejbul would have been the ancestor of some Khanzada families who might have embraced Islam during the reign of Firozshah Tughlaq. Thus, all these accounts, evidently drawn from local traditions about the Khanzadas, point to their conversion to Islam not earlier than fourteenth century, whether due to political pressures or not. Whatever and however disparate may have been their actual origins, the Khanzadas had forged their social identity as the local Muslim elite of Mewat by the end of the sixteenth century, as testified by their zamindari rights in many parganas of the region.[10]

According to Abul-Fazl's sixteenth-century chronicle, *Ain-i-Akbari*, the Khanzadas were divided in two social categories. One comprised of the Khanzadas of Mewat, chieftains from Bahadur Nahar to Hasan Khan who were descendants of Jadon Rajputs and converts to Islam. The other were former slaves of Firozshah Tughlaq.[11] The second category constituted mainly of the former Firozi slaves.[12] The title 'Khanazad' or 'Khanazadun' was given to those Firozi slaves who happened to be close and loyal to the Sultan.[13] As discussed in Chapter 1 of this volume, according to *Tarikh-i-Mubarak Shahi*, after Firozshah Tughlaq's death, a large number of former Firozi slaves, who opposed the new Sultan Muhammad Shah, were forced to leave Delhi and sought refuge with Bahadur Nahar, the Khanzada chief of Mewat, in his fortress at Kotla. These Firozi slaves, with their vast knowledge and experience in land revenue and military administration, were absorbed in the administrative structure of the infant Khanzada chiefdom and, in turn, must have played an important role in its consolidation. The key politico-administrative role of the Firozi slaves in the Khanzada chiefdom is attested by a traditional account of their ceremonial role of putting *tilak* (an auspicious mark) on the forehead of every new Khanzada chief—a role also performed by the Jats in Bikaner and the Meenas in Amber for the chiefs of these states.[14] Though a ceremonial practice, it reminded them that the state acknowledged their cooperation and contribution in state formation and administrative functioning. Significantly, the title 'Khanzada' was conferred on Bahadur Nahar by Firozshah after he had embraced Islam and been enrolled into the Sultanate nobility[15]—a title shared by the Firozi slaves as well. Hence, the fact that a section of the Firozi slaves were integrated into the Khanzada polity and shared the same title as their political patrons would have led to both constituting a composite ruling elite of the region known as Khanzadas. Not only did the Mewati ruling elite and the former Firozi slaves whom it inducted into its ranks share a common sociopolitical identity, but they also shared the religious identity of being Muslims, thereby giving impetus to Islamization in the region.[16] The Khanzadas were the first Muslim ruling elite to not only induce the Meo tribes to give up their predatory lifestyle, relocate from hills to plains and take up agriculture,[17] but also introduce Islamic culture in Mewat. Thus, processes of peasantization and Islamization ran parallel during this period. One of the agents of Islamization was the building of mosques by the Khanzadas in the region. The archaeological survey of the region by Alexander Cunningham shows that they had constructed many mosques in the towns and villages of the region. For instance, Bahadur Nahar built a fine stone mosque at Kotla in 1399 during the reign of Muhammad Shah;[18] Hasan Khan Mewati, at Tijara in the early sixteenth century;[19] and Jalal Khan Khanzada at Indori.[20] Similarly, mosques were constructed in other towns like Shahbad, Bhindusi, Nimali, Sarheta, Mandha, Masit Palah, Jewano, Sohna, Bhondsi, Pinangwan and Malab during the early sixteenth century.[21] The Non-archival Records of the Alwar State, too, mention that forty-one mosques were constructed by the Khanzadas in the villages and towns of Alwar *sarkar*.[22] The large number of mosques also reflects the size of the Muslim population in the region.

Another important agent of diffusing Islamic culture in Mewat region were the *qazis* appointed by the Khanzadas to maintain the Islamic law (*Sharia*) among the Muslim population and settle local disputes (criminal and civil) between the Muslims (Khanzadas) and the non-Muslims (mainly the Meos). The Islamic laws, during the period of the Khanzada rule, must have also influenced the social life of the Meos who came from a tribal background. But the Meos, while being profoundly affected by Islamization, did not give up their pre- or non-Islamic practices and lived with an ambiguous religious identity that they retained well into the twentieth century. This is corroborated by Powlett who writes:

The Meos are now all Musalmans in name; but their village deities . . . are the same as those of Hindú Zamíndars. They keep, too, several Hindu festivals. Thus the Holí is with Meos a season of rough play, and is considered as important a festival as the *Muharram, Id,* and *Shabíbarát;* and they likewise observe the *Janam ashtmí, Dasehra* and *Diwálí.* They often keep Brahmin priests to write the *pílí chithí,* or note fixing the date of marriage.[23]

Cunningham adds that the Meos worshipped Sayyid Salar Masud with great respect, and the banner of Salar Masud was held in every Meo village at *Shab-i-barat.*[24]

Yet another impetus to Islamization would have been the matrimonial relations that the Khanzadas established with the Meos (as also with the Meenas) in order to strengthen their social base.[25] In the process, the Meos and Khanzadas would respectively have adopted Islamic and Hindu customs from each other, especially in the area of marriage which shows an array of Hindu rites around the core Islamic nuptial ceremony of *nikah.* Thus, the Khanzadas, despite being agents of Islamization, also did not assume a rigid Islamic identity. On the socio-religious position of the Khanzadas, Powlett writes:

[I]n social rank they are far above the Meos, and though probably of more recent Hindú extraction, they are better Musalmáns. They observe no Hindú festivals, and will not acknowledge that they pay any respect to Hindu shrines. But Brahmins take part in their marriage contracts, and they observe some Hindu marriage ceremonies. Though generally as poor and ignorant as the Meos, they, unlike the latter, say their prayers, and do not let their women work in the fields.[26]

In particular, this interesting blend of Hindu and Islamic customs in the Khanzada wedding rituals is vividly described in *Arzang-i-Tijara.* A Brahmin priest writes a *chithi* (note) fixing the date of a Khanzada girl's wedding after performing a customary puja, and ties as many knots of a red *naal* (thread) around the note as are the numbers in the date. Then, he, accompanied by a member of Muslim bardic caste (*mirasi*), carries the note to the groom's house. The groom's family keeps the note and sends them back with gifts. Three days before the wedding, the groom is smeared with a paste of turmeric, lemon and mustard oil, the note is opened and read by a Brahmin before everyone, and the groom is then carried back inside the house. On the day of wedding, the groom, wearing bangles in henna-decorated hands and red robes, goes to the bride's house on horseback in a procession (*baraat*). After the departure of the procession, rituals are performed for three days at the groom's house. As part of these rituals, *negs* (customary gifts) are given by the groom's father to married women, and members of various occupational castes such as *mirasi* (minstrel), *chamar* (leather-worker), *kumhaar* (potter), *khaati* (carpenter), *lohar* (blacksmith), *sakka* (water-carrier), *dhobi* (launderer) and *maniaar* (bangle-seller). In the meantime, the groom upon reaching the bride's house is welcomed on the doorstep by women singing songs and *aarti*. The groom then asks for the bride's hand in marriage seven times in lieu of a bride price. Thereafter, the *nikah* or wedding takes place with Islamic rituals.[27] Thus, on the one hand, conversion to Islam under the aegis of Delhi Sultans; involvement in the politics and exposure to the political culture of Delhi Sultanate; and sociopolitical assimilation of Firozi slaves—all led the Khanzadas to adopt and project their Islamic identity, as also spread Islamic culture in the region. On the other hand, matrimonial relations with local communities such as Meos and Meenas in their bid to expand their social base made them receptive to Hindu rites and customs without giving up their Islamic identity. Meos, too, would have undergone acculturation to Islam, though there is no clear documentary evidence of Meos assuming Islamic identity before the eighteenth century. Nevertheless, the religious identities of both would have remained fluid and far from being fixed and frozen, and thus made the growth of a syncretic culture in the region a corollary to Islamization.

III

The sociocultural life of Meos was profoundly affected by the twin process of peasantization and Islamization initiated by the Khanzadas in the late fourteenth century. Even after the end of Khanzada chiefdom,[28] these processes not just continued but accelerated from the sixteenth to eighteenth century under the aegis of the Mughal state which brought Mewat under its politico-administrative control after the decline of Khanzada chiefdom. From the late sixteenth century—although the Khanzadas had been integrated into the administrative machinery of the Mughal state since early sixteenth century—one section of Meos joined the Mughal administrative service as well and, due to their regular interaction with the Mughal state, began to adopt Islamic practices and way of life. However, one account in the medieval text *Waqiat-e-Mustaqi*[29] points to the employment of Meos in the pre-Mughal period. In this account from the reign of Sikandar Lodi, a horse stolen from the royal stable was recovered after three days from a Meo thief caught near Dholpur. The Sultan restrained his *wazir* Khan-i-Khana Nohani from awarding him death sentence on the ground that such a sentence would be un-Islamic, since the thief should have been put to death when he was committing the crime or when the stolen horse was recovered from him. The Sultan, instead, ordered him to be thrown in the prison. After seven years, when a list of prisoners to be pardoned was prepared, his name was included. The Sultan offered him freedom on the condition of embracing Islam. He said that conversion would have been relevant to him even a week after his capture, but not so after seven years of captivity; nevertheless he would still accept it for the sake of his life. When released after accepting Islam, he pleaded before the Sultan that he had nowhere to go, since he had forgotten the art of thievery and would be shunned by his family and relatives for converting to Islam. When asked about his skills, he offered to become a *khidmatiyya* (palace guard) and assured him of preventing any theft or, if one was committed, of finding and apprehending the culprit. After a few days, when cloth traders in the *bazaar* of Agra reported the theft of clothes from their shops, the Sultan summoned him and asked him to find the thief. He asked for all *khidmatiyyas* to be assembled (majority of Lodi *maliks* or *iqtadars* kept Meo *khidmatiyyas*). When about 400–500 *khidmatiyyas* were assembled, he detected some thieves from among them and managed to recover the stolen clothes, thereby earning the praise of Sultan. The story suggests that before Akbar's reign, Meos were in the service of Lodis as *khidmatiyyas*, and were known for thievery, a remnant of their predatory past; and that they had not converted to Islam in any significant number. Even if their induction in the administration can be considered to have begun in the pre-Mughal period, it was Akbar who attempted to accommodate them in the imperial service on a much larger scale.

In the *Ain-i-Akbari*, the Meos are broadly divided into two categories: (a) the agriculturists (peasants and primary zamindars), and (b) the Meoras and *khidmatiyyas* (post-carriers, spies and palace guards). During the Mughal period, it was the Meoras and the *khidmatiyyas* who played an important role in the diffusion of Islamic culture among the Meos of Mewat. The Persian and Rajasthani sources reveal that they were an integral part of Mughal postal and espionage system until the decline of the empire. About them, Abul-Fazl writes,

They are the native of the Mewat and are famous as runners. They bring from great distances with zeal anything that may be required. They are excellent spies, and well perform the most intricate duties. They are likewise always ready to carry out orders. The caste which they belonged to was notorious for highway robbery and theft; former rulers were not able to keep them in check. The effective orders of His Majesty have led them to honesty; they are now famous for their trustworthiness.[30]

Muhammad Arif Qandhari, the author of *Tarikh-i-Akbari*, adds,

Emperor Akbar employed four thousand foot-runners (Dak-carriers). They are experts in espionage also; they are on his majesty's service day and night so that news and reports reach everyday from all sides of the world. This class of men run as fast as lion, so that within ten days news comes from Bengal which is at a distance of seven hundred *kurohs* (*kos*) from Agra. His majesty gets all information of good or bad and profit or loss.[31]

Irfan Habib, in his analysis of the organization of Mughal postal communication system, has pointed out that it was not possible for a single *Meora* who could have run at a speed of 70 *kurohs*, about 158 mi., a day and night to reach his destination. Therefore, it must imply a relay system.[32] Indicating the existence of a relay system, Qandhari also states that Akbar established *dak chowkis* (postal stations) at every 5 *kurohs* (about 11 mi.), and at each *chowki* two horses were kept besides the Meora foot-runners.[33] It thus appears that Akbar enrolled strongly built young Meos into the Mughal postal system who could run fast and survive in hostile weather and terrain. In doing so, Akbar not only developed the postal system as an important institutional mechanism for ensuring the security and consolidation of the Mughal Empire, but also successfully transformed the Meo youth into loyal and faithful servants of the Mughal state. The following incident serves as an evidence of this new relationship that Akbar established with the Meos. In 1567, when Akbar came to know that Ali Quli Khan and his brother Bahadur Khan—nobles of the Turani faction of Mughal nobility—had rebelled, he organized a military campaign against them. Upon reaching Manikpur, he sent Hatwa Meora to find out the exact position of the rebels. According to Abul-Fazl, Hatwa Meora, a swift and intelligent courier, brought the much-needed news within 24 hours that the rebel nobles had constructed a bridge over Ganga near Singraur (modern Nawabganj) and crossed the river. When Akbar heard about this development, he immediately proceeded to take action against them. Abul-Fazl further adds that Hatwa Meora was loyal to Akbar and always accompanied him.[34] Channing, too, mentions that Akbar trusted the Meoras so much that he kept them as his bodyguards.[35]

Abul-Fazl observes that Akbar also posted Meo infantrymen, also called *khidmatiyyas*, outside the palace to watch, guard and see to it that his orders were carried out.[36] It seems that Akbar had understood the problems created by the isolation of the Meos who had been disparaged as trouble-makers in the earlier centuries. He thus not only administratively and politically integrated the Mewat region into Mughal state, but also brought about the social assimilation of the Meos. Once Akbar had developed the Mughal postal service with the help of the Meoras, the other Mughal emperors followed the same policy. For instance, chronicler Khafi Khan also points out that the Meoras were mainly *dak*-carriers during Aurangzeb's reign.[37]

Habib argues that the postal system was essential for a large centralized territorial entity like the Mughal Empire because news and orders had to be conveyed over great distances. The organization was essentially based on the twin methods of relay-runners and relay horses which were posted at various *dak chowkis* that had been set up along different routes throughout the empire. In one part of Gujarat alone, 94 Meoras were posted at the *chowkis* along the route from Khandap (Ajmer *suba*) to Ahmedabad and from there to Baroda and Broach. At least two Meoras were posted at each *chowki* because they had to be available round the clock. The Meoras were required to give a written undertaking that they would not carry along with the (official) *nalwas*, personal papers of individuals.[38] According to B.L. Bhadani, 164 *dak* Meoras were posted along the Agra-Ahmedabad route, of these 77 were stationed at the *chowkis*.[39] This shows that almost half of the Meoras remained on duty round the clock at the *chowkis* and presumably the remaining half always stood in reserve.

Dastur komwar, a set of documents pertaining to the Jaipur state, lists the names of more than 200 Meoras posted at *dak chowkis* on the routes from Delhi to Jaipur and from Jaipur to Agra.[40] Many of them were rewarded for their good services by the Amber state. For instance, Lalchand Meora and his son were known for their services as spies in the Mughal court during the reign of Aurangzeb.[41] Similarly, Khoja Avad Khan Meora was also rewarded with a jagir of three villages in pargana Jalalpur (Alwar sarkar) for his service by Aurangzeb.[42] Tara Meora and Ram Singh Meora were also rewarded with one village each in pargana Pahari and Bharkol on account of their services.[43]

The *Ain-i-Akbari* mentions that the monthly salaries of the *dak* Meoras ranged from 100 to 120 *dams* (Rs.2½–3) during the reign of Akbar.[44] An early eighteenth-century *dastur komwar* also informs us that generally the *dak* Meoras were paid monthly salaries ranging from Rs.2 to Rs.4.[45] However, it appears from the Rajasthani documents that the *dak* Meoras were not paid equally; some got perquisites for delivering politically crucial communication. For instance, in 1714, Bhoja and Madho Meoras were paid Rs.22 by the diwan of Amber for bringing a letter of Chhabela Ram from Allahabad.[46] Sunder and Chetan Meoras were paid Rs.14 for bringing a letter of Ruhla Khan (an imperial mansabdar) which assigned the ijara of the villages of pargana Chatsu to the Amber Raja.[47] Similarly, Hari Ram Meora and his ally—who brought a letter of an imperial mansabdar communicating that the zamindari rights of four parganas, viz., Averi, Bahatri, Niwai and Fagi were assigned to the Amber Raja—were paid extra money by the diwan of Amber.[48] Apart from monthly salary and perquisites for extraordinary services, the *dak* Meoras were also given concessions in the payment of land revenue on their personal land holdings by the Mughal state. The amils were asked to implement the state orders for such concessions after receiving them attested by the qazis.[49] Bhoja and Laad Khan Meoras, for instance, were respectively assigned 10 and 14 *bighas* of revenue-free lands (*muwafik bighas*) in pargana Bharkol

(Tijara sarkar).[50] But it is not clear whether the *dak* Meoras got revenue-free land in lieu of their salaries or as a reward. However, upon their retirement from the service of the Mughal state, such concessions were automatically terminated.[51]

The *dak* Meoras, like other Meos, came from the tribal background and their religious identity was in a state of flux. They found employment in the Mughal postal service socially and economically beneficial. From the economic point of view, they obtained a secure source of income by way of monthly salaries and other perquisites. Besides, they were also given concessions in the payment of land revenue on their personal land holdings. Socially, they now constituted a class superior to the ordinary Meo peasants. Therefore, whoever once got a job in the Mughal postal service, always tried to induct his family members into it.[52] It seems that the *dak* Meoras had always enjoyed an advantageous position in the Mughal state in terms of creating job opportunities for their sons and relatives. This is how they must have transmitted their professional knowledge and experience in the field of postal service and their loyalty and faithfulness to the Mughal state to the succeeding generations. British ethnographers, too, had observed this spirit of fidelity among the Meos towards their masters.[53]

Due to their regular interaction with the Mughal court as well as other imperial authorities, the *dak* Meoras found themselves closer to the Islamic culture and gradually began to follow certain Islamic customs and rituals associated with the Mughal court. The nature of the Islamic festivals and rituals was such that they involved a congregation of a large number of people. These festivals were Id-ul-fitr, Ramzan, Shab-i-barat, and the Urs of Sufi saint Khwaja Muin-ud-din Chishti with a large number of people, including palace staff and the emperor's bodyguards, all taking part in the celebrations.[54] In particular, the Urs of Muin-ud-din Chishti, celebrated in the Mughal court since the days of Akbar, witnessed the participation of a large number of people from all classes like nobles, officers, *khidmatiyyas*, bodyguards and the *dak* Meoras. They walked 228 mi. from Agra to the tomb of Khwaja Saheb in Ajmer passing through the Mewat region. They carried the holy flag of the saint and a large number of people paid their respects to the flag on their way to Ajmer.[55] The *dak* Meoras and *khidmatiyyas* reverently observed these festivals, and after retirement started celebrating these festivals in their own villages.[56] They even invited their relatives and friends to take part in these festivals. They started inviting qazis to perform *nikah* for their children and contracting marriages with Muslim peasants. Thus, in more ways than one, they started regarding themselves as part of the Muslim community. The *khatoot ahalkarans* also underline the role of qazi appointed by the Mughal state to resolve the disputes of the people. Devidas Harkara (a spy) complained to the diwan of Amber that the qazi did not attend his own duties; rather he visited the villages to perform *nikahs*. Devidas further stated that although the qazi got a salary of Rs.240 from the Mughal state, he was very greedy; and that he should have concentrated on his job. Finally, he pleaded with the diwan to speak to the *vakil* so that he could raise the issue at the Mughal court.[57]

As discussed in Chapter 1 of this volume, after the battle of Khanwa, the Khanzadas lost their principality; Mewat became part of the Mughal state while the Khanzadas became part of the Mughal nobility. However, with the decline of the Mughal Empire, the socio-economic position of the Khanzadas also declined. Muhammad Makhdum, the author of *Arzang-i-Tijara*, states that they migrated eastwards, i.e. to the adjoining states like Awadh, Lucknow and Bareilly, while some joined the military service of the Rajput Narukas of Alwar and the British.[58] The Khanzadas left in Mewat cultivated fields as *khudkashta* peasants with the help of family labour, although they had never touched the plough before.[59] Many Khanzadas were also displaced from their villages by some Meo pals who coveted the Khanzada-owned lands for their high soil fertility and sweet ground water for irrigation.[60] The social security of the Khanzadas was thus threatened by the rising power of the Meos, the Jats of Bharatpur state and the Naruka Rajputs of Alwar state in Mewat. In order to strengthen their social base, some Khanzadas began to enter into matrimonial relations with the former *dak* Meoras who had acquired a Muslim identity by then. *Arzang-i-Tijara* also adds that earlier Meos belonging to Gotwal and Duhlot clans had their matrimonial relations with the Khanzadas.[61] Corroborating this, Channing writes that the Meos belonging to Ghatawasan, Paul, Narainwas, Kherlikhurd and Mohammada Bas villages of pargana Firozpur Jhirka claimed that they were Khanzadas in the past, but merged with their identity with the Meo community as a consequence of their matrimonial relations with the Meos.[62] However, this does not mean that all Khanzadas had matrimonial relations with the Meos, though certainly the matrimonial relations between some Khanzadas and *dak* Meoras did encourage the Islamization of Meo community. It appears that the late-Mughal context of intermarriages between the Khanzadas and the Meos was substantially different from the pre-Mughal context of intermarriages between the Khanzada chiefs and their Meo subjects. In the former situation, the Khanzadas had been sociopolitically ascendant; while in the latter, they, having lost their political power long ago, now became socially insecure as well. Nevertheless, intermarriage remained a catalyst for Islamization in both situations. Significantly, in contrast to the period prior to eighteenth century when evidence for Meos assuming an Islamic identity is virtually nil, in the late Mughal period such identity of certain sections of Meos was becoming quite evident. Indeed, the *Jagga Records* show that by the early eighteenth century, the Meos had begun to adopt Muslim names (See Table 3.1).

Table 3.1: Genealogy of some Meo families

Family genealogy	Gotra	Name of the village	Date of establishment of the village
1. Mansingh ↓ Umed Singh ↓ Mukhtiar Singh ↓ Maan Singh ↓ Salar Singh ↓ Rai Mal ↓ Mohammad Khan, Nahar Khan	Shaugan	Maacha	VS 1524/CE 1467
2. Chuhar Singh ↓ Loot Singh ↓ Todar Mal ↓	–	Chuharpur	VS 1505/CE 1448

Table 3.1 (*contd.*)

Family genealogy	Gotra	Name of the village	Date of establishment of the village
Mawasi ↓ Mohar Singh ↓ Mehrab Singh ↓ Imam Baksh, Mlekhan			
3. Pithusamal ↓ Jaishwant Singh ↓ Hari Singh ↓ Dhan Singh ↓ Umrao Singh ↓ Khuda Baksh, Chote Khan	Ratawat	Pathrai	VS 1532/CE 1465
4. Chand Singh ↓ Ranbir Singh- Bhan Singh ↓ Vir Bhan ↓ Amar Singh ↓ Mangal Singh ↓ Rustam, Ismail Khan	Singhal	Chandauli	VS 1532/CE 1465

Source: *Jagga Records*, *pothi* no. 1.

However, the Meos, like the Khanzadas, never managed to assume a rigid Islamic identity, forsaking their pre-/non-Islamic practices. As discussed earlier, Powlett commented on the fragile and incomplete process of Islamization among the Meos, who, according to him, adopted Muslim names, but continued to worship Hindu village deities and observe several Hindu and Muslim festivals. Further, only eight out of fifty-two Meo villages in pargana Tijara had mosques.[63] Channing, too, made similar remarks about the Meos of Nuh-Firozpur Jhirka region:

They have been very lax Muhammadans sharing in most of the rites and customs of their Hindu neighbours, especially such as are pleasant to observe, their principle of action seems to have been to keep the feasts of both religions, and the fasts of neither. Recently some Meos now even observe the Ramzan fast, build village mosques, say their prayers, and their wives wear trousers instead of Hindu petticoat — all signs of a religious revival.[64]

Although the process of Islamization among the Meos remained slow up to the early twentieth century, it certainly created an Islamic identity of the Meos which distinctly separated them from other non-Muslim castes in the region. A case in point is an incident of 1905 that brought the Islamic identity of the Meos to the fore. In qasba Tapukada, about 5 *kos* to the north of Tijara, every year a fair was held near an old Sufi *khanqah* (hospice), where petty mobile traders, i.e. *bisaati*, both Hindu and Muslim, put up their shops and sold their ware. During the fair in the said year, one evening a Muslim *bisaati* who was staying in a *sarai* started giving a loud call (*azaan*) to prayer (*namaaz*), hearing which the local people as well as the Hindu *bisaatis* asked him to lower the volume. At this, the *bisaati* got angry and complained to the local Meo chaudhari. As the tension mounted up, the Meo chaudharis of neighbouring areas gathered and sided with him, while the Hindu *bisaatis* stood in opposition. Since the *qasba* was within the Alwar state, the news spread rapidly and the matter was taken to the Maharaja. However, the agitated Meo chaudharis deemed the opposition of Hindu *bisaatis* as an assault on their religion and, in retaliation, bought a house near a temple in the venue of the fair in order to build a mosque, and set about collecting money from every local Meo family and even a Meo butcher-usurer of Meerut. Eventually, in order to defuse the situation, the Maharaja of Alwar had to come in person and appeal the Meo chaudharis and influential local Hindu people to restore peace between the two communities.[65] This incident shows that even though the Meos observed several Hindu rituals and celebrated Hindu festivals, they were quite conscious of their Islamic identity.

IV

Many Meo oral accounts are centred on their Islamization under the influence of Sufi saints or, more often, their close interactions with these saints that may have acted as a stimulus to their Islamization. While the Indo-Persian and Rajasthani sources do not provide any information about the impact of Sufi saints on Meos, these stories—some of which are furnished by colonial land settlement and ethnographic reports— suggest that some interaction may well have taken place between the Meos and the Sufis in the medieval period, though such intercourse would have remained localized. These accounts of interaction between the Sufi saints and the Meos need not be taken as historical evidence for deliberate proselytization; rather, they indicate the Meo community's perception of the broader influence of Sufis on its sociocultural life. These stories can also be read as an attempt on the part of the Meos to convey to the Islamic world that they should not be considered a lower category of Muslims because their Islamization was sanctified by renowned Sufi saints. Such postulations were constructed to attain religious legitimacy as Meos were the latest converts to Islam.

Among the several beliefs prevalent among the Meos regarding their relation with the Sufis, one is that Khwaja Muin-ud-din Chishti, while passing through Mewat on his way to Ajmer, blessed them to become Muslims,[66] though there is no evidence to prove this linkage. However, Channing's land settlement report of Gurgaon district records a couple of charms used to cure scorpion bite by invoking the saint:

Hari dandi Munj ka baan;
Utr re bichu, Khwaja Muin-ud-din Chishti ki aan

[green stick, Munj rope, get out scorpion, I charge you by (lit. oath of) Khwaja Muin-ud-din Chishti]

Choti kothi, bara pahaan;
Utr re, Khwaja Muin-ud-din ki aan

[little granary with a big top (to it); get out by (oath of) Khwaja Muin-ud-din][67]

Another belief of the Meos is that they converted to Islam under the influence of Salar Masud, a semi-mythical figure who has been the subject of several stories recounted in oral traditions and textual sources. Abul-Fazl states in his *Ain-i-Akbari* that Salar Masud was one of the martyrs of the Ghaznavid army.[68] According to *Mirat-i-Masudi*, Salar Masud was the son of a sister of Mahmud of Ghazni. Born in 1015 in Ajmer, he participated in the Ghaznavid invasions of Hindustan at the age of 16, and died at the age of 19. A number of significant events were thought to be associated with Masud's life, and he was worshipped by both Hindus and Muslims.[69] According to a traditional account,[70] the formidable chief of a Meo village named Toda in the Kala Pahad region, together with a section of Rajputs, used to raid the neighbouring areas and hoard the spoils in his village. Thus, the Meos were held in awe and fear in the surrounding areas. After the end of the rule of Chauhan Rajputs and the establishment of Turkish rule in Ajmer and Delhi, Masud, in order to conquer Mewat, attacked Toda, the power base of Meos. After days of bitter fighting and heavy casualties on both sides, the Meo chief surrendered and begged for his life. Masud pardoned him, and he embraced Islam. He was, in turn, conferred the title of *malik*; his followers, too, converted to Islam. However, many Meos fled and went into hiding in the forests of Kala Pahad, and their depredations continued unabated. Their Rajput accomplices, too, remained active in these raids. Subsequently, during the reign of Firozshah Tughlaq, these Meos and Rajputs were captured and converted to Islam. Thereon, the Rajputs merged their identity with the Meos, and the latter began to trace their ancestry from the Rajputs. The Meo *pals* linked themselves to Rajput *gotras*, assuming such names as Dahgal pal Kachhwaha, Singal pal Badgujar, Kalesa pal Chauhan, etc.[71] Salar Masud, on the other hand, has remained a revered figure among the Meos, his name being invoked on occasions of conflict-resolution. During disputes, for instance on fixing the boundary between two villages, both disputant parties carried the banner of Masud while negotiating for a solution.[72]

Stories of two other Sufi saints appear in Channing's report: Shah Chokha and Murad Shah.[73] A marble mausoleum and *khanqah* (hospice) of Shah Chokha exists in village Khohri located between Firozpur Jhirka and Punhana as a testimony to his influence in the region. While no credible information about him—his original name, period or provenance—can be found in the medieval sources, the tomb is dated prior to sixteenth century. It is believed that he came from Herat, Afghanistan, and established his *khanqah* at Khohri in the fourteenth century, and that he belonged to the Chishti order (*silsila*).[74] Channing's report informs us that a week-long fair, beginning on a moonlit night in the month of *jeth* (5–7 April), was held on the occasion of Shah Chokha's Urs after the harvesting of rabi crops. Associated with the assemblage of lovers and wooers, the fair attracted thousands of Meo men and women—the figure was 10,000 in 1870, according to the report. At this fair, many couples from Meo and other castes were married by mutual consent. The legitimacy of such unions, particularly inter-caste ones between Meo men and women of other castes, was not questioned by the Meo community, since they were believed to have been blessed by Shah Chokha himself (in fact, the groom would introduce the bride to his family stating that she had been gifted to him by the saint himself). Non-Meo women married to Meo men in this fashion had full rights and status in their households, and (male) children born of such marriages were entitled to their patrimony. The Meo community showed some flexibility in marital norms insofar as it allowed the practice of *karewa*, *gharecha* or *gharijna* whereby a widow could remarry or a woman could abandon her first husband and marry another man in lieu of some money, but what was significant about the cult of Shah Chokha was that it sanctified cross-caste marriages without the intervention of state or society. This practice was also associated with the Urs of Murad Shah or Madar Saheb of Qalandar *silsila* at Hasanpur Bara near Tijara. As in the case of Shah Chokha's Urs, during the Urs of Murad Shah, men and women gathered on a moonlit night and forged nuptial ties. His cult was more popular among the non-cultivating sections of Meos such as *sapera* (snake charmers), *bazigar* (acrobats), *saqqa* (water bearers), *faqir* (mendicant), etc.[75]

While the authority of Sufi Saints such as Shah Chokha and Murad Shah is invoked to legitimize certain marital practices outside the ambit of community norms, popular perceptions about them in certain sections of the Meo community also show the links forged between these quasi-historical figures and the origin myths of communities. A case in point is the legend[76] concerning the role of Shah Chokha in the settlement and prosperity of Chhiraklot Meo pal in the Firozpur Jhirka region. According to the legend, Shah Chokha scattered (*chhirak*) three fistfuls of grain in the region and blessed them to settle down there, this being the reason why the Chhiraklot Meos are so named and why they are settled there. Both Shah Chokha's mausoleum and villages of Chhiraklot Meos are located in the Firozpur Jhirka valley where incidentally the soil is very fertile and produces a good yield of cotton. The Meos thus attribute their prosperity to Shah Chokha's blessing. The myth links the origin of Meo settlement and agricultural productivity of the area to the Shah's intervention, endowing the Meos with the sanctity of association with a saintly figure belonging to the well established tradition of Islamic mysticism. However, as discussed in Chapter 2 of this volume, Jagga records on the genealogy of Meo pals suggest that they earlier subsisted on predatory activities in the Kala Pahad region, and later migrated to this region, taking to sedentary life as peasants due to historical factors, particularly state pressure.

By far the most famous saint in Mewat was Shaikh Gadan of Tijara. He belonged to the Chishti order and is thought to have been a contemporary of Akbar. According to one account,[77] he was once on his way to Tijara with his disciples. As he entered the field of a Meo peasant, the latter's wife saw him and thought that he had picked the *sitta* (barley pods) for eating. She yelled at him and called her husband who in a fit of rage shot an arrow piercing his chest and killing him. Shaikh Gadan's tragic death at the hands of a Meo suggests that Meos were not drawn to him, even though he was a popular figure in the Tijara region, possibly among the Khanzadas. Nevertheless, the story does show that Mewat was a fertile ground for Sufi activity in the medieval period.

Besides the afore-discussed accounts of Sufis coming from outside Mewat, there are also those of local saints such as Peepa, Chuhad Siddh, Lal Das and Mohanram who are perceived to have deeply influenced the sociocultural life of Meos. One account given in the Rajasthani sources concerns Peepa whose tomb is in village Guvalada near Tijara and who is believed to have been a contemporary of Akbar. At the age of 18, he was engaged to a Meo girl of Sarheta village. But, unbeknownst to him, her father broke off the engagement and married her off to another Meo boy, since people thought him crazed for he roamed aimlessly in the forest. On the day of marriage, when the groom's party reached the bride's house, Peepa, too, reached there on horseback and carried her to his native village Sarheta. The groom's party chased him all the way, and near Guvalada killed both. Later, a tomb was built for him on that very spot, and the Meos of Dahgal pal would take the newly-wed couples to his tomb to offer worship, seek his blessings and perform the rite of untying the nuptial knot.[78]

The foregoing discussion points to several factors that would have facilitated the Islamization of Meos in the medieval period. In the Rajasthani sources, particularly the *dastur komwars* and *arsattas*, while there are no clear references to the Islamic identity of Meo peasants, references to the *dak* Meoras from the late seventeenth and early eighteenth centuries indicate the beginnings of the process of Islamization of Meos in terms of their observance of certain Islamic rituals, such as *nikah*, burial, celebration of festivals like *Id*, and adoption of Muslim names. This can also be viewed as changes in the cultural life of the *dak* Meoras on account of their long service in the Mughal administration. These changes would have spread the influence of Islam among the Meo peasantry. At the same time, the early initiatives of Khanzada chiefs in introducing Islamic culture in the pre-Mughal period and the impact of Sufis on their sociocultural life would have been instrumental in their acculturation to Islam, if not actual formal conversion. However, the religious identity of the Meos remained ambiguous, even as late as mid-nineteenth century, since the first statistical report prepared by the British in 1840 recorded that about one-third of the Meo population in parganas Firozpur Jhirka, Nuh and Taoru were unaware of whether they were Hindus or Muslims. Thus, it may be concluded that many among the Meos began to assume Muslim identity only towards the end of the eighteenth century and this process continued well into the twentieth century.

Notes

1. Richard M. Eaton, *The Rise of Islam and the Bengal Frontier, 1204–1760*, Berkeley: University of California Press, 1996; Richard M. Eaton, 'The Political and Religious Authority of the Shrine of Baba Farid in Pakpattan, Punjab', in *Moral Conduct and Authority: The Place of Adab in South Asian Islam*, ed. Barbara Metcalfe, Berkeley: University of California Press, 1983.

2. Alexander Cunningham, *Report of a Tour in Eastern Rajputana in 1882–83*, *Archaeological Survey of India Reports*, vol. 20, 1885; repr. Varanasi: Indological Book House, 1969, pp. 29–30. Channing adds that the ancestors of the Meos embraced Islam during the reign of Qutbuddin Aibak (1206–10); see F.C. Channing, *Land Revenue Settlement of the Gurgaon District*, Lahore: Central Jail Press, 1882, p. 28.

3. J. Forbes Watson and John William Kaye, eds., *The People of India*, vol. 4, London: W.H. Allen and Co. for the India Museum, 1869, item 202. Watson and Kaye think that the conversion of the Meos was 'probably the work of Sultan Firozshah Tughlaq in the 14th century, when so many tribes were forcibly made Mohammadans, and that Aurangzeb completed what was then begun'. The settlement report of 1878 puts the date of Meos' conversion somewhere around the time of Qutubuddin Aibak, while W.W. Hunter puts the date of conversion of the Meos at the time of Mahmud of Ghazni; see Channing, *Land Revenue Settlement of the Gurgaon District*, p. 28.

4. The story was narrated by Jagdish Jagga of village Khuteta Kalan, Ramgarh tehsil, Alwar district, in 2004.

5. Major P.W. Powlett, *Gazetteer of Ulwur*, London: Trübner & Co., 1878, p. 7.

6. Cunningham, *Report of a Tour in Eastern Rajputana*, pp. 15–16.

7. Sheikh Muhammad Makhdum, *Arzang-i-Tijara* (Urdu), Agra: Agra Akhbar, AH 1290/CE 1873, translated to Hindi by Anil Joshi, Alwar, 1989, pp. 15–16.

8. A. Fraser, *Statistical Report of Zillah Gurgaon*, Lahore: n.p., 1846, p. 14, note.

9. Makhdum, *Arzang-i-Tijara*, p. 6.

10. Abul-Fazl, *The Ain-i-Akbari*, vol. 2, tr. Blochmann, corr. and ann. Sir Jadunath Sarkar, 3rd edn., Calcutta: Royal Asiatic Society of Bengal, 1978, pp. 202–4.

11. Ibid.

12. Abul-Fazl says that the Khanzadas of Mewat belonged to Juhiya Rajput clan. Abul-Fazl, *The Ain-i-Akbari*, vol. 1, tr. H. Blochmann, 3rd edn., Calcutta: Royal Asiatic Society of Bengal, 1977, p. 354.

13. A.M. Husain, *Tughluq Dynasty*, Calcutta: Thacker, Spink, & Co., 1963, p. 336.

14. Powlett, *Gazetteer of Ulwur*, pp. 134–5.

15. Husain, *Tughluq Dynasty*, p. 336. After being given the title of Khanazadar Khanazadun by Firozshah, Bahadur Nahar became a powerful and respectable chief of Mewat. Later, the word 'Khanazad' changed to 'Khanzada'; see Makhdum, *Arzang-i-Tijara*, p. 3.

16. It is noteworthy that Khanzadas and Kayam Khanis, two contemporary Muslim ruling groups that established their control over parts of eastern Rajasthan in the late fourteenth century and had similar traditions of Rajput ancestry associated with them differed in the projection of their sociocultural identity. While the descent of the Khanzadas has been traced to Jadon Rajputs in oral traditions, there seems to have been no significant emphasis on their Rajput origins, nor evidence for any attempt on their part to forge their social identity with that of the Rajputs. Rather, assimilation of former Firozi slaves into their ranks foregrounded their Islamic identity which remained consistent throughout the medieval and early colonial periods. But at the

same time, a legend of the establishment of their rule in Alwar following their decisive victory over the Nikumbha Rajputs of Alwar fort suggests that attempts to valorize their military might at the expense of Rajputs and thereby legitimize their rule in Alwar were made. Thus, while they did not claim glory from their Rajput origins or Rajput culture of chivalry and maintained their Islamic identity, they did perhaps try to shape their own tradition of heroism as superior to the Rajputs'. Moreover, their subsequent matrimonial relations with the Mughals would have lent further legitimacy to their privileged political status in Mewat (for details, see Chapter 1 of this volume). In contrast, the Kayam Khanis, who ruled parts of eastern Rajasthan, claimed their descent from Chauhan Rajputs as well as their conversion to Islam towards the end of Firozshah Tughlaq's reign—just as the Khanzadas did—associated themselves more with the Rajput culture and even entered into matrimonial relations with them (Kavi Jana, *Kayam Khan Raso*, tr. Ratan Lal Mishra, ed. Dashrath Sharma, Agarachand Nahata and B.L. Nahata, Jodhpur: Rajasthan Prachyavidya Pratisthan, 1996). The difference in the sociocultural identities of both, forged in part by their choice of alliances and associations, suggest that different political imperatives guided their attempts at self-legitimation as dominant groups in their respective regions.

17. For details, see Chapter 2 of this volume.
18. Cunningham, *Report of a Tour in Eastern Rajputana*, p. 16. The date of construction of the mosque is written on the gateway to the mosque in Kotla. In the courtyard of the mosque, there is a fine tomb, which is said to be that of Bahadur Nahar himself.
19. Ibid., p. 117.
20. Ibid., p. 134.
21. Ibid., pp. 118–19, 127, 135–7.
22. Non-archival Records of Alwar State, Rajasthan State Archives, Bikaner, *Bandhak* no. 3, *granthank* no. 66.
23. Powlett, *Gazetteer of Ulwur*, p. 38.
24. Cunningham, *Report of a Tour in Eastern Rajputana*, p. 23.
25. See Chapter 1 of this volume.
26. Powlett, *Gazetteer of Ulwur*, p. 40.
27. Makhdum, *Arzang-i-Tijara*, pp. 5–6.
28. See Chapter 1 of this volume.
29. S.A.A. Rizvi, *Uttar Timur kaalin Mughal Bharat*, vol. 1: *1399–1526*, tr. S.A. Rizvi, Rajkamal Prakshan, 2010, pp. 112–14.
30. Abul-Fazl mentions that 1000 Meoras were employed as *dak*-carriers by Akbar, see *The Ain-i-Akbari*, vol. 1, p. 262.
31. Muhammad Arif Qandhari, *Tarikh-i-Akbari*, tr. Tasneem Ahmad, Delhi: Pragati, 1993, p. 62. He says that Akbar employed 4000 Meos in the *dak* system.

32. Irfan Habib, 'Postal Communication in Mughal India', *Proceedings of the Indian History Congress*, 46th Session, Amritsar, 1985, pp. 236–52.

33. Qandhari, *Tarikh-i-Akbari*, p. 62.

34. Abul-Fazl, *Akbarnama*, vol. 2, tr. H. Beveridge, 1902–39; repr., New Delhi: Low Price Publications, 1993, pp. 427–8.

35. Channing, *Land Revenue Settlement of the Gurgaon District*, p. 30.

36. Abul-Fazl, *The Ain-i-Akbari*, vol. 1, pp. 261–2.

37. Muhammad Hashim Khafi Khan, *Aurangzeb in Muntakhab-al Lubab*, vol. 1, tr. Anees Jahan Syed, Bombay: Somaiya, 1977, p. 147.

38. Habib, 'Postal Communication in Mughal India'. The letters that the couriers transmitted, whether on foot or mounted, used to be put in a tube made of a section of hollow bamboo cane called *nalwa* (ibid.).

39. B.L. Bhadani, 'The Mughal Highway and Post Stations in Marwar', in *Proceedings of the Indian History Congress*, 52nd Session, Delhi, 1992, pp. 439–48.

40. *Dastur Komwar Mutfarkat*, vol. 23, vs 1774/CE 1717, pp. 59–140.

41. *Arzdasht, Mah Vadi 6*, vs 1744/CE 1687.

42. *Arsatta*, pargana Jalalpur, vs 1744/CE 1687.

43. *Arsatta*, pargana Pahari, vs 1793/CE 1736.

44. Abul-Fazl, *The Ain-i-Akbari*, vol. 1, pp. 261–2.

45. *Dastur Komwar Mutfarkat*, vol. 23, vs 1774/CE 1717, pp. 59–140.

46. *Khatut-ahalkarn, Asaj Sudi*, vs 1771/CE 1714.

47. *Arzdasht, Bhadva Vadi 13*, vs 1740/CE 1683.

48. *Arzdasht, Chet Vadi 1*, vs 170/CE 1683.

49. *Arsatta*, pargana Kotla, vs 1722/CE 1665; pargana Jalalpur, vs 1722/CE 1665; pargana Bharkol, vs 1722/CE 1665; pargana Pahari, vs 1793/CE 1736.

50. *Arsatta*, pargana Bharkol, vs 1722/CE 1665.

51. Complaints were lodged by some *dak* Meoras against the amils who denied them concessions in the payment of land revenue on their personal holdings. The amils, in turn, argued that the concession was valid till the *dak* Meoras remained in the service of the Mughal state. See *Chithi* to the amil, pargana Pahari, *Asoj Vadi 9*, vs 1804/CE 1747.

52. *Arzadasht, Mah Vadi 6*, vs 1740/CE 1683.

53. Major-General Sir John Malcolm, *The Political History of India from 1784 to 1823*, vol. 2, London: John Murray, 1826, p. 174. Malcom says that the Meos happened to be faithful and courageous guards and servants to their masters.

54. Muhammad Umar, *Muslim Society in Northern India during the Eighteenth Century*, Delhi: Munshiram Manoharlal, 1998, pp. 145–55.

55. *Arsatta, pargana* Uzirpur, vs 1771/CE 1714, vs 1774/CE 1717, vs 1776/CE 1719, vs 1777/CE 1720, vs 1778/CE 1721, vs 1780/CE 1723.

56. *Khatoot ahalkaran, Asad Sudi 4*, vs 1780/CE 1723.

57. Ibid.; Devidas cited the instance of Noor Khan Meora inviting the qazi to perform *nikah*.
58. Makhdum, *Arzang-i-Tijara*, p. 5.
59. Ibid.
60. For details, see Chapter 1 of this volume.
61. Makhdum, *Arzang-i-Tijara*, p. 33.
62. Channing, *Land Revenue Settlement of the Gurgaon District*, p. 30.
63. Powlett, *Gazetteer of Ulwur*, p. 70.
64. Channing, *Land Revenue Settlement of the Gurgaon District*, pp. 37–8.
65. Non-archival Records, Alwar State, Historical Section, *granthank* 3, *bandhak* no. 83.
66. Muhammad Habibur Rahman Khan, *Tazkirah-i-Sofiya-i-Mewat: Islami Hind ki Tarikh ka Bhula Hua Ek Aham Baab*, Gurgaon: Mewat Academy, 1979, pp. 39–44.
67. Channing, *Land Revenue Settlement of Gurgaon District*, p. 37.
68. Abul-Fazl, *The Ain-i-Akbari*, vol. 1, p. 153
69. Abdur Rahman Chisti, 'Mirat-i-Masudi', in *The History of India as Told by Its Own Historians*, ed. H.M. Elliot and John Dowson, vol. 2, Delhi: Low Price Publications, 2001, pp. 513–49.
70. Non-archival Records, Alwar State, Historical Section, *granthank* 1, *bandhak* no. 81.
71. Ibid.; and Makhdum, *Arzang-i-Tijara*, pp. 3–4: both mention that during Firozshah's reign, many Rajputs merged their identity with the Meos.
72. Non-archival Records, Alwar State, Historical Section, *granthank* 1, *bandhak* no. 81.
73. Channing, Land Revenue Settlement of the Gurgaon District, p. 37.
74. Khan, *Tazkirah-i-Sofiya-i-Mewat*, pp. 313–20.
75. Ibid., pp. 39–44.
76. Shail Mayaram, *Against History, Against State: Counterperspectives from the Margins*, Delhi: Permanent Black, 2004, p. 38.
77. Makhdum, *Arzang-i-Tijara*, p. 13.
78. Non-archival Records, Alwar State, Historical Section, *granthank* 12, *bandhak* no. 89.

4

Conflict over Social Surplus

Problems of Revenue Farming in Eighteenth-Century North India (Mewat)

ISTORIANS HAVE CRITICALLY examined the ijara or revenue farming system in the Mughal period from different perspectives. On the one hand, it has been viewed as a practice of the Mughal state that violated the norms of the regular land revenue system and led to the exploitation of peasantry in the sixteenth and seventeenth centuries CE.[1] On the other hand, it has been projected as a progressive practice insofar as it led to an increase in the agricultural production and the consolidation of intermediate classes of the society, i.e. townsmen and service gentry.[2] For instance, it has been argued that the ijara in the territory under the Marathas (particularly under the Peshwa's rule in the late eighteenth century CE), was 'one of the organizational means of agrarian restoration and expansion, internal as well as external', and that it 'did not normally have a destructive effect upon agriculture in either the short or the long term'.[3] In a study, based on the archival records of the Jaipur state, it has been argued that 'it would be misleading to assume that the ijara grants invariably led to profit. The officials did not regard ijara as a sound revenue arrangement. The state initially resorted to ijara only in order to rehabilitate old ruined and desolated villages and with a view to increasing the jama of unlucrative villages.'[4] Another study explains the working of the ijara system in terms of the territorial expansion of the Jaipur state in the early eighteenth century CE.[5] In the light of such studies offering such divergent assessments, and on the basis of hitherto understudied Rajasthani documents, viz., *arsattas*, *arzdashts*, *chithis*, *khatoot-ahalkarans*, reports of vakil, *dastur-al amals* and *dehai ferhashtis*, this chapter attempts to reassess the working of the ijara in the Mewat region during the late seventeenth and early eighteenth centuries CE; its impact on the regional economy, particularly agriculture, on peasants, on their relation with the state and the local political elite, and on the power equations between the various political entities of the region.

I

In the medieval period, Mewat was, and still is, inhabited predominantly by Meos and other cultivating castes like Jats, Gujars, Ahirs, Malis, and Meenas. The sixteenth-century text *Ain-i-Akbari* by Abul-Fazl details the territorial distribution and caste composition of the zamindaris in the region. Around 1600, the Meo and the Khanzada zamindars had the maximum number of parganas under their jurisdiction. More specifically, they had their zamindaris in 30 out of 43 parganas in Alwar sarkar, and in 16 out of 18 parganas in Tijara sarkar. Similarly, the majority of parganas in Sahar sarkar were under the jurisdiction of the Meo zamindars; the Khanzadas, however, did not possess any zamindari rights in this sarkar.[6] But during the seventeenth century, significant changes took place in the position of zamindars belonging to various castes and clans of the Mewat region. The Meos and the Khanzadas were gradually replaced by the Rajput and Jat zamindars. The former could not safeguard their politico-economic interests due to the growing influence of the Kachhwaha Rajputs of Amber who followed a policy of systematically expanding their territorial control in the parganas of Mewat that were contiguous to their watan jagir. As the Kachhwaha chiefs acquired political leverage at the Mughal court, they used their position to extend their influence in the Mewat region by carving out new Rajput zamindaris and displacing the Meo and Khanzada zamindars. The Mughal emperors, too, regarded the Rajputs as more reliable and worthy supporters than the Meos and the Khanzadas.[7]

II

The ijara constituted a kind of contract for the farming out of revenue of a pargana, a *mauza* (revenue village) or a part thereof.[8] The contract called *patta* or deed of lease was between the state and the ijaradar (revenue farmer), or between the imperial jagirdar/mansabdar and the ijaradar.[9] The *patta* spelt out the amount of revenue to be realized from the territory assigned on ijara, as also other terms agreed upon by both parties.[10] The ijaradar had to pay a fixed amount of revenue as stipulated in the *patta* and give his *qabuliyat* (acceptance) of this obligation.[11] The *patta* was usually drawn by a *sahukar* or *mahajan* (money-lender), though sometimes the latter themselves obtained the ijara of villages from the jagirdars by giving personal surety.[12]

The practice of assigning territories on ijara was present in the seventeenth century,[13] but not to a significant extent. Rajasthani sources inform that the usefulness of the practice was limited to ruined or deserted villages, i.e. jagirdars assigned such villages on ijara for the purpose of their rehabilitation. The practice, however, began to acquire greater currency in the early eighteenth century, especially after the death of Mughal emperors Aurangzeb and Bahadur Shah, and became widespread during the reign of Farrukh Siyar. The growth and spread of the practice was the result of agrarian disturbances in the Mewat region during the late seventeenth and early eighteenth centuries.[14] In the post-Aurangzeb era, due to factional politics at the Mughal court, the political authority of the emperor gradually eroded. As a result, the functioning of the land revenue administration was adversely affected, and the rules and regulations regarding the land revenue assessment and collection and were brazenly flouted by the central and provincial officials alike. The Rajasthani *arsattas* show that the land revenue was supplemented by various customary and non-customary taxes, and this increased the total revenue demand manifold. The middle and small peasants, who constituted the bulk of the rural population, had to bear the growing revenue burden and the resulting hardships, more than their relatively richer counterparts did.[15] All these developments ultimately provoked peasant protests in various forms in the region during the early eighteenth century CE. The Rajasthani text *Kiyam Khan Raso*, too, informs us that in the period of unrest following Aurangzeb's death, the imperial mansabdars found it increasingly difficult to collect revenue from the jagirs assigned to them in lieu of salary since the many of these jagirs were located in far-flung areas and local zamindars regularly created hurdles in the revenue collection.[16] In these unsettled conditions, the imperial mansabdars began to farm out their jagirs to various powerful local bidders, notably the Amber chief and Churaman Jat. According to *Kiyam Khan Raso*'s testimony, the practice became so widespread that even the smaller mansabdars resorted to it; the Amber chief Jai Singh hugely benefitted from it, taking a large number of jagirs on ijara.[17]

Broadly, ijara in the Mewat region may be divided in two categories: the ijara of the jagirs of the imperial mansabdars assigned to the Amber Raja and the Jats; and the ijara of the villages sub-assigned by the Amber Raja to his Rajput *chakars* (servants), mahajans and land revenue officials. The Rajput *chakars* were mainly the Rajawats, the Narukas, the Kilanots, the Panchnots, the Hamirdekas, the Kumbhanis and the Nathawats, all belonging to the Kachhwaha clan. An *arsatta* reveals that the majority of the sub-assignees belonged to the Kachhwaha Rajput clan that also inhabited most of the villages whose ijara was assigned to them. The other sub-assignees, i.e. the mahajans and officials like qanungos and chaudharis, were granted ijara on account of their local connection with the *raiyati* (peasants),[18] since they belonged to the localities where these villages were situated or neighbouring ones. Thus, on account of their strong local connections, the majority of these sub-assignees who held ijara for a long period consolidated their position as local potentates. The sub-assignees were also required to pay a fixed amount of money as *peshkash* annually to the Amber Raja in two seasonal installments.[19] In 1704, the Amber Raja acquired the ijara of five parganas, including Shonkhar-Shonkhari, from the imperial mansabdar Mukhtiyar Khan, and sub-assigned them to his Rajput *chakars*.[20] In the same year, Ramchander—the diwan of the Amber state—informed the Amber Raja that he had acquired, on the Raja's behalf, the ijara of parganas Niwai, Fagi and Uniyara from the imperial mansabdar Husain Ali Khan. The diwan added that he had to pay Rs.1,25,000 as peshkash to Husain Ali Khan, since 'this *musalman* [was] very greedy'.[21] In 1712, the Raja received the ijara of the entire Khohri pargana comprised of 342 villages that came under the jagirs of the imperial mansabdars. He, in turn, sub-assigned the ijara of these villages to his Rajput *chakars*.[22] In 1714, he obtained the ijara of two more parganas, Piragpur and Atela Bhabra, from the imperial mansabdars.[23] The *dehai-ferhashtis* and *chithis* reveal that the ijara of villages was also sub-assigned to mahajans, qanungos and chaudharis.[24]

Another type of ijara that the Raja obtained involved the transfer of zamindari and thanedari rights of several parganas from the imperial faujdar. Such rights, which entailed the responsibility for maintaining law and order, were granted to local potentates like the Raja, in the wake of serious agrarian disturbances in many parganas of Mewat. For instance, in 1702, the Raja got the thanedari of five parganas, including Mojpur and Bharkol, in Alwar sarkar from Mughal faujdar Vazhadi Khan.[25] In 1704, the Raja got the zamindari of parganas Alwar, Khilohra, Bharkol, Mungana, Baroda Meo and Khohrana from the Mughal faujdar of Mewat.[26] In the same year, diwan Ramchander informed the Amber Raja of his success in securing the zamindari and thanedari of seven more parganas of Alwar sarkar in ijara from faujdar Sakurla Khan. In particular, he pointed out that he had acquired these rights from the faujdar in Narnol with great difficulty: he had to pay Rs.700 to the faujdar's *munshi* and Rs.500 to Qanungo Pranath of Narnol for their help in getting these rights and would have to continue sending Rs.500 in advance every year to the qanungo for such help in future.[27]

It was through the exercise of the zamindari and thanedari rights granted to him on ijara that the Amber Raja managed to remove the Meo and Khanzada zamindars from the parganas of Alwar sarkar on the pretext of the latter's administrative incompetence or seditious activities. Consequently, there was a drastic decline in the number of Meo and Khanzada zamindaris—a change borne out by the Rajasthani documents of the period under study. A more significant development was the creation of new zamindaris and the enlargement of the existing ones by various segments of the Kachhwaha Rajput clan. Thus, in the late seventeenth and early eighteenth centuries CE, by cashing in on their influence at the Mughal court and securing the ijara, thanedari and zamindari rights of the jagirs of imperial mansabdars and faujdars, the Amber chiefs systematically tried to expand their territorial control over the parganas of Alwar sarkar that were contiguous to their watan jagir and thereby increase their economic gains. This, in effect, destroyed the socio-economic base of the Meo and Khanzada zamindars and rendered them incapable of offering any effective resistance to the Amber chiefs, as also to the Jats, who had also gained zamindaris in the region at their expense.

As pointed out earlier, the Amber Raja Jai Singh Sawai's move of taking the ijara of the jagirs of imperial mansabdars was based on strategic economic and political considerations. In many cases, the Amber Raja's desire to take the ijara of the parganas in the Mewat and Agra regions contiguous to his watan jagir was crucially motivated by his desire to expand the sphere of his territorial control beyond his watan jagir. This motive is well-reflected in a report written to him by his vakil:

O *Majarajaji*, the *jagirs* of imperial *mansabdars* Badshahzada Ayaz-ud-din Khan, Khan Jahan Bahadur, Azam Khan Bhahadur, Khan-i-daura Bahadur, Khan Jahan Bahadur's son, and Khan-i-daura Bahadur's son are in Mewat. We have been trying to take these *jagirs* on *ijara*. We have spoken to Khan Jahan Bahadur's *mutsadi* (clerk or scribe) and tempted him by offering to pay the revenue of three months in advance. For this reason, Khan Jahan Bahadur has agreed to assign us the *ijara*. These *jagirs*, spread from Mewat to Agra are contiguous to our *watan* (the Amber state), and our concerted attempt should to acquire their *ijara*. It is known to all in the Mughal court that you are not on good terms with the emperor. We should try to obtain the *pattas* (deeds of lease) of as many *parganas* as we can get on *ijara* for three years because even the *mansabdars* are hesitant to assign us these *jagirs* on *ijara*. We can sort out the political problems with the emperor later, but first we should take the *parganas* adjoining our *watan* on *ijara* so that we can extend our control over these neighboring territories. To this end, we have taken the *parganas* of Firozpur Jhirka, Tonk, Lalsot, Jaitpur and Mauzabad on *ijara*; we have agreed to pay the revenue of three months in advance to the *mutsadis* of the *jagirdar*s, as also obtained the *pattas* from them. [28]

According to another report, the Amber Raja, in a letter to his vakil Jagjivan Das Panchole at the Mughal court, had also advised the latter to secure the ijara of as many parganas adjacent to his watan jagir as possible. Further, he had emphatically asked him to try to get the ijara of the parganas Chatsu, Mauzabad, Niwai, Toda Bhim, Toda Rai Singh, etc. It thus appears that the Amber Raja was keen on expanding his watan jagir, and at the same time expected to reap the economic benefits out of the ijara grant.[29]

The *Kiyam Khan Raso* also details how Raja Jai Singh gradually enlarged the state of Amber by acquiring many parganas of the imperial jagirs on ijara. For instance, the Raja obtained the entire ijara of mansabdar Shujat Khan's jagir, which included parganas Amarsar, Mauzabad, Bhairana and Nagina. In 1728, he acquired the entire *suba* (province) of Ajmer except Tappa Haveli on ijara for a year. The ijara of parganas Sambhar and Didwana, too, became his. Sometime later, parganas Gawdi, Bawai, Jhunjhunu, Udaipur, Narhad and Panchmahal were assigned to him on ijara by mansabdar Muzaffar Khan. In 1732, he sent Shardul Singh of Udaipur and Shiv Singh of Sikar to expel the ruling Kayamkhani family from southern Fatehpur. Given the scale of territorial expansion through ijara, the Amber emerged as one of the biggest states in India and remained so till 1743. Its vast area of 20,000 sq. mi. included 9,000 sq. mi. of the Raja's watan jagir as well as several parganas such as Shekhawati (5,200 sq. mi.), Macheri (3,000 sq. mi.), Tonk (1,800 sq. mi.), Gazi ka Thana, Khohri, Pahari, Narnol, Kanod, etc.[30] Corroborating the evidence from Rajasthani documents, the *Raso* further reveals that these jagirs were sub-assigned on ijara to petty zamindars for 1–3 years.[31]

Other compelling reasons for the Amber Raja to take the parganas of imperial jagirs on ijara were the threats posed by the growing political ascendancy of Churaman Jat in the Mewat and Agra regions, and the need to provide the Raja's Rajput clansmen a source of income. Pointing this out, a vakil's report states that Churaman had already moved into these regions and got the ijara of many parganas from the imperial mansabdars, thereby making it all the more critical for the Amber Raja to acquire the ijara of the jagirs of imperial mansabdars so that he could extend his territorial control in these regions, as also provide a source of income, by way of sub-assignment of ijara, to his Rajput *chakars*.[32] Yet another report also reveals that the Raja's Rajput *chakars* had been plundering the jagirs of the imperial mansabdars and had thus turned into a menace. Commenting on this, the vakil wrote: 'Not only these activities of our *chakars* defame us in the Mughal court but these *chakars* also defy the law and order of the Amber state; they become selfish and disobedient and do not bother about the economic interests of the Amber state.'[33] This made acquiring the ijara more essential for the Amber Raja in order to provide a source of income to his unruly clansmen and check their depredations, as also to contain the expansion of Jat power.

Expectedly, the Amber Raja's move of sub-assigning the ijara of villages to his clansmen brought him into direct confrontation with the Jats. The root cause of the conflict was their desire to appropriate the larger share of the agricultural surplus through the exercise of ijaradari rights at the expense of each other. In the changing political scenario of the Mughal court, Churaman received open support from the influential Sayyid brothers and Nawab Khan-i-daura.[34] This support continued to be extended to Churaman till the fall of the Sayyid brothers in the

Battle of Hasanpur (1720). In this period, Churaman received from the imperial mansabdars the ijara of many parganas that were within their jagirs, not only in the Mewat region but also in the Agra-Mathura region.[35] His main motive, thus, was to gain control over these regions and their agrarian resources by convincing the imperial mansabdars at the Mughal court that he could better manage the land revenue collection of their jagirs than the Amber Raja would.

The vakil of the Amber state expressed his concern in a report to the Amber Raja that Churaman Jat was becoming a favourite of the Mughal court and that through the influence of the Sayyid brothers he had got the ijara of not only all the parganas within the Agra region, but also some parganas of Alwar sarkar like Kathumbar, Bhushawar and Devati-sanchari out of the jagirs of imperial mansabdars.[36] Further, Churaman had encouraged the Jat peasants to settle and colonize the old deserted villages of these parganas. It is thus evident from the Rajasthani documents that the Jats had widened their social base in the Agra-Mathura and Mewat regions through the ijara system during the reign of Farrukh Siyar.[37] The rising influence of Churaman Jat in the Mughal court was detrimental to the economic interests and political status of the Amber Raja, and this conflict of interest led to a fierce competition between Churaman Jat and the Amber Raja over the acquisition of ijara of the parganas belonging to the jagirs of the imperial mansabdars.

Their widening socio-economic base as well as growing military power and political leverage at the Mughal court even emboldened Churaman and his men to launch assaults on and exact revenue from the territories taken on ijara by the Amber Raja. For instance, in 1715, the Jats removed all the *thanas* (police posts) of the Amber Raja in the villages and qasbas of pargana Khohri, set up their own *thanas* and collected revenue from the entire pargana. Following is the vakil's report expressing concern about these incidents and their repercussions:

O *Maharajaji*, news has come from Akbarabad (Agra) that last year Churaman Jat had collected land revenue from half of the *pargana* Khohri (i.e., 171 out of 342 villages); and this year he has forcibly removed your *thanas* from the *pargana*, established his own *thanas* and collected revenue from the entire *pargana*. Khan-i-daura's *diwan* has summoned me as your *vakil* and conveyed that if Churaman Jat continues to forcibly collect revenue from the *pargana* assigned to you on *ijara* (in other words, if you cannot stop Churaman from appropriating the revenue), then you better leave (i.e., give up the *ijara* of) this *pargana* and he will assign it to Churaman Jat. The *diwan* has further said that everyone at the Mughal court is surprised at Churaman's audacity in forcibly collecting revenue from the *pargana* assigned to you. We are being asked whether we would give up the *pargana* out of the fear of a Jat. If we leave this *pargana*, we will also have to leave the adjoining *pargana* of Devati-Sachari, as Churaman exercises his influence there as well. Moreover, if we leave *pargana* Khori out of fear, we will be laughing stock of the Mughal court. Therefore, it is imperative to punish Churaman.[38]

Subjected to exactions and harassment by both Amber Raja and Churaman Jat, the peasants complained to the Mughal emperor at Shahjahanabad against their highhandedness. For instance, in 1712, the peasants of parganas Firozpur Jhirka and Khohri, which had been taken on ijara by the Amber Raja from the imperial mansabdar Ayaz-ud-din Khan, declined to pay revenue to the Raja and pleaded before the emperor that they were being oppressed by the Jats and the Raja and forced to pay land revenue to both, and that they could not withstand this state of affairs and would be forced to leave their villages if they continued to be maltreated. When the peasants of both parganas remained adamant on not paying revenue despite much cajoling by the Raja's amil, Mukand Ram Vakawat was sent with a big force to help the amil collect land revenue from the villages, but as the contingent reached Khohri, it found the villages deserted.[39] In 1716, again, peasants deserted several villages of pargana Khohri, fearing assaults by the armies of the Amber Raja and the Jats.[40] In another instance, many Meo villages of parganas Khohri and Pahari, which had paid their land revenue to Churaman Jat were set to fire and their cattle was captured by the army of the Amber faujdar.[41] Evidently, as a result of the rivalry between the Churaman Jat and the Amber state, the condition of the peasants became miserable.

III

The peasants' discontent with the ijara system chiefly consisted in the opposition to additional arbitrary taxes imposed by the Amber Raja, the main ijaradar in the Mewat region. For the latter, such irregular levies served as a convenient way to transfer the burden of peshkash to the peasants. Customarily, the Amber Raja had to pay peshkash to the imperial mansabdars in lieu of the ijara; and in the situation of a fierce contest between him and Churaman Jat over the acquisition of ijara, the imperial mansabdars demanded hefty peshkash from both. Instead of paying it from his own treasury, the Amber Raja collected this amount from the peasants by way of a special cess called *virar*. Clearly, *virar* was not a customary levy on the peasants who were coerced into paying it over and above the regular land revenue. On the one hand, the Amber Raja claimed that as he had got the right to collect land revenue for the parganas of Mewat from the imperial mansabdars which were part of the jagirs of these mansabdars, the peasants should pay revenue to him only. The plea of the peasants, on the other hand, was that many new taxes like *virar*, *nyota* and *bhomi* that were imposed on them were non-customary and forcibly exacted from them by the Amber Raja. The Rajasthani sources record several peasant complaints against the grant of ijara to the Amber Raja, the excesses of his revenue officials and troops and the heavy burden of irregular levies like *virar*. The following report of the Raja's vakil illustrates the peasant discontent:

O *Maharajaji*, *diwan* Khan Jahan Bahadur has written to us that the *raiyati* (peasants) of *pargana* Firozpur Jhirka came with the complaint that their *pargana*, which is part of Badshahzada Ayaz-ud-din Khan's *jagir*, has been assigned on *ijara* to Mirza Raja, and that the latter's men plunder them and extract non-customary taxes from them. It is, therefore, their plea that Ayaz-ud-din Khan be asked to take away the *ijara* of the *pargana* from Mirza Raja, who sends his *amil* to collect land revenue as well as other non-customary taxes from them. Further, the *diwan* has forwarded this complaint to the emperor, and the emperor has ordered Mirza Raja not to send his *amil* to collect land revenue from the *pargana* and instead let the imperial *amil* do the same. [42]

Further, from the peasant's perspective, the root of his discontent and conflict with the state lay not merely in the amount that he had to pay to the state as regular revenue and/or irregular levies, but in the fact that he had little surplus to part with. It was the insufficient surplus and his consequent inability to satisfy the state's demand that made the imposition of non-customary levies under the ijara system particularly galling and burdensome for the peasant.

A sharp reaction of the peasants against the ijara system was noticed in 1712 in pargana Firozpur Jhirka. Amber Raja had taken the ijara of the pargana from the imperial mansabdar, Sarfaraz Khan Badshahzada.

The Meo peasants went to the Mughal court and filed a petition demanding that the emperor issue an order to Sarfaraz Khan, cancelling the assignment of the ijara of his jagir to the Amber Raja because 'the men of the Amber Raja rob and plunder us. We have been subjected with many non-customary illegal taxes. Therefore, under ijara system, we will not pay land revenue to the amil of the Amber Raja.' Further, the peasantry pleaded that they would pay their land revenue only to the amil of the imperial mansabdar, Sarfaraz Khan.[43]

A major difference between the rates of taxes under the regular land revenue system and those under the ijara system indicated that the additional levies increased the tax burden manifold. For instance, in 1712, according to the amil's report, after the parganas Khohri, Tijara and Bahadurpur were taken in ijara by the Amber Raja from the imperial jagirdar, the zamindari or *bhomi* tax was revised (or rather increased) and the new rate was authenticated by the seal of *qazi*: under the regular systems of land revenue assessment based on crop-sharing (*batai-jinsi*) and cash rates of crops (*zabti*), the state's share in the produce amounted to 1 *ser* per *maund* and *zabti* of Rs.2 per Rs.100, respectively, while under the ijara system, it rose to a *zabti* of Rs.2½ per Rs.100.[44]

There are several documentary instances of peasants pleading their inability to pay *virar*, which constituted a heavy sum of money over and above the regular land revenue. In 1728, the peasants and the patels of the villages of pargana Khohri went to Shahjahanabad and sought audience with the Mughal emperor, reporting to him that a sum of Rs.17,300 had been demanded from them as *virar* and that the demand was not only unjust but totally beyond their capacity to meet.[45] A similar protest was lodged by the peasants of pargana Shonkhar-Shonkhari with the emperor. In their petition, they complained that the Amber Raja had collected land revenue worth Rs.52,000 from the rabi harvest; out of this sum, the actual amount of land revenue was only Rs.38,000 and the balance of Rs.14,000 was *virar*.[46] The peasants of pargana Sahar complained that the amil of the Amber Raja had forcibly collected total land revenue of Rs.26,624 of which the actual revenue amounted to Rs.19,624 while Rs.7,000 were levied as *virar* in order to meet the army expenditure.[47] The peasants of two villages of pargana Pindayan, too, complained that the ijaradar had collected land revenue of Rs.7,441 of which Rs.1,436 was levied as *virar* to meet military expenses.[48] In 1740, the actual land revenue of kharif and rabi produce of the villages in pargana Khohri assigned to the Amber Raja on ijara was Rs.11,551 and Rs.10,000, respectively, but the Amber Raja collected additional Rs.4,000 and Rs.2,300 rupees as *virar* in order to meet military expenses.[49] In 1730, the peasants of Pipal Khera, Kithwara and other villages in pargana Khohri protested against the ijaradars, Karan Singh and Deep Singh Narukas, who had tried to force them to pay as much land revenue (i.e. Rs.12,551 from both kharif and rabi produce) as was paid in the previous year despite crop failure.[50] Similarly, the peasants of 85 villages of pargana Pawta opposed the imposition of *virar* by the ijaradars, Hasan Khan Pathan and Surti Ram Naruka.[51] These and numerous other instances prove that *virar* was so heavy and oppressive that it became unbearable for the peasantry.

Besides petitions, the peasant opposition to the practice of ijara and the heavy tax burden often took the form of armed rebellions and non-payment of taxes, which, in turn, was met with repressive measures. Such violent unrest adversely affected the revenue collection in many cases as well. For instance, a massive peasant protest broke out in parganas Firozpur Jhirka and Tijara whose ijara had been taken by the Amber Raja. The amil of the Amber state went with a big force to collect the land revenue from the rebellious peasants, but the entire Meo peasantry led by the patels resisted the armed assault. A fierce battle took place, in which 60 peasants were killed and many wounded on the one hand, and Daulat Khan, the deputy commander of the Amber army, along with many soldiers, was killed by the peasants on the other hand. The peasants belonging to Jaisar, Alipur, Khohra Mora, and Kamohera villages ran away to Kala Pahar (Aravali hills of Firozpur Jhirka and Ramgarh). Eventually, the Amber army managed to crush the revolt and collect 3,000 maunds of grain and 13 horses from the villages.[52] According to the reports of the amils from parganas Bharkol and Jalalpur, the peasants did not pay their land revenue of rabi crops.[53] In 1725, Hasan Khan Koka, the imperial mansabdar of pargana Alwar, complained that 26 villages had not paid the land revenue of the rabi harvest to his amil. The faujdar was ordered to crush these rebellious villages with heavy hand.[54] In 1726, the Amber Raja secured the ijara of 109½ villages of pargana Khohri from the imperial mansabdars, but the amil managed to collect Rs.70,445 out of the total amount of Rs.97,010 from them.[55] A *dehai-ferhashti* of 1732 from pargana

Khohri throws further light on the unrest in the villages assigned in ijara. When the peasants of Bamrauli village refused to pay their land revenue under the ijara system, the faujdar's army seized their entire harvest and cattle. Similarly, when the peasants of Doli and Badkhera villages refused to pay the land revenue to the amil of the ijaradar, army was sent to punish them. The army of the faujdar was sent to seize the harvest and cattle of the peasants in other *raiyati* villages on account of their non-payment of land revenue.[56]

Similar conditions prevailed in pargana Pahari as well. In 1716, the Amber Raja obtained the ijara of 59½ villages of the pargana from the imperial mansabdar, but the amil managed to collect the land revenue only from 42 villages; 7 villages were deserted by the peasants.[57] In 1724, the peasants of 21 villages of the pargana did not deposit the land revenue to the ijaradar.[58] In 1731, the Amber Raja obtained the ijara of 110 villages of the pargana from the imperial mansabdars, but managed to collect only Rs.2,892,023 out of the total stipulated amount of Rs.4,460,823 from 63 villages.[59] The amil of the Amber Raja could not collect the land revenue from the 28 rebellious Meo villages whose peasants had plundered and burned other villages in protest against the ijara. The amil, in his report to the Amber Raja, emphasized the need to keep a watch on the Meo peasants who were used to cutting the standing crops of other peasants and even advised against taking the ijara of Meo villages in future.[60] He further recommended that since most of the rabi crops were grown by the peasants with the help of well water (*lao charas*), the ijara be fixed on the basis of *lao charas* rather than on the basis of the harvested crop.[61]

Besides petitions and armed rebellions, another form of peasant resistance to the excessive revenue demand of the ijaradars was the desperate act of deserting villages and giving up cultivation to evade the payment of revenue. The Rajasthani documents testify to the increasing incidence of desertions of villages, which adversely affected agriculture. In 1712, 97 out of 312 villages of pargana Khohri got deserted at the time of rabi harvest. They had paid only Rs.10,696 out of the total land revenue of Rs.23,992.[62] In 1716, when the faujdar of the Amber Raja went to collect the land revenue from the peasants of pargana Khohri, 127 villages were deserted due to the fear of the army.[63] The peasants of 7 villages of the pargana Mojpur ran away to *thoon* (Jat fortress), seeking protection from the Amber army.[64] Desertions were also reported from pargana Pahari which comprised 209 villages. According to an *arsatta* from this pargana, the peasants deserted 24 villages due to the fear of the Amber army.[65] In 1742, when the Amber Raja secured the ijara of 138 villages in the pargana from the imperial mansabdars, the peasants deserted 25 villages in that same year and 41 more villages in the following year due to fear of the army.[66]

The enormity of peasant resistance can be gauged from the amil's report on the dismal state of villages in pargana Bayana whose ijara was secured by the Amber Raja from the imperial mansabdar Amir Khan. According to the report, out of 138 villages granted on ijara, 33 were deserted, 48 were *zortalab* and 25 were those that had not raised the rabi crop. The amil further mentioned that he could manage to collect the land revenue only from 31 out of 138 villages. In his words:

Not a single peasant is willing to come to us to pay his *hasil*. There is need to send some wise men to the villages to persuade the peasants to pay the land revenue to us. The *patels* of the Daang *tappa* in *pargana* Bayana have been taken into custody and the cattle of many villages have been captured. The *rabi* crop has ripened, [but] the peasants of many villages cut the standing crops and carry them to their villages. We require more army so that the land revenue of the *rabi* crops may be collected from the peasants of some more villages.[67]

The aforementioned instances clearly show that the ijara turned into an oppressive practice for the peasants in the late Mughal period. It was clearly in contravention of the norms of the Mughal revenue system insofar as various types of non-customary taxes were imposed on the peasants by the ijaradars (even the fiscal burden of the peshkash paid by the ijaradars to the imperial jagirdars/mansabdars in lieu of the ijara rights was passed on to the peasants in the form of a non-customary levy, viz., *virar*). Thus, not only did the peasants consider it as a violation of the *rajdharam* (royal duty)[68] on the part of the king and, therefore, an unjust, unethical and immoral practice, but they also found the total tax burden and the coercive measures of collection increasingly unbearable. Thus, various forms of peasant resistance to the practice, such as petitions at the Mughal court, armed uprisings against the ijaradars, non-payment of taxes or desertion of villages and fields, became common during the late Mughal period, resulting in a marked decline in the agricultural production in areas controlled by the ijaradars during the early eighteenth century.

This oppressive practice of ijara and the peasant protests against it were not just limited to Mewat but manifest in many parts of India as well. For instance, in 1714, a powerful protest of Ahir peasants against the oppression of the ijaradars broke out in the Narmada river valley in Gujarat. In the same year, peasant revolts broke out in parganas Kalanaur, Batala, Ropar, Bhatta, and Lahore of Lahore *suba*; Abdul Samad Khan was sent with big army to crush these revolts in which a large number of peasants were killed.[69] The peasants of pargana Jahangirabad in Bengal *suba* rose in protest against the high-handedness of the ijaradar when the latter raised the land revenue demand.[70] In the wake of peasant protests, the diwan and bakshi of Kuch (Kamrup) were dismissed on grounds of unlawful enhancement of revenue and negligence.[71] Aurangzeb had ordered the jagirdars in Kashmir not to give their jagirs on ijara, but to collect land revenue through their own amils.[72] The peasants of pargana Mandu in Malwa *suba* complained against the high-handedness of the ijaradar who had been forcing them to pay more land revenue.[73] A powerful peasant revolt reportedly took place under the leadership of Shabha Chand Jat in the Hardwar region. Nawab Amirul Umaro was sent with a large force to crush the revolt, but his two younger brothers were killed in the fighting and Shabha Chand Jat, along with his men, ran away to the hills of Srinagar.[74]

IV

While revealing the widespread discontent and unrest among the peasantry against the practice of ijara, the vakil reports also inform about the depredations of many imperial mansabdars and rebel zamindars in the countryside. Several imperial mansabdars, in alliance with the rebel zamindars of various localities, indulged in plundering villages and thereby compounding the misery of the helpless peasantry who often sought redressal of their grievances from the Mughal emperor.[75] In 1714, a powerful revolt of zamindars took place in the Awadh region. In the resultant battle between Sarbuland Khan (the subedar of the region) and the zamindars, more than 1,000 men were killed.[76] In another instance, Syed Kabir Khan (the faujdar of Muradabad) and Garh Mukteshwar were invited by the Syeds to attack the rebel zamindars of the region. Eventually, Kabir Khan along with his 4,000 soldiers crushed the zamindars.[77] The vakil further reported that in the absence of the Mughal emperor who had gone towards Deccan for hunting, the imperial mansabdars were plundering and oppressing the peasantry. The hapless peasantry was in distress, but not much attention was paid towards their grievances at the Mughal court.[78]

On the other hand, many imperial mansabdars complained to the Mughal emperor that the Rajput Bhomias (zamindars) were creating disturbances in their jagirs in order to extract the ijara rights from them. For instance, Ruhlaimat Khan, the imperial mansabdar of pargana Shonkhar-Shonkhari, accused Udai Singh and Vijayram Narukas of creating disturbances in the villages of his jagir.[79] Other imperial mansabdars, too, accused Panchnot Rajput Bhomias of not depositing the *hasil* (land revenue) of rabi harvest.[80] Nawab Shipehdar Khan and Bahadar Khan, the imperial mansabdars of Alwar sarkar, complained that the Chauhan and Panchnot Rajput Bhomias used to cut the standing crops of rabi harvest in the villages of their jagir and carry them away to their *garhis* (fortresses).[81] Mir Shahab-ud-din, mansabdar of pargana Sahar complained that Abheram, a *chakar* of the Amber Raja who was assigned Javan village of Shahab-ud-din's jagir on ijara, had deposited only Rs.300 out of a total of Rs.700 due from him.[82] Qazi Mohammad Akaram, the imperial mansabdar of pargana Sahar, complained that he had incurred big losses due to the disturbances caused by the Meos.[83] The imperial mansabdars of parganas Todathek and Pindayan complained that Naruka Rajputs were creating disturbances in their jagirs.[84] Pargana Mandawar was reported to be thoroughly disturbed by the depredations of Badgujar Rajput Bhomias. The amil of the Amber state informed that the agricultural production in 27 parganas of Alwar sarkar was adversely affected by such disturbances.[85] Dildar Khan, the imperial mansabdar of pargana Lalsot, also complained to the Mughal emperor that the Amber Raja had not paid 48 lakh *dams* for the ijara of his jagir.[86] Thus, as the Rajput Bhomias sometimes created disturbances, putting pressure on the imperial mansabdars to assign them the ijara of their jagirs, the imperial mansabdars had no option but to capitulate to their demands.

V

The ijara system was marked by a rather loose control of the central authority over the land revenue administrative mechanism, which not only resulted in anarchy in the rural society but also adversely affected the commercial and trading activities in the region during the early eighteenth century CE. The Rajasthani sources shed some light on the impact of the high-handedness of the ijaradars on trade and traders. In 1721, the community of traders in Sanganer town complained to the Amber Raja that the ijaradar had set up a *chautra* (police post) at the centre of the town and had started collecting *rahdari* (road tax) from traders without any *dastur* (custom). Due to the high rate of this tax that had never been charged earlier, the traders from other towns had stopped coming to Sanganer. They urged the Amber Raja to intervene in this matter, as otherwise the trade of the town would be badly affected.[87] Sharing this concern of the Sanganer traders, the amil too informed the Amber Raja that due to the high rate of *rahdari*, few traders were coming from Gujarat to Sanganer. An *arzdasht* mentions that Baloch traders from Bhera and Kasab in Punjab (modern-day Pakistan) when subjected to the new *rahdari* tax by the ijaradar decided not to come to Sanganer and instead to unload their merchandise (mainly Potassium Alum or *phitkari*) at Kotputali town.[88] Further, the vakil of the Amber Raja wrote from the Mughal court that due to the high rate of *rahdari* and other harassments by Churaman Jat and his men, the traders and shopkeepers had shut their shops in Agra and closed all the city gates as an act of protest. As a result of the traders' protest and breakdown in trade, the grain prices had soared, six *sers* costing as high as Re.1 in Agra.[89] The traders of Chatsu town complained to the diwan of the Amber Raja that they were being charged Rs.6,501 as *rahdari* by the ijaradar.[90] In 1709, the *amil* wrote to the Amber Raja that traders and *banjaras*[91] were not coming to Averi, Sanganer, Dosa, Fagi, and Mauzabad due to the fear of the Rajput Bhomias, and unless and until the faujdars would protect the trade routes, the traders would not dare to come to these towns.[92] The *banjaras* were further charged a tax (*hasil ghas charai*) for grazing their cattle, and the tax was raised to Rs.5 per 100 heads of cattle.[93]

The ijara system also dented the customary privileges of the Brahmins. The Brahmins complained to the diwan of the Amber Raja against the illegal and non-customary revenue demands of the ijaradars. The Brahmins used to get concession in the land revenue charged on their personal landholdings on the basis of the local customary practices during the Mughal period. This is evident from the *dastur-al amals*, which mention that the peasants belonging to high castes such as Brahmins, Rajputs and mahajans, were customarily charged the land revenue at lower rates than were the other castes by the Amber state.[94] For instance, in 1738, Bhudhar Das Brahmin of Chandpur village complained to the diwan of the Amber state that he had always paid the land revenue at the rate of 25 per cent on his personal landholdings to the state, but he was now being forced by Kharagsingh and Devisingh Shekhawats, the ijaradars of Atela Bhabhra, to pay the revenue at higher rates.[95] Mayaram Brahmin of Atela Bhabhra qasba similarly complained to the diwan that he was being forced by the ijaradar to pay the land revenue at higher rates.[96] To redress such grievances, the amil was ordered by the diwan to take the undertaking (*zamini*) from the sub-assignees (ijaradars) that they should not demand the revenue at higher rates from the Brahmins.[97]

VI

The ijara was not always granted by the state on political and economic considerations alone. Sometimes, it was granted for the purpose of rehabilitating deserted villages. In 1664, the ijara of 11 deserted villages of pargana Khohri was assigned by the imperial mansabdar in order to rehabilitate them. Similarly, in 1665, the ijara of six deserted and ruined villages of pargana Chalkaliyana was assigned by the imperial mansabdar to rehabilitate them.[98] In 1704, the amil of the Amber state submitted a report on the deserted villages of pargana Averi to the diwan. The peasantry of pargana Averi had deserted the villages due to the harassments by the Rajput Bhomias and emigrated to the villages of parganas Tonk and Boli. Thereafter, for eight to ten years these villages lay deserted. The ijara of these villages was then assigned to facilitate their rehabilitation, and seven of them, including Rangwar, Palai, Khanda, and Ramsingh pura, were rehabilitated. Subsequently, the others, viz., Mukandpur, Bhakti, Sherohi, Jugalpur Bujarak, Mandap, Vijaypur, Karod, Badthal, Sirsi, and Sumail, whose peasants and patels had emigrated to the villages of pargana Chatsu were also rehabilitated. The peasants settling in the deserted villages were given *patta votka* (concession in the land revenue), as per the agreement between them and the state prepared by the qanungo.[99] The amil wrote that 100 deserted villages in pargana Pahari had been rehabilitated by the peasants of Ahir caste;[100] many deserted villages of pargana Khohri by the peasants of Ahir caste; and many deserted villages in parganas Mojpur, Jalalpur, Naharkhoh, Khilohra, Harsana, and Pindayan by the *pahikasht* peasants.[101]

The rehabilitation of the deserted villages, however, brought about a new kind of conflict within the peasant community, i.e. between the old émigrés and the new settlers. For instance, when many Meo peasants returned to their native villages, they found that their villages had been already occupied by the Ahir peasants. This brought about confrontations between the Meo and the Ahir peasants in many villages of parganas Khohri and Pahari. The Ahir peasants from several villages of pargana Khohri, such as Taharpur, Bhada, Nikatpur, and Chanderpur, complained to the diwan that they had been brought by the amil to recolonize or rehabilitate these villages that had been lying deserted a few years ago, but were now being threatened and pressurized to leave by the Meos who had returned to these villages.[102] Similarly, the Ahir peasants from the villages of pargana Khohri, such as Verdu, Palko, Alamshahko, Palki, Jaishree, Shuketi, Jaishro, Varkero, Bhurakho, Vadkheri, and Paral, complained to the Amber Raja that two years ago they had recolonized these villages and built their mud houses (*chhapparbandi*), but were now being threatened by the Meo peasants.[103] On the other hand, the Meo peasants argued that these villages are their native villages, their ancestors had settled these villages long ago and they had been recently forced to abandon them only a few years ago in the wake of severe and prolonged drought. Actually, since the Amber Raja secured the ijara of these deserted villages, his *amil* rehabilitated them by settling the Ahir and *pahikasht* peasants in order to increase the agricultural production and the land revenue for the Amber Raja. Thus, besides being an exploitative and repressive system, the ijara system, even where it was meant to effect the rehabilitation of deserted villages and resumption of cultivation, created tensions and conflicts within the peasant communities.

VII

According to Alam and Wink, the ijara system led to a dislocation in the pre-existing agrarian relations, as many hereditary zamindars were replaced by bankers and speculators from the cities.[104] However, the *arsattas* show that in the Mewat and Brij regions, the Amber Raja and the Jats emerged as the chief ijaradars. By virtue of their superior social standing and military might, replaced the hereditary Meo and Khanzada zamindars. The Amber Raja used to sub-assign the ijara of the villages to his Rajput *chakars*, who mostly belonged to his own clan, the Kachhwahas. The pargana-level officials, such as chaudharis, qanungos and mahajans, who had been already engaged in the land revenue administration, were also sub-assigned the ijara of the villages.[105] For instance, in 1716, the Amber Raja secured the ijara of 134¾ villages in pargana Khohri from the imperial mansabdar and sub-assigned their ijara to his Rajput *chakars* in the following manner: 60, 41¾, 17¾, 4, 2, and ¾ villages were distributed among the Rajawats, the Narukas, the Kumbanis, the Rathores, the Chauhans, and the Hamirdekas, respectively; and the remaining 11¾ villages were sub-assigned to the land revenue officials.[106] Similarly, in 1724, the ijara of the entire pargana Khohri was assigned to the Amber Raja and others by the imperial mansabdar. The Amber Raja, in turn, sub-assigned the ijara of 127¼ villages to his own Rajput *chakars*—mainly the Narukas, the Kilanots, the Hamirdekas, the Vakawats, the Shaurampotas, the Rajawats and the Banbirpotakas—and the remaining 48 villages to Badan Singh Jat and Firoz Khan Khanzada.[107] The main difference between the patterns of ijara sub-assignment of 1716 and 1724 was the changing social position of the different groups of the sub-assignees. Among the Kachhwaha Rajput *chakars*, the Narukas, the Kilanots and the Hamirdekas were the dominant sub-assignees in 1724, while earlier, the Rajawats had secured the larger share of ijara villages. This change occurred for two reasons: first, after the death of Churaman Jat (1722), the Jats led by Badan Singh accepted the overlordship of the Amber Raja; second, the Narukas and the Kilanots gave up their plundering activities and rebellious attitude and were reconciled with the Amber Raja. Among the other sub-assignees too, notable ones from pargana Pahari were Mukand Ram Vakawat, the amil of pargana Khohri; Gujarmal Qanungo; Vijayram Chaudhari, Mohan Ram Mahajan; and Moti Ram Mahajan.[108] According to B.R. Grover, the Mughal state discouraged the revenue officers—chaudharis, qanungos and muqqadams—from acting as revenue farmers, because they did not possess adequate resources for the payment of the ijara instalments and resorted to dishonest practices. For instance, they would spend away the revenue collected, and in order to make up for the loss exempt their own lands from revenue assessment and coerce the ryots to make the excess payment, often excommunicating them from their villages in case of non-payment. Thus, these officials, in many cases, were instrumental in the oppression of the ryots.[109]

The erstwhile Meo zamindars fiercely resisted the encroachment of their traditional rights by the Amber Raja and Jats, but evidently they were fighting a lost battle. For instance, when in 1712, the Amber Raja got the zamindari of pargana Khohri, the Meo zamindars rose in revolt, but had to retreat and finally give up their zamindari in the face of the superior military strength of the Raja. In many cases, the Meo zamindars were removed ostensibly on the ground of their inability to make timely payment of revenue. For instance, the Meo zamindars in the villages of Neekatpura, Todarpur, Prannath, Bhada, and Jaisingpura in pargana Khohri were deprived of their zamindaris, since they had failed to deposit the land revenue to the ijaradar, i.e. the Amber Raja.[110] Many Meo zamindars were also replaced on account of their seditious activities. The diwan of the Amber state ordered the amils of parganas Khohri and Pahari that the ijara of none of the villages in these parganas be assigned to the rebel Meo and Jat zamindars, and those villages whose ijara had been already assigned to them be vacated.[111] It appears that the Amber Raja sought to systematically undermine the socio-economic base of the Meo zamindars so that they could not offer any effective resistance to his growing political ambitions in the Mewat region. The ijara system was the only means by which the Amber Raja could expand his territorial possessions and accommodate his Rajput *chakars* in the rural society by way of assigning them the revenue collection rights in villages and thereby create a strong foothold for them vis-à-vis the Meos. Under these circumstances, the Naruka Rajputs, who were already socially dominant, further strengthened their position by acquiring zamindaris in many villages of Alwar sarkar through the ijara system. The Jats, too, acquired zamindaris in many villages of parganas Khohri, Pahari Hodal, Deeg, Kama, Devti Shanchari, Kathumbar, and Bhashawar.[112]

In the Mewat region, as noted earlier, the majority of sub-assignees were the Rajput *chakars* who owed their grant of ijara to their membership of the Kachhwaha clan to which the Amber Raja belonged as well. After getting the ijara, the new zamindars, i.e. Rajput *chakars* (mainly Narukas and Kilanots) and the Jats, invested their resources in consolidating their social, political and military position in the villages by raising *jamiyats* (contingents of soldiers belonging to their own sects or clans) and constructing *garhis* (fortresses), rather than in trade and commerce. There are no references to the new zamindars being involved in trade and commerce in the Mewat region. On the contrary, the Rajasthani sources refer to them establishing their *bhomi* rights over many villages in Alwar sarkar by constructing *garhis*.[113] There are also many references to the construction of new *gharis*, the raising of *jamiyats* and the mobilization of war weapons. The amil wrote to the Amber Raja that Naruka Bhomias had constructed *gharis* between parganas Mandawar and Banawar and had forcibly collected Rs.12,000 from the peasantry for the maintenance of their own *jamiyats*.[114] Similarly, as the amil reported, the Panchnot Rajput Bhomias had forcibly collected *rahdari* and *nyota* from the traders and peasants, respectively, constructed new *gharis* in the villages, raised their own *jamiyats*, and collected war materials in their *garhis*.[115]

In an another letter, the amil wrote that the Chauhan and Panchanot Bhomias had constructed *garhis* in the ijara villages of Baghari, Mundawari, Maharawar Vachhochh, Phulwara, Batota, and Jharoda in pargana Liwali. The peasants of these villages were forced by these Bhomias to pay more money.[116] The amil further noted that the Naruka and Kilanot Bhomias had constructed new gharis in most of the villages in the parganas of Mundawar, Naharkhoh, Punkhar, Bharkol, Umarni, Manbhari, Hasanpur, and Rori parganas of the Mewat region. Thereafter, they had even ceremonially celebrated the construction of new *garhis* in the villages with their own men by organizing *nangal* (feasts).[117] It was reported that the faujdar of Hindaun had attacked the *garhis* of Kishna and Daula Narukas and seized 12,000 maunds of grain, 20 horses, 100 *ramchangis* (local guns), and four *rahkallans* (small cannons).[118]

Thus, it was these efforts of the new zamindars to build and consolidate their power base in the Mewat region in the early eighteenth century CE by expending most of the revenue collected for raising and maintaining military contingents and constructing their *gharis* that laid the social, political and military foundations for the formation of the Alwar state in the late eighteenth century CE. Therefore, while it is true that the ijara practice eroded the power of hereditary zamindars, such as the Meos and the Khanzadas, as has been pointed out by Alam, in the Mewat region, the old zamindars were not replaced by the 'bankers and speculators' but by the Rajput *chakars* of the Amber state or the Jats who were more interested in consolidating their politico-military base than increasing agricultural production and productivity.

Commenting on this exploitative character of the ijara system during the early eighteenth-century CE Mahrashtra, Wink rightly points out that 'it would be seen as "oppressive" where the legitimate kings share (*rajbhag*) of the agricultural produce no longer represented the limit of a demand which was increased arbitrarily by an uncontrolled revenue farmer imposing extra taxes or raising assessment rates'.[119] Wink cites Peshwa Madav Rao I who wrote in his will of 1772 that the *raiyat*s were oppressed in Konkan and Desh due to revenue farming, and made a plea for its abolition and substitution by 'regular management' in order to give protection to the subjects.[120]

VIII

From the discussion in the foregoing sections, it is clear that in the wake of the weakening of Mughal revenue administration and the growing incidence of agrarian unrest in the late seventeenth and early eighteenth centuries CE, the imperial jagirdars/mansabdars found it increasingly difficult to collect land revenue from their jagirs and hence started assigning them on ijara to local zamindars, and particularly to the emergent political powers, the Amber Raja and Churaman Jat. Some did so even when there were no disturbances in their jagirs because it had become more of a fashion and convenience to assign territories on ijara. Some zamindars, on their part, created disturbances in the jagirs of the imperial mansabdars to compel the latter to grant them ijara rights. Nevertheless, the practice turned out to be profitable for both the mansabdars who assigned their jagirs on ijara and the zamindars who received them. The mansabdars found it a convenient—and rather irresponsible—way to ensure revenue collection and derive an income greater than the regular revenue. In this sense, they acted like absentee landlords shifting the responsibility of revenue administration to the local zamindars. The latter sought to increase their own income, as well as raise money for paying peshkash to the mansabdars and remunerating the revenue officials and contingents who were required in large numbers to assess and collect revenue. To this end, they imposed and collected various irregular levies. Thus, both mansabdars and zamindars promoted and hugely profited from this practice, which amounted to a flagrant violation of the norms of the Mughal land revenue administration and led to a ruthless exploitation and immiseration of the peasantry. The peasants, in turn, considered the practice of ijara unethical, unjust and non-customary; they resorted to various acts of resistance, such as petitioning at the Mughal court, armed rebellions, non-payment of taxes and wilful abandonment of cultivation and desertion of villages. It created discontent not only among the peasants but also among other sections of the society, such as traders, Brahmins and *banjaras*. Further, it also resulted in the phenomenon of military fiscalism in the region. In the wake of a fierce rivalry between the Amber Raja and Churaman Jat for the acquisition of jagirs on ijara, zamindars, both Jat and Rajput, constructed fortresses, mobilized troops, and arranged for the manufacture and storage of ammunitions. By doing so, they strove to build, consolidate and assert their politico-military power in their respective localities, as also convince the mansabdars of their capacity to collect revenue and protect their revenue-collection rights by military might. Politically, the phenomenon established the base for a military fiscal state in the early eighteenth century. But economically, it diverted the crucial resources away from productive activities, such as agriculture, artisanal manufacture and trade; and socially, it intensified the exploitation of the peasantry.

The social unrest caused by the widespread practice of ijara can be understood at multiple levels. First, the position and role of zamindars and primary producers, i.e. peasantry, underwent a visible change and realignment in terms of access to resources and social privileges. Second, a major shift in the perceptions of power and authority is discernible. Amidst the growing political turmoil, the legitimacy of the rights of different claimants to the surplus produce was continuously contested as reflected in the rivalry between the Amber state and the Jats over the acquisition of ijara. At the same time, the traditional claims of the Mughal state to the land revenue, as also its political and administrative control, were progressively eroded. This, in turn, led to the overall weakening of the mechanisms of grievance redressal at the village level, this further affecting the peasantry. These developments eroded the customary rights of the peasants and placed a heavy burden on their already meagre resources. The hapless peasantry was left with no alternative but to satisfy all the demands of the multiple claimants on the agricultural surplus. In order to cope with this abnormal situation, the peasantry resorted to invoking higher moral justifications, such as *ruh-nyaya* (conscientious justice), and began mobilizing themselves on caste lines.

To sum up, the ijara in the late seventeenth and early eighteenth centuries CE, unlike the other pre-existing Mughal administrative structures, such as mansabdari, jagirdari or the revenue administration, was not an institution created by imperial policy, nor was it a progressive instrument of reinvigorating and expanding agricultural production. Rather, it was an ad hoc mechanism co-created by the mansabdars and zamindars to reap short-term fiscal benefits. But it, in turn, created disorder, tension and conflicts in the rural society, leading to debilitating impacts on various sectors of the economy, chiefly agriculture where it led to shrinkage in the area under cultivation and fall in the output. Judging by its intent, practice and effect, the ijara was not a political success in the long run either. On the one hand, it could not arrest the demise of the Mughal Empire, rather by heightening the rural unrest, particularly the peasant protests, it hastened its collapse. On the other hand, as a mechanism conceived and used by the emergent regional political entities to maximally appropriate the agricultural surplus for self-aggrandizement in a short span of time, it could not function as a stable institution for sustaining a military-fiscal state in the long run.

Notes

1. Irfan Habib, 'The Eighteenth Century in Indian Economic History', in *The Eighteenth Century in India*, ed. Seema Alvi, New Delhi: Oxford University Press, 2002, pp. 55–82; B.R. Grover, *Land and Taxation System during the Mughal Age*, vol. 4, *Collected Works of Professor B. R. Grover*, ed. Amrita Grover et al., New Delhi: Low Price Publications, 2009, pp. 27–8.

2. C.A. Bayly, *Rulers, Townsmen and Bazaars: North Indian Society in the Age of British Expansion, 1770–1870*, Cambridge: Cambridge University Press, 1983, pp. 14–15; André Wink, 'Maratha Revenue Farming', *Modern Asian Studies*, vol. 17, no. 4, 1983, pp. 591–628; Muzaffar Alam, *Crisis of the Empire in Mughal North India: Awadh and the Punjab, 1707–48*, Delhi: Oxford University Press, 1986, pp. 39–40.

3. Wink, 'Maratha Revenue Farming'.

4. Dilbagh Singh, *The State, Landlords and Peasants: Rajasthan in the 18th Century*, New Delhi: Manohar, 1990, pp. 129–36.

5. S.P. Gupta, 'Ijara System in Eastern Rajasthan (c. 1650–1750)', in *Medieval India: A Miscellany*, vol. 2, New Delhi: Centre of Advanced Study, Department of History, Aligarh Muslim University and Asia Publishing House, 1972, pp. 263–74. According to Gupta, the imperial mansabdars were unable to collect land revenue from their jagirs situated in the periphery of the Jaipur state due to the weakening of the Mughal revenue administration and began to assign the ijara of their jagirs to the Amber chiefs. Thus, after 1712, Maharaja Sawai Jai Singh or Jai Singh II came to acquire the ijara of several parganas within the imperial jagirs, and the area thus acquired far exceeded that of his *tankhwah jagir* (land in lieu of salary). Not only did he retain control over this area for life, but he also had them administered by his subordinate ijaradars to whom he had sub-assigned the ijara of these parganas.

6. Abul-Fazl, *The Ain-i-Akbari*, vol. 2, tr. H. Blochmann, corr. and ann. Sir Jadunath Sarkar, 3rd edn, Calcutta: Royal Asiatic Society, 1978, pp. 202–6.

7. Satish Chandra, 'Mughal Relations with the Rajput State of Rajasthan: The Foundations', in *Essays on Medieval Indian History*, New Delhi: Oxford University Press, 2003, pp. 357–407; Iqtidar Alam Khan, 'The Nobility under Akbar and the Development of His Religious Policy, 1560–80', *Journal of the Royal Asiatic Society of Great Britain and Ireland*, vol. 100, no. 1, 1968, pp. 29–36.

8. Singh, *The State, Landlords and Peasants*, p. 129.

9. Ibid., p. 129. The Mughal state assigned the ijara of a portion of its *paibaqi* lands comprising a single village or a few villages or a single pargana to a *mustajir* on terms stipulated in the *patta*. Similarly, a *tankhwah jagirdar* or a *madad-i-maash* grantee could give a portion or whole of his land grant to a *mustajir*. The lease contract would be for a single crop or two crops grown in a year, or for a period of three years or so. Under the Mughal ijara system, the tenure of ijara grant was never permanent, but short-term ijara assignments were renewable.

10. Grover, *Land and Taxation System during the Mughal Age*, p. 26.

11. Singh, *The State, Landlords and Peasants*, p. 129.

12. Grover, *Land and Taxation System during the Mughal Age*, p. 26.

13. Some scholars trace the origins of the system to earlier periods. For instance, in his *Land and Taxation System during the Mughal Age*, Grover locates the roots of the ijara system in the Sultanate period. The Dutch merchant Francisco Pelsaert who visited Mughal India in the seventeenth century CE, noted that even during Emperor Jahangir's reign, the jagirdars had begun to

assign the ijara of their jagirs due to the inability of their agents to collect revenue. See Francisco Pelsaert, *Jahangir: India: The Remonstratre of Franscisco Pelsaert*, tr. W.H. Moreland and P. Geyl, Cambridge: W. Heffere, 1925, p. 54.

14. *Arsatta*, pargana Pahari, vs 1788/CE 1731; *Dehai-ferhashti*, pargana Khohri, vs 1769–1807/CE 1712–50.

15. *Dastur-al amal*, pargana Khohri, vs 1723/CE 1666; *Dastur-al amal*, pargana Shonkhar-Shonkhari, vs 1773/CE 1716; *Dastur-al amal*, pargana Atela Bhabhra, vs 1767/CE 1710; *Chithi* to the amil, pargana Khohri, dt. *Asadh Sudi* 7, vs 1784/CE 1727; *Chithi* to the amil, pargana Khohri, *Asadh Vadi* 9, vs 1784/CE 1727.

16. Ratan Lal Mishra, *Kiyamkhani Vamsh ka Itihasa evam Samskriti*, Jodhpur: Rajasthani Granthagar, 2002, 2nd revd edn, pp. 99–100.

17. Ibid.

18. *Arsatta*, pargana Khohri, vs 1781/CE 1724, vs 1783/CE 1726.

19. *Arzdasht*, *Asadh Sudi* 2, vs 1761/CE 1704. *Chithi* to the amil, pargana Pahari, *Vaishakh Sudi* 4, vs 1783/CE 1726; pargana Atela Piragpur, *Chet Vadi Amavash*, vs 1784/CE 1727. The sub-assignees were asked to give their undertaking (*jamini*) to the main ijaradar at the rate of 1½ rupees on 100 rupees in order to get the ijara of the villages.

20. *Arzdasht*, *Mah Vadi* 6, vs 1761/CE 1704.

21. *Arzdasht*, *Posh Vadi* 15, vs 1761/CE 1704.

22. *Arzdasht*, *Chet Vadi* 14, vs 1769/CE 1712.

23. *Arzdasht*, *Sawan Sudi* 3, vs 1771/CE 1714.

24. *Chithi* to the amil, pargana Pahari, *Vaisakh Sudi* 4, vs 1783/CE 1726; pargana Khohri, vs 1782/CE 1725. *Dehai-ferhashti*, pargana Khohri, vs 1767–1807/CE 1710–50 (this document mentions the names of the sub-assignees).

25. *Arzdasht*, *Kartik Sudi* 9, vs 1759/CE 1702.

26. *Arzdasht*, *Mah Vadi* 4, vs 1761/CE 1704.

27. *Arzdasht*, *Chet Vadi* 4, vs 1761/CE 1704.

28. *Vakil's* Report, *Asoj Vadi* 2, vs 1769/CE 1712.

29. *Vakil's* Report, 9th *Ramzan* 51st, vs 1764/CE 1707.

30. Mishra, *Kayamkhani Vamsha*, pp. 99–100.

31. Ibid.

32. *Vakil's* Report, *Asoj Vadi* 8, vs 1769/CE 1712.

33. *Vakil's* Report, *Jeth Vadi* 3, vs 1769/CE 1712.

34. *Vakil's* Report, *Fagun Sudi* 2, vs 1767/CE 1710.

35. *Vakil's* Report, *Asadh Vadi* 17, vs 1771/CE 1714.

36. *Vakil's* Report, *Jeth Sudi* 11, vs 1771/CE 1714.

37. *Arzdasht*, *Asadh Sudi* 3, vs 1773/CE 1716.

38. *Vakil's* Report, *Jeth Sudi* 12, vs 1772/CE 1715.

39. *Arzdasht, Asadh Sudi* 2, vs 1769/ce 1712.
40. *Arsatta, pargana* Khohri, vs 1773/ce 1716.
41. *Arzdasht, Asadh Vadi* 15, vs 1766/ce 1709.
42. *Vakil's* Report, *Asoj Vadi* 7, vs 1769/ce 1712.
43. *Vakil's* Report, *Bhadva Vadi Amavash*, vs 1769/ce 1712.
44. *Arzdasht, Vaishakh Sudi* 7, vs 1769/ce 1772.
45. *Chithi* to the amil, *pargana* Khohri, *Vaishakh Sudi* 9, vs 1785/ce 1728.
46. *Arzdasht, Asadh Vadi* 5, vs 1744/ce 1685.
47. *Arsatta*, pargana Sahar, vs 1749/ce 1692.
48. *Arsatta*, pargana Pindayan, vs 1786/ce 1729.
49. *Chithi* to the amil, pargana Khohri, *Mah Vadi* 6, vs 1797/ce 1740.
50. *Chithi* to the amil, pargana Khohri, vs 1787/ce 1730.
51. *Chithi* to the amil, pargana Pawta, *Asoj Sudi* 14, vs 1787/ce 1730.
52. *Arzdasht, Asadh Vadi* 5, vs 1744/ce 1685.
53. *Arzdasht, Asadh Vadi* 2, vs 1768/ce 1711.
54. *Arsatta*, pargana Alwar, vs 1782/ce 1725.
55. *Arsatta*, pargana Khohri, vs 1783/ce 1726.
56. *Dehai-ferhashti*, pargana Khohri, vs 1789/ce 1732.
57. *Arsatta*, pargana Pahari, vs 1773/ce 1716.
58. *Arsatta*, pargana Pahari, vs 1781/ce 1725.
59. *Arsatta*, pargana Pahari, vs 1788/ce 1731.
60. *Chithi* to the amil, pargana Pahari, vs 1788/ce 1731.
61. *Chithi* to the amil, pargana Pahari, vs 1788/ce 1731.
62. *Arsatta*, pargana Khohri, vs 1769/ce 1712; pargana Khohri, vs 1770/ce 1713.
63. *Arsatta*, pargana Khohri, vs 1773/ce 1716.
64. *Arsatta*, pargana Mojpur, vs 1771/ce 1714.
65. *Arsatta*, pargana Pahari, vs 1771/ce 1714.
66. *Arsatta*, pargana Pahari, vs 1799/ce 1742, vs 1800/ce 1743.
67. *Arzdasht, Fagun Vadi* 13, vs 1752/ce 1695; *Bhadva Vadi* 6, vs 1752/ce 1695.
68. For details on the peasant conception of *rajdharam*, see Chapter 6 of this volume.
69. *Vakil's* Report, *Chet Vadi* 10, vs 1771/ce 1714.
70. Grover, *Land and Taxation System during the Mughal Age*, p. 28.
71. Ibid.
72. Ibid.
73. Ibid., p. 36, n. 64.
74. *Vakil's* Report, *Vaishakh Vadi* 1, vs 1771/ce 1714.
75. Ibid.
76. *Vakil's* Report, *Sawan Vadi* 1, vs 1771/ce 1714.

77. *Vakil's* Report, *Mangsir Vadi* 9, vs 1769/CE 1712.

78. *Vakil's* Report, *Mangsir Vadi* 11, vs 1771/CE 1714.

79. *Arzdasht, Asadh Vadi* 5, vs 1742/CE 1685.

80. *Arzdasht, Asadh Sudi* 6, vs 1739/CE 1682.

81. *Arzdasht, Posh Vadi* 7, vs 1743/CE 1686.

82. *Khatoot-ahalkaran, Asadh Sudi* 3, vs 1750/CE 1693.

83. *Arzdasht, Kartik Sudi* 12, vs 1755/CE 1698.

84. *Arzdasht, Sawan Vadi* 11, vs 1747/CE 1690.

85. *Arzdasht, Asoj Sudi* 5, vs 1742/CE 1685; *Asoj Sudi* 7, vs 1742/CE 1685.

86. *Vakil's* Report, *Chet Sudi* 13, vs 1768/CE 1711.

87. *Arzdasht, Kartik Sudi* 13, vs 1778/CE 1721.

88. *Arzdasht, Fagun Sudi* 4, vs 1755/CE 1698.

89. *Vakil's* Report, *Mangsir Vadi* 9, vs 1769/CE 1712.

90. *Arzdasht, Vaishak Sudi* 3, vs 1758/CE 1701.

91. *Banjara*s were, and still are, itinerant tribes trading in and transporting various commodities.

92. *Arzdasht, Mangsir Sudi* 12, vs 1766/CE 1709.

93. *Arsatta, pargana* Khohri, vs 1769/CE 1712.

94. *Dastur-al amal,* pargana Khohri, *Hizari San* 1044/CE 1639–40; pargana Atela Bhabhra, vs 1767/CE 1710; pargana Sonkhar Sonkhari, vs 1773/CE 1716; pargana Mojpur, vs 1770/CE 1713.

95. *Chithi* to the amil, pargana Atela Bhabhra, *Chet Sudi* 13, vs 1795/CE 1738.

96. *Chithi* to the amil, pargana Atela Bhabhra, *Sawan Sudi* 1, vs 1792/CE 1725.

97. *Chithi* to the amil, pargana Bharkol, *Jeth Sudi* 7, vs 1786/CE 1729.

98. *Yaddashti Hal Bail,* pargana Chalkaliyana, vs 1722/CE 1665.

99. *Arzdasht, Asadh Sudi* 2, vs 1761/CE 1704.

100. *Arzdasht, Fagun Sudi* 12, vs 1746/CE 1689.

101. *Arzdasht, Asoj Sudi* 7, vs 1732/CE 1675; *Fagun Sudi* 9, vs 1745/CE 1688. *Chithi* to the amil, pargana Khohri, vs 1797/CE 1740; pargana Khohri, *Mah Vadi* 6, vs 1797/CE 1740.

102. *Chithi* to the amil, pargana Khohri, vs 1797/CE 1740.

103. *Chithi* to the amil, pargana Khohri, *Sawan Sudi* 7, vs 1807/CE 1750.

104. Alam, *Crisis of the Empire,* p. 39; Wink, 'Maratha Revenue Farming'.

105. Singh, *The State, Landlords and Peasants,* pp. 129–30.

106. *Arsatta,* pargana Khohri, vs 1773/CE 1716.

107. *Arsatta,* pargana Khohri, vs 1781/CE 1724.

108. *Arsatta,* pargana Pahari, vs 1781/CE 1724, vs 1782/CE 1725, vs 1786/CE 1729.

109. Grover, *Land and Taxation during the Mughal Age,* p. 27.

110. *Chithi* to the amil, pargana Khohri, *Asadh Vadi* 4, vs 1797/CE 1740.

111. *Chithi* to the amil, pargana Khohri, *Asadh Vadi* 5, vs 1791/CE 1734; pargana

Pahari, *Posh Vadi* 6, vs 1784/ce 1727; pargana Khohri, *Bhadva Sudi* 2, vs 1791/ce 1734.

112. *Arzdasht*, vs 1747/ce 1690; *Mangsir Sudi* 13, vs 1754/ce 1697; *Vaishakh Sudi* 7, vs 1755/ce 1698; *Asoj Sudi* 7, vs 1740/ce 1683; *Mangsir Sudi* 2, vs 1745/ce 1688. *Chithi* to the amil, pargana Khohri, *Bhadva Sudi* 7, vs 1743/ce 1686; pargana Khohri, vs 1795/ce 1738.

113. *Arzdasht*, vs 1761/ce 1704.

114. *Arzdasht, Asadh Vadi* 5, vs 1742/ce 1685.

115. *Arzdasht, Asadh Sudi* 6, vs 1739/ce 1682.

116. *Arzdasht, Posh Vadi* 7, vs 1743/ce 1686.

117. *Vakil's* Report, *Chet Sudi* 13, vs 1768/ce 1711; *Arzdasht, Bhadva Vadi* 7, vs 1742/ce 1685.

118. *Arzdasht*, vs 1761/ce 1704. However, S.P. Gupta has argued that the ijara was sub-assigned by the Amber Raja to the jagirdars in his service, who qualified for the grant either by their local standing or by their capacity to hold their own amidst a turbulent population; see Gupta, 'Ijara System in Eastern Rajasthan', pp. 263–74.

119. Wink, 'Maratha Revenue Farming'.

120. Ibid.

5

Changing Dynamics of Peasant-State Relation in Mewat

Conflicts, Conciliations and Incipient Class Consciousness

THE NATURE OF PEASANT protests/rebellions in medieval Indian history has been discussed by many historians, although the nature of class consciousness, if any, underlying such protests has not been adequately studied. Irfan Habib points out that the peasants in medieval India lacked the kind of class consciousness that the peasants in medieval Western Europe, especially England and Germany, had cultivated in their conflict with the feudal landlords for protecting their economic interests and rights.[1] He concedes that Indian peasants did revolt against the Mughal state, but contends that the peasant protests/rebellions were divided along caste, communitarian and religious lines and that the development of a distinct class consciousness among the peasants was impeded by the class of zamindars or landlords. The zamindar class managed to subsume the conflict of the peasants with the Mughal state within its own conflict with the state by merging its grievances against the state with those of the peasants, and thereby exploited the peasants' discontent to subserve its own interests. Thus, the zamindars' contradictions with the state became primary and the peasants' secondary, and their exploitation continued in the same manner even after the decline of the Mughal Empire.

Linking the social conflict between the peasant and the state to a peculiar characteristic of the Indian production system, Harbans Mukhia argues:

In early medieval western Europe social conflict inhered in the very process of production, in which all the different strata of the rural society had a degree of involvement; consequently, a resolution of it was possible in the transformation of the production system and redistribution of the means of production, giving rise to new classes. In medieval India, on the other hand social conflict was limited to the distribution and redistribution of the surplus; the means of production did not get redistributed.[2]

In other words, the production process of the peasantry by itself was free from extraneous control, but it was only after the process had been completed that the exploitation of peasantry came to be centred on revenue collection and the peasant-state conflict surfaced over the distribution of surplus.[3] This is why, as Mukhia observes, the class struggle between the Indian peasantry and state was different from that between the west European peasantry and lords.

Commenting on R.S. Sharma's and Debiprasad Chattopadhyaya's views on the role of ideology in shaping the peasant's mind in early and medieval Indian society, Mukhia states that they 'tend to treat it as a kind of conspiratorial creation of the ruling class implanting its own ideology on to the peasants' (or artisans') mind and thereby impeding the growth of peasants' class consciousness and consequent class struggle'.[4] He, in particular, cites Sharma's observations at length in this regard:

Classes with conflicting interests were kept together through the performance of *puja* [worship], *japa* [repeated uttering of a sacred name or verse], *vratas* [fasts or domestic rituals], *tirthas* [pilgrimages], *samskaras* [rituals connected with life cycle], *prayaschitas* [penances] and through the prospects of heaven and hell. The all-pervasive influence of astrology (*jyotisa*) and that of the doctrine of Vedanta kept the people reconciled to their lot. All factors brought people of opposite interests together.[5]

Mukhia critiques this view as a rather 'partial vision, for it does not explain why the peasants came to accept an ideology so alien to their interests' and 'tacitly assumes' that the ruling class, with considerable intellectual, among other resources, 'develops a sophisticated ideology to defend its own interest which it then imparts to the peasantry', while the peasantry with no similar intellectual resources at its command, is unable to resist the alien ideology.[6] Further, this view, in Mukhia's words,

amounts to considerable disrespect to the intelligence of peasants to treat them merely as victims of ruling class conspiracy. This is not to deny the influence of the ruling class ideology on peasant's minds, but to suggest that peasants accept that part of the ruling class ideology which corresponds to their daily experience; they do not accept all of alien ideology. Thus, for example, the medieval Indian peasant was renowned for his fatalistic attitude, an attitude which would reconcile him to considerable adversity. . . . But the peasant would accept the notion of fatalism only when his crop had failed, for he had no one else to blame for it. Unlike the medieval European peasant whose process of production was under control of the lord and who therefore had a visible target in case of crop failure, the Indian peasant's process of production being free from such extraneous control . . . he could hardly lay the responsibility for it at the door of any individual or institution; an invisible factor such as fate then came handy as an explanation. But the same peasant refused to blame this fate if the state or its agent demanded more revenue than was customary; he stood up for his rights, sometimes by submitting petitions, at other times by threatening to give up cultivation, at still others by actually migrating to other areas or into forests and finally by taking up arms. This time his enemy stood before him, and one could hardly trace a sign of the fatalistic attitude in him.[7]

In explaining why the medieval Indian peasant demonstrated a fatalistic attitude in certain situations and did not do so in others, Mukhia not only points to a selective absorption of the ruling class' ideology by the peasant who accepted crop failure or bad harvest as fait accompli but not the non-customary exactions by the state, but also locates the root of conflict between the peasant and the ruling class in the redistribution of surplus outside the production process.

Following Sharma's contention, it is difficult to deny that the medieval Indian peasant was in the grip of superstitions and fatalism: he believed in evil spirits, sorcery, omens, life cycle rituals, fasts and vows, penances, etc. Indeed, the late-nineteenth-century British ethnographer P.W. Powlett records the immense popularity of religious texts such as *Satyanarayan ki Katha* and astrological texts such as *Shanichar ki Katha* in eastern Rajasthan,[8] the area under the purview of this study. The texts differ in their essence: the former stresses on the importance of keeping fasts for securing good results, while the latter warns against the ill-effects of selling or buying cattle, or of sending wife to her natal home or bringing her back from there on Saturday. Similarly, the peasant took recourse to sorcery in the hope of alleviating his pain or physical ailments and those of his cattle. At the same time, he feared the sorcerer or witch doctor lest the latter unleashed evil spirits to possess or afflict him. Further, he worshipped the *bhomia* or *bhaiya*, a platform with stones placed on it so as to protect a lamp, sacred to the *khera devata* (guardian deity) of the locality, in order to invoke his protective blessings for the locality or village.[9] Several big and small fairs were also held at regular intervals and served to anchor the religio-cultural life of the rural society.

Notwithstanding his fatalism and belief in the supernatural, the peasant was a realist: he acquired considerable pragmatic knowledge, insight and wisdom from his day-to-day experiences. For instance, he inherited from his ancestors and bequeathed to his successors precise experiential knowledge about agriculture: when to sow seeds of a particular crop and in what quantity, when to reap its harvest, how to practice crop rotation or multicropping, etc. He similarly developed a keen foresight about nature's behaviour, for instance, occurrence of droughts or good rains.

In this respect, while I concur with Mukhia's contention that the peasant did not accept the ideology of the ruling class entirely and was selectively fatalistic (as he is now), I argue that the fatalistic attitude demonstrated by the peasant was not necessarily the part of the ruling class' ideology that he imbibed, but was the result of a profound lived experience of struggle with nature's fury and gratitude to nature's bounty. This is especially so, the peasant's agricultural wealth was completely dependent on nature. His gaze was always fixated at the sky in the hope of rains. Every time he managed to reap a good harvest and safely bring it back home, he got a fresh lease of life and happily paid the revenue due to the state. And every time the standing crops withered owing to insufficient rains or drought, or were ruined by hail, or devoured by locusts invading from the west or other pests; or the reaped harvest was blown away by strong winds, he blamed his ill fate and worried himself to death over feeding his family. Thus, he lived in perpetual fear of nature's erratic behaviour. Capturing this plight of the peasant are the following Haryanvi couplets from a *bhajan* by late Hardhyan Singh, addressed to the peasant:

> पट-पट कै दिन-रात कमाया, फरि भी भूखा सोया रै।
> अन्नदाता, तेरा हाल देखकर मेरा जीवड़ा रोया रै ॥
> तेरे बैरी बहोत जगत मैं, तुँ क्यूकर रहै रुखाला रै।
> सूसा, भूसा, चड़िया, बईयां, गादड़ कर गया चाला रै ॥

आंधी, धूंध, फूल नै खोदे, बुरी आग तैं पाला रै ।
औले, बिजली, फसल फूंकदे, रुखां तक का गाला रै ॥
पीपी, डीडी, सुन्डी, रोली कड़िा कान्दरा यो रोज काढ़लै कोया रै ।
अन्नदाता तेरा हाल देखकर मेरा जीवड़ा रोया रै ॥

O peasant, you earn by toiling in the field day and night,
yet you sleep unfed.
O food-giver, seeing your plight rends my heart.
Many are your enemies in this world; how do you stop them [from
damaging your crops]?
Rodents, hares, sparrows, weaver birds and jackals play their 'tricks' [i.e.,
devour the crops],
winds and fog spoil them,
hail and frost consume them like fire,
insects feed on them.
O food-giver, seeing your plight rends my heart.[10] [Translation mine]

It was this fury of nature in varied forms that made the peasant fatalistic. Further, in his worldview and thinking, the peasant significantly differed from the ruling class. He accepted the ideology of the ruling class to the extent he found it just and beneficial, in other words, corresponding to his interests and social situation. Folk musical-cum-theatrical performances, such as *sang/svang* and *tamasha*, played an important role in shaping the peasant's worldview. These performances were based on the life stories of legendary rulers. While credible information on the history of such performances in the peasant society of medieval north India is inadequate and fragmentary because of their fluid, oral character, there must have been a well established, long-standing performative tradition in one form or the other in the medieval period, considering their survival in the nineteenth century (and even to this day).

As early as the sixteenth century, Narsingh Meo of Kajhota village composed a ballad 'Hasan Khan ki Katha'[11] on Hasan Khan Mewati, a Khanzada ruler of Mewat. Kishanlal Bhat, who is regarded as the father of the *sang* tradition, is placed in the first half of the eighteenth century, more precisely between 1730 and 1750. Three of his *sangs* that narrate the stories of Guru Guga, Raja Gopichand and Raja Nal have been discussed by the British civil servant and folklorist R.C. Temple in his late-nineteenth-century three-volume work, *The Legends of the Panjab*.[12] In the eighteenth century, Saadulla Khan composed 'Pandun

Ko Karo',[13] a Mewati rendition of the Sanskrit epic *Mahabharata*, sung by wandering bards/minstrels (*mirasis*) in the region. It recasts the ancient epic story of a fratricidal conflict between two collateral branches of a ruling family into that of a struggle of the dispossessed Pandavas for their legitimate rights and against the oppressions of their cousins, the Kauravas, and, by implication, into a conflict between the forces of justice/righteousness and injustice/unrighteousness. In the second half of the nineteenth century, there emerged two other famous exponents of this folk tradition, Ali Baksh (*c.*1854–91) and Pandit Deepchand. The former is credited with the composing 'Nal-Daman',[14] a tale of the trials and tribulations of a mythical king Nal and his wife Damayanti, drawn from the *Mahabharata* and popular in the Mewat region. Deepchand is said to have wandered in the villages of Haryana, popularizing his *sangs*, the most notable of which are those on Raja Bhoj and Sarande, Nal-Damayanti, Gopichand Maharaj and Raja Harishchandra.[15] Besides, in the late nineteenth century, Alexander Cunningham also reported that stories of the Badgujar Rajput chiefs, well known for their justice, had been popular in the Alwar region of eastern Rajasthan since the early Sultanate period.[16] Among these, the stories of King Mordhvaj were particularly popular among members of the Meena caste. Similarly popular was the tale of two brave Chandel Rajput warrior-brothers, Alha and Udal of Mahoba (present-day Uttar Pradesh) in thirteenth–fourteenth century, sung by wandering *jogis* throughout north India. In the nineteenth century, in Haryana and eastern Rajasthan, performances based on such folk tales attracted thousands of peasants from many villages, near and far. While one or the other of these tales individually may well have been relatively more popular among or more reflective of the aspirations of particular rural groups/communities of certain areas, the tales were/are not or, at least, not seen as being exclusively associated with specific groups. Rather, they were known in various renditions over a wide area of north India and thus constituted a body of oral traditions shared in common by the rural communities/groups notwithstanding caste/communitarian differences.

The historicity of many of the protagonists (male and female) of these folktales remains dubious at best, and is an issue of secondary importance. What is of primary importance is that the folktales project these characters, real or mythical, as exemplars of the ideals of justice, morality, duty, sacrifice, struggle, forbearance and truthfulness. These stories when recounted through enlivening musical-cum-theatrical performances must have left a deep impression on the minds of the peasant-audience, as they still do. They could relate their everyday struggles, sorrows and miseries with those of the mythical characters and thereby empathize with them. (From a comparative perspective, the peasant's psyche in the early nineteenth century, as reflected in the *sangs*, would not have been very different from that in the Mughal period.) For instance, the stories of royal male personages, such as Harishchandra, Prahlad, Dhruvbhakt and Nal, suffering or making sacrifices in steadfast defence of their convictions, moral values or the cause of justice, or those of women like Damayanti and Savitri undergoing tribulations out of unwavering devotion to their husbands Nal and Satyavan—have been deeply inspiring for the peasants, as also for the rural society at large in medieval north India across generations. A performative popular culture was thus created on the perceived affinity between the lived experiences of the peasant-audience and the life-stories of these characters, enacted or sung. This culture not only served to ameliorate their pains, but also, as will be discussed later in the chapter, gave expression to their class struggle against injustice at the hands of the oppressive ruling class. Further, these tales conveyed in a clear and forthright fashion the binaries of right and wrong, just and unjust, moral and immoral, virtue and sin. Such ethical ideas were derived from the ancient texts of Brahmanical literary tradition, such as epics, Puranas and Dharmashastras, but integrated with the folk rendition of the life-stories of the epic-Puranic heroes. Thus presented in a language and form that was familiar and appealing to the peasants, these ideas came to be imbibed by them as essential components of their culture and value system.

The strong ethical content of the performances profoundly influenced their thinking and conduct in the realm of familial and social relations and obligations. It is this ethical wisdom, inculcated by the folktales over generations, that the medieval rural communities used to regulate the behaviour of and relations among their members, for example, in dealing with commonplace cases of disputes over land, cattle-lifting, grain-theft, etc. More importantly, the ethical content of these stories or songs also shaped the peasant's perception of an ideal ruler and his ideal relation with the state (personified by the ruler).

Hence, stories celebrating some rulers for their proverbial justice and concern for their subjects, such as Vikaramaditya, Mordhvaj, Puranmal and Raja Bhoj, underscore the desirable qualities of a ruler and hence were quite popular among the peasants. For instance, Narsingh Meo's 'Hasan Khan ki Katha' praises King Vikaramaditya for his justice that made him popular among his subjects, especially peasants, and a memorable figure for successive generations. In Narsingh Meo's words:

परदुख भंजन राइ अजीत । राजा बड़ौ वकि्रमाजीतु ॥
पर दुख भानै याको रै । तांको आकु दुनी महि फिरै ॥
कति-कति हुए भौवाल । मै उपरझिाड़े करवाला ॥

> At different points of time, there have been kings who have ameliorated the pains and miseries of others [i.e., their subjects] and never caused pain to them. The greatest of them is Vikramaditya.[17] [Translation mine]

But at the same time, the author condemns Ibrahim Lodi for his injustice, arrogance and misdeeds which eventually resulted in his defeat at the hands of Babur in the Battle of Panipat (1526). Other popular stories of rulers like Harishchandra, Prahlad, Dhruvbhakt and Nal presented them as victims of injustice by state who emerged victorious through their trials and tribulations. In doing so, the stories would have provided inspiration and mental strength to the medieval Indian peasants not only in waging their everyday struggle of survival, but also in confronting and demanding justice from oppressive rulers. It was these stories—whether of benevolent, just rulers or dispossessed, suffering ones—that the peasants would have internalized and thereby conceptualized the duties of the ruler and the subjects and the relation between them. This made the medieval Indian peasant mentally beholden to his *prajadharam/prajadharma*, i.e. his moral duty (*dharam/dharma*) as subject (*praja*) to pay a share of his produce as revenue to his ruler (*raja*) or the state—a duty that he had inherited and imbibed from his ancestors. At the same, he held the state beholden to its *rajdharam/rajadharma*, i.e. its duty to govern the subjects 'justly'. In times of good harvest, the peasant paid the land revenue to the state based on customary rates. It was the imposition of non-customary levies, along with crop failures, that roused his ire: he considered such demand unjust, illegitimate and a transgression of *rajdharam*, and resorted to protests or revolts. Thus, historically, a tradition of rebellion/protest against the perceived injustice of the state or the ruling class had always been present in the peasant society. In the peasant's worldview, his ideal relation with the state, based on the reciprocal adherence to their respective customary duties (*rajdharam, prajadharam*), and the benevolence of the omnipotent but capricious nature was the recipe for a content and happy life. Capturing his vision of an ideal life—marked by good harvests (thanks to nature's timely benevolence), adequate means of production, sufficient food for a comfortable life and surplus produce for paying customary dues to the ruler—is the following Haryanvi couplet:[18]

दस चगें बैल देख, वा दसमन बेरी ।
हक हिसाबी न्याय, वा साकसीर जोरी ॥
भूरी भैंस का दुधा, वा राबड़ घोलणा ।
इतना दे करतार, तो बोहरि ना बोलना ॥

[The peasant prays:] May there be strong oxen for farming,
and (enough) grain to eat.
May revenue be paid to the king as per custom.
May there be *rabri*[19] and buffalo-milk (to savour).
Just give me this much, O lord; I ask no more. [Translation mine]

Although the characters in the *sangs* were drawn from the ruling class and represented, to an extent, its ethical and cultural norms, their acceptance and exaltation by the rural society was not in any way based on some kind of cultural compromise with or emulation of the ruling class. In other words, the stories of rulers, while percolating down from the 'high' literary traditions of the ruling class to the unlettered peasant class did not inculcate submissiveness and passive obedience in the peasant. Rather, they were appropriated by those who composed their musical renditions and popularized them by moving from village to village and staging performances based on them. Many of these poets and artistes in the nineteenth-century north India emerged out of peasant communities and hence could act as key players in the making of the peasant worldview. These poets and artistes reinterpreted or refashioned the life stories of the royal characters in terms of the peasant's own life experiences, and rendered them in cultural forms (i.e. poetry, songs, and theatrical performances) and vernacular idioms or parlance familiar to the peasant. In the course of their performance as well as reception by the peasant-audience, these compositions were thus dynamically transfigured by the peasant into vehicles of his own class consciousness and his class struggle with the ruling elite. More specifically, they enabled the peasant: (a) to intimately relate the tensions in his own social and familial relations and the hazards and struggles of his everyday occupational life to—and thereby draw inspiration from—the moral predicaments and dilemmas, sufferings and struggles of the royal protagonists of these stories; (b) to conceive an idea of his own customary entitlements from and duties towards the state, the ethics of governance and the limits of the state's rights over him—in other words, a customary reciprocal relation between his class (as *praja* or subject) and the state (personified by raja or the king), based on their respective adherence to *prajadharam* and *rajdharam*; and (c) to emphasize and celebrate such moral values as forbearance in suffering, courage in making sacrifices, justness, truthfulness, etc., which he implicitly identified as those of his own class but whose epitomes he found in these legendary rulers.

The folk legends of rulers while appearing to be borrowings from the self-legitimizing ideological apparatus of the ruling class actually reflect the peasant's worldview: his own concerns, interests and ethics, as well as perception of his socio-economic situation, class position and his relation with the state or the ruler. If seen from this perspective, paradoxically, the ideology of the ruling class was so thoroughly re-oriented and reformulated in the hands of the rural bards-cum-performers to represent the peasant worldview and transmit it among the peasantry across generations, that it developed the potential to prepare the peasant to wage a class struggle against the state in medieval India, when in the former's perception the customary reciprocity between him and the state broke down, owing to the latter's transgression of the norms/rules of 'just' governance. Thus, the notion of an almighty state was eroded and seeds of a class struggle along with it were sown as the peasant absorbed the stories of heroic struggles of righteous individuals against powerful adversarial circumstances and people. Such a process of cultural appropriation 'from below', as it were, enabled the Indian peasant to conceive and articulate his class ideology in contradistinction to that of the ruling elite, however uniquely, through the medium of folk songs and theatrical performances.

Against this backdrop of the peasant's worldview, especially his class consciousness, in medieval north India, this chapter addresses certain fundamental questions with regard to peasant protests in the late Mughal period (late seventeenth and early eighteenth centuries) in the context of the Mewat region: whether any class consciousness was manifest in the peasant protests; if it was, what form it assumed; and what sort of ideology and historic circumstances hindered its development and thereby the potential of the peasants' class struggle, and obligated them—notwithstanding their pitiable plight—to continue paying revenue to the state while being oppressed by it. These questions have not been explored at length so far. On the basis of hitherto understudied Rajasthani documents, viz., *arsattas, arzdashts, chithis, khatoot-ahalkarans, vakil's* reports, the chapter essentially argues that peasants of Mewat, led by patels (village headmen),[20] fought against the state, or rather its revenue-collecting intermediaries (ijaradars) and their officials (amil, faujdar, sehna), for the redressal of their *own* grievances and the protection of their *own* economic interests, and in doing so demonstrated a certain class consciousness.

I

In light of the introductory section on peasants' notion of their customary reciprocal relation with the state or the ruler and in order to understand the roots of their class struggle in the late Mughal period, it is important to explore if the state-peasantry relationship was limited to the former's standard or routine demand for land revenue from the latter, or it exceeded customary limits of this demand. In other words, did the state, if it sought to appropriate more than its customary share of the peasants' produce, have any accountability towards the peasants? From the Rajasthani sources, it appears that generally the peasants did not oppose the state's demand for what they deemed as 'customary' land revenue and other levies, but according to the reports of the revenue officials, they (especially the Meos) rose against the state under the leadership of the patels only when the state forced them to pay such taxes and levies as they perceived 'non-customary' and hence 'illegitimate', 'unethical' and 'immoral', or when the state, in contravention of custom, gave the revenue-collection rights of the territories under its rule to such intermediaries who, in turn, raised the revenue demand manifold by adding many non-customary levies to it. More specifically, one such intermediary to emerge in the late seventeenth and early eighteenth centuries was the Raja of the Rajput state of Amber in the Alwar region of eastern Rajasthan. He acquired from the imperial mansabdars/jagirdars and faujdars the ijara (revenue collection rights), zamindari and thanedari of many parganas of Mewat falling under their jagirs, and imposed numerous non-customary imposts on the Meo peasants of those areas. It was particularly the spread of this practice of granting ijara and the consequent imposition and exaction of non-customary levies that intensified the exploitation of peasantry and thereby played a crucial role in provoking peasant protests and rebellions in the region.

The growth of ijara, in turn, was the direct result of a crisis in the jagirdari system. Imperial mansabdars, unable to realize revenue from their jagirs in the wake of uncertainties in collection, were forced to farm out their jagirs to various bidders for revenue collection rights. In particular, the mansabdars who held jagirs in Mewat resorted to assigning their ijara to the Amber rulers and Churaman Jat. Upon obtaining the ijara of many parganas of their jagirs from the imperial mansabdars, the Amber rulers set up a large number of thanas (police posts) in the villages and qasbas (towns) of these parganas in order to control the Meo peasants and consolidate his hold over the area. The peasants and patels were forced to submit their *muchalka* (undertaking) to the amils (pargana-level revenue officials) promising that they would duly deposit the revenue and other dues. The Amber faujdars (pargana-level administrators) were ordered to confiscate the entire property (crops and cattle) of those peasants who did not pay land revenue and other taxes under the ijara system. Various new, non-customary taxes were imposed over and above with the standard land revenue, on the peasants of these parganas granted in ijara; such taxes had never been collected from the peasants before. Among them, the most burdensome was *virar*, a cess levied on the peasants to collect the amount customarily paid by the Amber chiefs as peshkash to the imperial mansabdars for holding the ijara rights. Another cess was *nyauta* or *nyota* that had been customarily collected as present on the occasion of any marriage in the royal house of Amber from peasants residing in the Amber chiefs' watan jagir (hereditary jagir), but was arbitrarily extended to the parganas granted in ijara to the Amber chiefs.

Expectedly, not only did the Meo peasants consider ijara or

the practice of farming out revenue-collection rights to the new intermediary between them and the Mughal state, i.e. the Amber chief and his officialdom, as illegitimate, but they also deemed the non-customary levies exacted from them as such. Hence, on numerous occasions since the late seventeenth century, the Meo peasants from many parganas of Mewat, together with their patels, petitioned to the Mughal emperor, complaining against the assignment of the villages on ijara, the taxes imposed under it and the highhandedness of the Amber officials; and pleading that the practice and the taxes be discontinued and the imperial mansabdars be ordered to cease granting ijara of their jagirs to the Amber rulers. Occasionally, they did manage to secure certain concessions from the emperor. As a counteracting measure, the imperial mansabdars instructed their revenue officials to dissuade the discontented peasants from approaching the emperor. The Amber chief too instructed his diwan (chief financial minister) to stop, through the intermediation of his amils, the peasants from lodging their complaints, as attested by the vakil's reports. For instance, in 1683, the Meo peasants of pargana Firozpur Jhirka submitted a petition at the Mughal court in Shahjahanabad (Delhi) against the non-customary taxes imposed by the chief of Amber. According to the report sent by Devidas, a *harkara* (spy), to the Amber Raja:

The *raiyati* [revenue-paying subjects] of *pargana* Firozpur Jhirka have become stubborn; no one can make them understand. No one can instill sense into them. They have stooped down to pig-headedness and treachery. Their refusal to pay certain taxes is causing us a great deal of loss every day. The *raiyati* of many villages of *pargana* Firozpur Jhirka had gone to Shahjahanabad to plead before the Mughal emperor. After hearing their plea, the emperor waived off *jajiya* [or *jizya*, a tax on non-Muslims] and ordered that *jajiya* be collected from the *jagirdar* instead of the *raiyati*. Besides, the *raiyati* also refused to pay *nyauta* and *gara* [tax on cart]. The *diwan* of the Mughal *darbar* sent a letter to the *ukil* [*vakil*] stating that the *raiyati* of the *pargana* of Firozpur Jhirka had approached the emperor with a complaint against the Amber Raja. Therefore, try to pacify the *raiyati* and get a contract of conciliation signed by them.[21]

Again in 1683 the Meo peasants of pargana Khilohra lodged a similar complaint with the emperor against the imposition of *nyauta* by the Amber Raja. The Meo peasants' plea was that since the villages of pargana Khilohra were not a part of the Raja's watan jagir, but of the imperial jagir and they were subjects of the Mughal emperor, *nyauta* was a non-customary tax that the Raja could not force them to pay. On the other hand, Bhawani Shankar, the amil of the pargana, argued that since the Amber Raja had been assigned the ijara of this pargana by the imperial mansabdar, the peasants should pay *nyauta* to the Amber Raja, just as the peasants of the Raja's watan jagir did. As soon as Vimal Das, the diwan of Amber, came to know that the peasants and their patels of pargana Khilohra were ready to go to the Mughal court with their complaint against the Raja, he ordered amil Bhawani Shankar to stop them at any cost and pacify their grievances immediately, the reason being: 'It is necessary for us to stop the peasants from going to the Mughal court, otherwise our image in the Mughal court would be spoilt and it will be difficult for us to get the *ijara* of the royal *jagirs* from the imperial *mansabdars*.'[22] In another report to the Amber Raja, diwan Vimal Das informed that the peasantry of pargana Salawad had refused (*nat gai*) to pay *nyauta* to amil Bhawani Shankar, arguing that they were not the *raiyati* of the Amber Raja, but that of the Mughal emperor, and had they been the former then only levying *nyauta* on them would be justified: 'The *raiyati* refused to pay *nyauta* and said that they were the *raiyati* of the emperor, and that if they had been the *raiyati* of his [Amber Raja's] *watan jagir* they would have paid *nyauta*. *Diwan* Vimal Das came to *pargana* Salawad and tried to reason with them, but they refused to pay *nyauta*.'[23] The peasants and their patels proceeded towards the Mughal capital Shahjahanabad to lodge their complaint with the emperor. When they reached Sherpur, Bhawani Shankar intercepted and tried to placate them, but the peasants insisted that the diwan give a written undertaking promising them exemption from *nyauta* and *bhomi* levies.[24]

In 1685, a similar protest was lodged by peasants of pargana Shonkhar-Shonkhari with the Mughal emperor. In their petition, they complained that the Amber Raja had collected land revenue of Rs.52,000 out of which the actual amount of land revenue was Rs.38,000 and the balance of Rs.14,000 was collected as *virar* from them.[25] A sharp reaction of peasants against the ijara system was noticed in 1712 at Firozpur Jhirka pargana, after the Amber Raja had taken the ijara of the pargana from the imperial mansabdar, Sarfaraz Khan Badshahzada. The Meo peasants submitted a petition at the Mughal court demanding that the emperor issue an order to Sarfaraz

Khan, cancelling the assignment of the ijara of his jagir to the Amber Raja. Describing this incident, the vakil of the Amber Raja wrote from the Mughal court:

The peasants and the *patels* of *pargana* Firozpur Jhirka had come to the Mughal court in Shahjahanabad to present their petition before Munim Khan (*diwan* of the Mughal state). [The petition stated:] 'The army of the Amber Raja loot and plunder us by imposing various arbitrary and non-customary taxes on us. Our villages lie in the *jagir* of Shahzada Sarfaraz Khan and their *ijara* had been assigned to the Amber Raja'. Therefore, the peasants requested Munim Khan to speak to Sarfaraz Khan for the cancellation of the *patta* (lease) of *ijara* of his *jagir* granted to the Amber Raja.[26]

Describing the incidence of peasant complaints in parganas Firozpur-Jhirka and Khohri in 1712, vakil Khanzad Nandala reported:

O *Maharajaji*, the subjects (*raiyati*) of *pargana* Firozpur-Jhirka (which, along with *pargana* Khohri had been taken on *ijara* by the Amber Raja from the imperial *mansabdar* Ayaz-ud-din Khan) came to the Mughal court in Delhi to appeal to the emperor that an *amil* be sent to their *pargana* from the court because the Amber Raja had sent his *vakil* to collect land revenue from them without the imperial *amil*'s consent. On the other hand, your *amil* wrote to us that the subjects of the *pargana* had refused to pay the revenue (*bad-amali karai chhai*) and stooped to complete insubordination. Similarly, (as the *amil* further informed) the subjects of *pargana* Khohri were refusing to pay the revenue. The *amil* claimed to have made his fullest efforts to reason with them (i.e. persuade them to pay the revenue), but they remained adamant on not paying the revenue. We then sent Mukand Ram Vakawat with a big force to Firozpur, while the *amil* stayed in Tijara. Thereafter, the subjects of *pargana* Firozpur-Jhirka again come to the court and pleaded: 'the forces of Jats and the Amber Raja oppress us; both the Jats and the Amber Raja demand land revenue from us. We cannot live like this.' Meanwhile, the peasants [of *pargana* Khohri] declined to pay the revenue to our *amil*. When Mukand Ram and his force reached the villages of Khohri, he found the residents absconding and the village deserted.[27]

In 1714, after the ijara of parganas Piragpur and Atela Bhabra was taken by the Amber Raja, the peasantry of these parganas, as per the amil's report, refused to pay *bhomi*, a non-customary cess, and when forced to do so went to Shahjahanbad to lodge their complaint with the Mughal emperor. Sent by the diwan to pacify them, the amil tried to reason with the peasants at qasba Pawata where they had assembled to proceed to the Mughal capital. But the peasants insisted that they would return to their villages only if the Raja withdrew the *bhomi* cess by a written agreement. They eventually returned only when the diwan gave them the undertaking.[28] In 1728, the peasants of 15 villages of pargana Khohri lodged their complaint at the Mughal court against the imposition of *virar* by the Amber Raja. They reported to the emperor that a sum of Rs.17,300 had been demanded from them as *virar*, which, they argued, was unbearable and non-customary.[29] Here, a wide difference between the amount of *virar* demanded from the peasants and their actual capacity to meet the demand can be observed. In 1729, the peasants of parganas Atela Bhabhra and Piragpur complained to the Mughal emperor that the Amber Raja's amil had compelled them to pay land revenue at the rate of 40 per cent on both rabi and kharif crops and *sehangi* cess at the rate of one *ser* of grain per maund, while they had been customarily paying land revenue at the rates of 40 and 30 per cent on rabi and kharif crops, respectively, and *sehangi* at the rate of half-a-*ser* of grain per maund.[30]

The foregoing instances of peasant complaints show that the Meo peasants were well aware of the fact that their villages were a part of the jagir assigned to the imperial mansabdar by the emperor, not that of the Amber Raja's watan jagir, and that the mansabdar had, in turn, assigned the ijara of their villages to the Amber Raja. Thus, whosoever happened to be their jagirdar, they could precisely understand that the emperor was their highest appellate authority and that the Amber Raja had no legitimate right to collect non-customary taxes from them. That is why they retained faith in the justice administered by the Mughal state, expected the emperor's intervention in redressing their grievances, and did not lodge their complaint with the imperial mansabdar or the Amber Raja, but with the Mughal emperor himself. They clearly perceived Amber Raja as a disruptor of their customary relationship with the Mughal state, and the imposition of non-customary taxes by him as a violation of *rajdharam* so exalted in their oral traditions. While Irfan Habib has rightly pointed out that the medieval Indian peasants cannot be compared with their medieval west European counterparts in terms of class consciousness,[31] it is true, as evident from the peasant complaints, that the Meo peasants understood the behaviour of the ruling class and expected the state to perform its *rajdharam*, its duty of administering justice to its subjects. Clearly, class consciousness had not a single but several forms.

While it is amply evident that peasant protests often erupted over non-customary imposts, such protests were occasioned as much by the perceived illegitimacy of the state's demand as by their incapacity to meet it, especially in times of bad yields, crop failures, droughts or famines. There are, however, some instances to show that peasants did not resist paying the revenue when he was capable of doing so because of good harvests and when the state demanded the customary revenue. Illustrative of this pliant behaviour of the peasants is the following report by the amil:

O *Maharajaji*, this year the *pargana* has received good rains, as a result of which harvest has been good. Peasants themselves came to us and expressed the desire to pay the land revenue. This is why the measurement of yield (*lata*) for the assessment of revenue under the crop-sharing system (*batai*) was to be promptly carried out. Accordingly, we had the harvested crop measured for assessing the revenue due from all villages in the *pargana*. When the peasants (*raiyati*) came to the court for this purpose, we also proposed to prepare the *jamabandi* (document containing the particulars of the amount of revenue and the method of assessment). Accordingly, we prepared the *jamabandi* for the *rabi* crop, wherein the revenue on *polach* land (i.e. superior land under continuous cultivation and yielding two crops) was fixed at half of the produce, and that on *banjar* land (waste or fallow land, fit for cultivation) at 40 per cent (*pachduva*) of the produce where such land was cultivated. Alongside, where *kaccha kuan*s were dug (for irrigation), peasants were given concession (in revenue) and the revenue (on produce from lands irrigated by such wells) was fixed at 40 percent of the produce. Where land was irrigated by *dhenkli* (water-lifting device), revenue was fixed at 50 percent, though there are more *kaccha kuan*s than *dhenkli*s in the area. We have also carried out investigation of the Rajputs and Brahmins to ascertain which Brahmins know the Gayatri *mantra* (a sacred Vedic chant) and which Rajputs possess guns (so that they can be given concessions in revenue; in other words, concession would not be extended to those Brahmins who did not know the Gayatri *mantra* and those Rajputs who had no guns). Undertakings (*muchalka*) for the preparation of *jamabandi* were taken from *patel*s and *patwari*s too. *Amil*s were instructed that if *ghughri* of *sehna* had been collected at a rate more than one *ser* per *maund* of grain, the excess amount should be returned to the peasants. Further, order was issued to *amil*s and *amin*s that *jogi*s (a mendicant caste in Rajasthan) and not their own men (*chakar*s) be appointed to ward off pests from the fields.[32]

As the afore-cited report shows, the peasant did accede to the state's revenue demand as long as it was not illegitimate in his eyes and was within his capacity to meet. Even if the state's and the peasant's interests in the sharing of surplus were fundamentally at odds with each other, the relation between the two at least in this respect was not always conflictual but based on a compromise that required both to abide by certain customary norms.

The relation between the state and the peasants, in the latter's view, was not limited to the sharing of agricultural surplus; they had several expectations from the state, including a sympathetic treatment of their pleas/complaints, administration of justice and protection of their interests. In fact, the *arzdashts* and the *hasil farohi* column of *arsattas* inform us about numerous instances of state intervention in the peasants' sociocultural life. Such instances are those of state officials adjudicating cases of petty quarrel, rape, theft of cattle and food grains, breach of informal contracts/promises and murder, as well as awarding penalties, mostly *taqsir* (fines) to offenders. One Muslim was fined Rs.9 for throwing a *baniya*'s son into a well;[33] Nanda, a *chamar*, was fined Rs.6 for selling cow—sacred to the Hindus—to a butcher;[34] Gobinda, an Ahir of Nainapur village was fined Rs.11 for eloping with the wife of a fellow Ahir, Maina;[35] a Meo named Tara, of Jhorada village in qasba Pahari was fined Rs.20 for arranging his daughter's engagement with the son of a fellow Meo, Hansa, and then marrying her off to someone else;[36] a Brahmin, Jayaram, of *mauza*[37] Kakroli was imprisoned and fined Rs.301 for killing a Gujjar in a fight during the reaping of kharif harvest; another Brahmin, Khadgo, and his son belonging to *mauza* Jhadu in *tappa*[38] Chidi were fined Rs.151 for killing Sukha, also a Brahmin, in an altercation that erupted when the former grazed their oxen presumably in the latter's field; Svikaran, a Brahmin of Chapar Khurd village was imprisoned for killing another Brahmin, Jaisa, in a fight that broke out among the villagers of pargana Balahara.[39] Besides these instances, several cases of cattle theft are also reported in the *arzdashts*. For instance, in one *arzdasht*, the amil reported to the Amber Raja that while on his tour through villages to collect the state's share of produce as revenue under the *batai* system, he was informed that Madho Meena and his companions indulged in cattle-lifting; he immediately sent *sawars* (horsemen) to arrest him, but the patel of his village got wind of this news and alerted him, and even as he fled from the village, the horsemen managed to apprehend his brother, nephew and wife and seize 83 heads of cattle stolen by him.[40] Further, resolution of larger disputes involving villages or social groups by officials reflects the state's mediatory (but not punitive) role. For instance, a boundary dispute between two villages, Delavaas and Shri Kisanpura, was resolved after the patels of neighbouring villages testified before the amil and Shri Kisanpura's jagirdar and patel accepted the guilt of trespassing into Delavaas and illegally seizing 68 *bighas* of land.[41] In another case, Pathans of pargana Averi appealed to the Amber Raja for protection, when Nathawat Rajputs attacked some Pathans fishing in a *johad* (pond) within a Meena locality and killed three of them. The diwan advised them to stay in the locality but refrain from committing such an act in future, since fish was sacred to the Meenas and killing it was considered a sin.[42]

While such cases testify to the vertical penetration of state authority down to the smallest administrative unit, i.e. the village, interestingly, there does not appear to be any caste discrimination in awarding penalties. At the same, the penalty for *chamchori* (rape) on zamindars, mahajans (moneylenders) and revenue officials belonging to the upper strata of the rural society was usually heavier than that for offenders who were of the same caste as the victims. This was so perhaps because the conduct of those from the upper castes/classes was expected to be exemplary and any misdemeanour on their part was thought to impair the moral fabric of the society. For instance, zamindar Jai Singh of *mauza* Kotdi was fined Rs.61.4*an.* for raping a Meena's wife,[43] and Bansi Chaudhari of *mauza* Sakat in *tappa* Haveli was fined Rs.151 for raping a Meena woman,[44] while the fine imposed on an offender of the same caste as the victim's ranged from Rs.5–10.

II

When the peasants failed to get relief through the routine method of petitioning, they resisted the payment of taxes as a last resort. Instances of peasant defiance and rebellions and ensuing conflicts with the Amber state abound in the Rajasthani sources of the late Mughal period.[45] In 1709, the amil of pargana Khilohra reported in alarm that the peasants of many villages[46] had consumed the entire harvest payable to the state as *hasil* (revenue) and asked the diwan to send a big force of *sawars* (cavalrymen) to exact revenue from the remaining villages.[47] In 1712, when the ijara of Firozpur Jhirka and Tijara parganas was taken by the Amber Raja, the peasantry refused to pay revenue to his amil and instead decided to pay the same to the amil of the Mughal state (i.e. of the imperial mansabdar). When they, led by their patels, rose in revolt, the amil of Amber was sent with a big force to collect land revenue from the rebellious peasants. This led to a fierce battle, in which sixty peasants were killed and many left wounded on the one side, and on the other, the deputy commander-in-chief of the Amber army, Mohammad Daulat Khan was killed along with many soldiers. Many peasants and patels were arrested by the army, while the peasants of Jaisar, Alipur, Khora, More and Kamohera villages fled to Kala Pahar (Aravalli Hills of Firozpur Jhirka and Ramgarh). Eventually, the army managed to collect 3000 maunds of grain and 13 horses from these villages.[48] At around the same time, peasant protests broke out in parganas Khohri and Bahadurpur when the amil of the Amber Raja, who had taken the ijara of these parganas, imposed a new cess, viz., *bhomi*, at the rate of Rs.2.8*an.* per *zabti* Rs.100 under the *zabti* system and one *ser* per maund of grain under the *batai-jinsi* system (the regular land revenue till then had been assessed at the rate of Rs.2 per Rs.100 *zabti* and half-a-*ser* per maund of grain). The rebellious peasants argued that the parganas were not part of the Raja's watan jagir nor were they his *raiyati*, but that of the Mughal emperor; that taxes imposed under the ijara system were not part of the regular land revenue system and hence non-customary; that the Raja had no legal or moral right to impose such taxes; and that on these considerations they had decided not to pay the new cess. The Amber sent 1000 cavalrymen to aid the amil in crushing the revolt. In the ensuing armed conflicts that took place between the peasants and the army in many villages, a large number of peasants were killed.[49] In 1716, when the ijara of pargana Bayana was taken by Amber Raja from the imperial mansabdar Amir Khan, the peasants' protest was so strong that the army of the Amber faujdar managed to collect land revenue from only 31 of 138 villages.[50] In 1731, the amil of pargana Pahari reported to the diwan of Amber that Meo peasants of 44 villages had not deposited their land revenue in protest against the transfer of the pargana in ijara by imperial mansabdar Hasan Khan to the Amber Raja.[51] In 1734, a *harkara* sent his report to the diwan of Amber, stating that the army of faujdars Wazid Khan and Kishan Singh Naruka had destroyed and plundered a large number of Meo villages in parganas Khohri and Pahari. While many peasants were wounded and arrested, others fled (*bhajari*). Eventually, the army managed to capture 78 horses and many cattle. The report provides a detailed village-wise description of the depredations of the faujdars' forces.[52]

There may have been many more such conflicts, not recorded in the available documents. On the other hand, as discussed in the previous section, there are a few instances where the amil of Amber worked out compromises with the affected peasants and dissuaded them from petitioning at the Mughal court with the promise that the Amber state would not collect non-customary taxes from them. Historically, no peasant community, however defiant and rebellious, could afford to engage with the state by way of physical resistance alone. In normal times, it would find ways and means of negotiating with the state and expressing its grievances before its authorities to get concessions and relief, as did the peasants of Mewat by complaining to the Mughal emperor or extracting concessions from the Amber Raja.

Instances of peasant protests in Mewat need not be seen in terms of resistance to state's authority per se, but rather in terms of non-acceptance of what was perceived as its illegitimate revenue demand (in the form of non-customary taxes). A recent study on the folklore of Meos[53] posits their perpetual anti-state stance. It argues that the Meo *pals*, lineages or clans claiming common ancestry, characterized by a strong sense of fraternity and led by *chaudharis* (chiefs), have been traditionally hostile to monopolistic centralized state, whether Mughal or Rajput, and have retained their relatively autonomous and self-governing character. However, as I have argued elsewhere,[54] the Meos were brought under the ambit of Mughal politico-administrative control subsequent to their peasantization and integration of Mewat into the Mughal Empire. As the archival evidence shows, the state-appointed amils played a key role in resolving their day-to-day mutual disputes and conflicts; the chaudharis, far from being like sovereign rulers of their *pals*, do not even figure in such decision-making and adjudicatory roles, and were possibly reduced to the position of petty zamindars collecting revenue from peasants. The rural communities on their part, too, looked up to the state (especially the Mughal state) for justice and conflict-resolution, not to the *pal* chaudharis. When after the decline of the Mughal state, the chaudharis were not inducted in the power structure of the states (e.g. Bharatpur, Amber) in which their region had been subsumed, they would have taken advantage of the unsettled conditions to begin (re-)organizing their *pals*. Further, it was in the backdrop of the weakening control of the Mughal state that the frequency of peasant uprisings, including those of the Meos, increased in response to the exactions and excesses of the Amber chiefs and the Jat chiefs of Bharatpur. But only after the eighteenth century did these chaudharis attain a somewhat 'sovereign' position within their *pals*. The Meo oral tradition exalting the autonomy of decentralized *pal* polity, banditry/plunder and perpetual conflict with the centralized state as features constitutive of Meo identity formation was the result of the growing tendency of the chaudharis to patronize the composition of laudatory oral histories of their respective clans by the *mirasis* (bards) in the late eighteenth and early nineteenth centuries, i.e. well into the colonial period. These oral histories are reflective of the newly gained sociopolitical power of the chaudharis, not testimonies of any supposed autonomy of self-governing communities. Thus, the concocted tradition of resistance to state was the outcome of particular political circumstances of this period. The British ethnographers-cum-administrators who documented such traditions also lent credence to them, thereby bolstering the image of self-sufficient, changeless rural communities existing in India outside the purview of state control. At the same time, they sought to induct these chiefs into the colonial administration to handle law-and-order problems and revenue collection at the local level. According to them, space in the colonial state would have made a case for highlighting such traditions that posit the communities' traditional antagonism to the precolonial state. Thus, a singular colonial perception of rural communities, which found justification in certain oral traditions, was projected back into the precolonial (in this case Mughal and Sultanate) period. In contrast to such oral traditions, the archival evidence, as discussed throughout this chapter, bears out more complex and multifaceted engagements of the Meos (and peasants in general) with the state. These diverse engagements involved, on the one hand, acceptance of punishments meted out by state officials for social crimes, and, on the other hand, opposition to the state's unbearably heavy revenue demand by way of petitions, compromises and armed uprisings. Such engagements essentially rested on their perceptions of legitimacy or illegitimacy of a ruler's conduct towards his subjects, and on their cognizance of the state itself as a stratified ensemble of power relations going all the way up to the Mughal emperor.

III

Besides their conflict with the Amber Raja in the parganas of Mewat that were assigned in ijara to him, the hapless peasantry of Mewat was also caught up in the protracted conflict between the Amber Raja and Churaman Jat for acquiring the ijara rights of the parganas in Mewat from the imperial mansabdars—a conflict that was aggravated by the factional politics at the Mughal court after Aurangzeb's death (1707). Churaman Jat received continued support from the 'king-makers', viz., Sayyid brothers, and Nawab Khan-i-Daura at the Mughal court until the fall of the Sayyid brothers in the Battle of Hasanpur (1720).[55] The Rajasthani documents testify that Churaman obtained from the imperial mansabdars the ijara of many parganas that were part of their jagirs in the Agra, Mathura and Mewat regions.[56] As a consequence, the Jats, led by Churaman, widened their social base in these regions through the ijara grants particularly made during the reign of Mughal Emperor Farrukh Siyar (r. 1713–19).[57] The rising influence of Churaman at the Mughal court and in the Mewat region proved detrimental to the economic interests and political status of the Amber Raja. Understandably, this conflict of interest led to a fierce competition between the two over the acquisition of ijara of the parganas in the Mewat region from the imperial mansabdars.

The main motive of Churaman Jat was to establish his control in the Mewat region by convincing the imperial mansabdars at the Mughal court that he could better manage the land revenue collection than the Amber Raja would. In 1714, he removed all the *thanas* (police posts) of the Amber Raja in the villages and qasbas of pargana Khohri and Mojpur, and set up his own *thanas*.[58] The amil of the pargana reported to the Amber Raja that Churaman Jat had forcibly collected land revenue from 171 of 342 villages, which were under the zamindari of the Amber Raja.[59] The amil further stated: 'The Jats have become very powerful in the Mewat region. They have removed our *thanas* in the villages of pargana Khohri and Mojpur and have beaten up our men.'[60] In another letter, the vakil reported to Amber Raja: 'At the Mughal court, everybody is stunned at how the Churaman Jat has forcibly collected land revenue from pargana Khohri which was assigned to the Maharaja [Amber Raja]'.[61] In retaliation, the Amber Raja sent a big force to help amil Mukundram Vakawat to collect land revenue from the villages of pargana Khohri. The peasants of 27 villages ran away to *thoon* (Jat stronghold), while many were arrested by the Amber army.[62]

Commenting on these developments, the vakil, in his report to the Amber Raja, pointed out two reasons why securing the ijara of imperial jagirs in Mewat was crucial for Amber. First, a large number of Rajput *chakars* (servants) of Amber had become unemployed due to a reduction in the mansab of the Raja. As a consequence, they had become disloyal and many of them had resorted to looting in the areas under imperial jagirs. Only when the Raja obtained the ijara of the imperial jagirs in Mewat from the mansabdars and sub-assigned them to his Rajput *chakars*, he would be able to satisfy their aspirations. Second, Mewat was very close to the Amber Raja's watan jagir; hence, securing the ijara of the imperial jagirs in Mewat would facilitate the territorial expansion of Amber and curb the growing power of the Jats. The vakil further suggested that unless and until the Amber Raja improved his relations with the Mughal emperor Bahadur Shah I (1707–12), he would not get the ijara of many parganas that were part of the imperial jagirs from the mansabdars in Mewat.[63]

In 1712, the Amber Raja obtained the zamindari of pargana Khohri and in the following year the ijara of parganas Firozpur Jhirka and Tijara in Tijara *sarkar*.[64] This move of the Amber Raja brought him into direct confrontation with the Jats. The basic cause of conflict between them was their desire to control the larger part of the surplus agrarian produce through ijara at the cost of each other. Following these developments, the peasants and patels of many villages in pargana Khohri went to the Mughal court at Shahjahanabad to lodge their complaint against the high-handedness of the Amber state and the Jats. Their plea was that they were being subjected to new, non-customary and illegal taxes by both Amber Raja and Churaman Jat. While they had already paid the *bhomi* tax to the amil of Amber state, they were now being forced to pay the same to Churaman Jat. In their petition, they voiced their grievance: 'We are being penalized both by the Jats as well as the Amber state. Land revenue is being extracted from us by the Amber state and Churaman Jat. We cannot live like this. We are totally helpless. Kindly do justice to us.'[65] They also sought to remind the Mughal emperor of his duty towards his subjects: 'We are the *raiyati* (subjects) of the Mughal emperor, not of Amber Raja and Churaman Jat; we are in stress, kindly help us.'[66] They further argued that they could not pay land revenue twice on the same crop: they had already paid land revenue to Churaman Jat, but were being persecuted by the Amber Raja to pay revenue to him, since he claimed that he had got the right to collect revenue in pargana Khohri from the Mughal authority and, therefore, the peasants should have paid their revenue to him only. Finally, expressing their desperation, they stated that if they continued to be harassed, they would be forced to leave their villages. Indeed, in 1716, according to the amil's report, the peasants deserted 127 out of total 342 villages in pargana Khohri fearing the assaults by the Amber army and the Jats.[67] In the same year, the peasants deserted 24 out of 209 villages in pargana Pahari, fearing repression by the Amber army.[68] The peasants of many villages in Mojpur, Jalalpur and Bharkol parganas followed suit.[69] On its part, the Amber state continued with the repression of Meo peasants in the region. Many villages that had paid revenue to Churaman Jat were set to fire and their cattle were captured by the faujdars' troops. For instance, in pargana Khohri many peasants were arrested, many wounded and 78 horses, along with a large number cattle, were seized by the army of the faujdar.[70] The vakil's report, too, mentioned an accusation leveled by Yarali Khan, the imperial jagirdar of Kol (Aligarh), against the Amber Raja that he, like Shivaji, had unjustly captured the jagirs of others (i.e. imperial mansabdars) and organized military campaigns to punish the poor and helpless peasants and raise funds to meet the expense of his own army.[71] On their part, the peasants, failing to get succour from the Mughal emperor, adopted desertion as a desperate means of resisting the competing claims of the Amber Raja and Churaman over their produce surplus and violent exactions.

Colonization and desertion of villages due to disturbed political conditions, unbearably heavy taxation, and natural calamities like droughts or famines was a recurrent feature of Mewat's agrarian history during the Mughal period and indicates the massive mobility of peasantry. The Rajasthani documents of the late Mughal period do not testify to any legal constraint on peasant mobility, even during droughts or famines when the peasants were forced to emigrate in search of livelihood. Rather, they amply testify to the efforts of amils to persuade, and not coerce, the emigrating peasants to stay back and, in the event of desertion, resettle the desolate villages by bringing in migratory landless peasants (*pahikashts* or *pahis*). In medieval India, there was a sizeable population of *pahikashts* who wandered from village to village in search of livelihood, and usually cultivated the arable wastelands or the lands abandoned by the permanent land-owning peasants, though they themselves could not become permanent residents of these villages or proprietors of the lands they cultivated. These *pahikashts* were brought in by the amils to resettle the abandoned villages— they could build their hutments, cultivate the fields and pay revenue at concessional rates. On the other hand, the landowning peasant, though mobile, had a sense of deep attachment to his land because it constantly reminded him of not only his own labour in cultivating it, but also the hard labour and long struggles of his ancestors in clearing forests and making land cultivable. Thus, although there was no land market in medieval India and land was never the issue of conflict with the medieval state for the peasant (as it indeed was for his medieval west European counterpart), fertile, cultivable land kept the peasant emotionally bound to it, which was also economically important as his prime source of livelihood. This is evident from several instances of peasants emigrating from their ancestral villages in dire circumstances, such as droughts, and returning to them later, only to get into conflicts with the new settlers over their ancestral lands. For instance, when the Meo peasants belonging to the villages of Prannathpura, Jaisinghpura, Paliko, Ram Singhpura and Chandpura in pargana Khohri left their villages during drought and migrated elsewhere to earn their livelihood, the amil of the pargana rehabilitated these Meo villages by settling the Ahir *pahikasht* peasants there. The lands of these villages were also allotted to them and patels were appointed from among them. After some time, when the Meo peasants returned to their ancestral villages and found that their land and *pateli* had been given away to the Ahir peasants, they attacked the Ahirs and demanded that they evacuate. The Meos also lodged a complaint against the Ahirs with the diwan of Amber, arguing that the Ahirs be evicted from their villages and their land and *pateli* be restored to them, since these were their ancestral property.[72] The *amil*, in turn, argued that the Meos themselves had deserted their own villages and it was his duty to rehabilitate the deserted villages; therefore, he had transferred the land and the *pateli* to the Ahir settlers. He further argued that the Ahirs had been paying land revenue to the state regularly and hence could not be evicted.[73]

While the efforts of the peasants to reclaim their ancestral land from the state indicate a sociocultural, economic and emotional dimension to their relation with land, they also constitute a form of peasant resistance to the state's practice of land resettlement. Underlying this practice was state's interest in ensuring uninterrupted revenue collection, which came in conflict with the peasant's interests in protecting his usage rights to his ancestral land. In this sense, the emigrant peasants' conflicts with the new occupant-tillers of their ancestral land and with the state patronizing the latter add a crucial political dimension to their relation with land.

IV

Between the extremes of formal petitioning and open defiance, rebellion or desertion of villages lay a covert form of peasant resistance to the state's revenue demand, at a stage prior to the completion of the production process itself, i.e. during the assessment of the state's share in the produce. The peasant paid revenue either in cash under the *zabti* system of assessment, or in kind under the *batai-jinsi/ghalla-bakshi* system, or in both cash and kind for different sets of crops under both systems.[74] The peasant would try to 'misappropriate' the share of crop yield payable to the state and, in turn, reduce his own fiscal burden by: (a) willfully misinforming the revenue officials about or concealing from them, certain standing crops or the area of land under cultivation of certain crops; or (b) stealing part of the harvested crop or removing part of the standing crops. Such acts when detected by the state officials, viz., *sehna* and *amil*, were deemed as 'theft of revenue' and punished by way of levying fines, as amply attested in the Rajasthani sources, particularly the *arsattas*.

Under the *zabti* system, the peasant would try to avoid getting land under the cultivation of certain crops (mainly cash crops) measured, since such crops were assessed at higher rates and thereby increased the state's revenue demand. For instance, Harji Patel of Kherli village in pargana Alwar did not get the land under sugarcane cultivation measured and was fined Rs.27 by the amil.[75] The Meo peasants of Jora Khera village in the same pargana concealed the fields under rabi crop cultivation and were collectively fined Rs.81 by the amil.[76] One Nathu Meo evaded the measurement of the part of his field under paddy cultivation and was fined Rs.25.[77] Ghasi Jat of Sihchan village in pargana Mundawar concealed the part of his field under rabi crop cultivation and was fined Rs.81.[78] Parsa Patel of *mauza* Dhanoli was fined Rs.181 for not getting the part of land under kharif crop cultivation measured.[79] Similar practices were also prevalent under the *batai-jinsi* system of crop-sharing. The state official *sehna* was appointed for every village and charged with the task of ascertaining the kind of crop cultivated by the peasants and watching over the standing crops to prevent their concealment, theft or destruction till the time they were harvested and state's share was taken as revenue. To reduce his revenue burden, the peasant would get an inferior crop (i.e. food crop) mentioned in the patwari's records in the place of a superior crop (i.e. cash crop) that he actually cultivated, since the revenue on the former would be assessed at lower rates. In case of mixed cropping, he would only inform about an inferior crop, the revenue on which would be assessed at a lower rate, and conceal another superior crop, which when assessed at a higher rate would raise the state's share. For instance, in case of *gochani*, a mix of *gehun* (wheat) and *chana* (gram); *gojaro*, a mix of wheat and *jau* (barley); or a mix of *bajra* (millet) and *moth* (kidney bean), he would only get inferior crops like chickpea, barley and millet recorded. In pargana Mundawar, Pohkar Mali had *moth* recorded instead of *bajra*, and when his fraud was exposed he was fined Rs.31 by the amil.[80]

It was a customary practice for the peasant to uproot the crop that had not grown properly (*chhidi*) and then either sow seeds of another crop or leave it uncultivated so that he would not have to pay revenue on it. This he often did without getting the crop duly inspected by the sehna and seeking his permission for uprooting it. Doing so, by implication, amounted to a violation of the state law, punishable with fines. For instance, in pargana Narayana, Chokha Patel uprooted or destroyed the sugarcane crop on 5½ *bighas* of land when the yield was not to his satisfaction, but he did so without the sehna's inspection or permission. When informed about this act, the sehna with his men reached Patel's field, but faced much abuse and insult from Patel. At this, the state imposed a fine of Rs.231 on him.[81] In three other instances from the same pargana,[82] fines amounting to Rs.14, Rs.7.8*an.*, and Rs.11 were respectively levied on Karma Patel of *mauza* Sakhoni for uprooting his sugarcane crop, Asa and Khema Jat of *mauza* Morda for destroying their *makka* (maize) and *kodon* crops on 4 *bighas* of land, and Dhalu Patel of Dhanoli village for destroying his mustard crop, since such acts were committed without the sehna's permission.

Besides attempting to falsify the official records of the crops grown, the peasant would tend to surreptitiously cut a part of the standing crops, or steal a part of the harvested crop. Several such cases of grain-theft were reported from various parganas, especially in the early eighteenth century. In pargana Narayana, Bihari Rajput of village Chharihar was caught stealing grains by the sehna, and the amil imposed on him a fine of Rs.81.12*an.*[83] Similarly, Harji Baradval Jat, Bhuro Jat, Bhuro Jat's sister-in-law, Sundara, Kanho Kumhar and Manroop Jat were caught stealing grain and had to collectively pay a fine of Rs.41.[84] A fine of Rs.35 was imposed on Prasanna, Heera, Tira Mahajan and Lekha for grain-theft.[85] In pargana Mundawar, the sehna caught the Meena peasants stealing grain and complained to the amil, wherefore they were collectively fined Rs.92.7*an.*[86] The Meena and Mahajan peasants in the same pargana when caught stealing gram were collectively fined Rs.15.2*an.*[87] In pargana Harsana, Pusa Jat and a few fellow peasants were caught stealing grain by the *sehna* and a fine of Rs.101 was imposed on them.[88] Nathu Meo and Luchha Meo of Jona Khera village in pargana Mojpur,[89] Nathu Meo in pargana Alwar[90] and another Meo peasant of village Amarpur in pargana Alwar[91] were fined Rs.45, Rs.51 and Rs.8, respectively, for stealing grain. In pargana Wazirpur, the Gujars of Behad village were arrested for cutting off standing crops (*zirayati*).[92]

The peasant's constant efforts to evade the payment of revenue posed a great challenge to the sehna. Hence, only such persons who had a social base and standing in the rural community, were acutely aware of and alert to the peasants' activities, and could exercise both influence and coercion on them to extract the state's share in the produce were appointed to the post. However, sehna's constant vigilance and frequent intervention in the interest of the state to prevent and penalize the 'misappropriation' of revenue occasionally strained the peasant's forbearance to the breaking point and made him the peasant's biggest foe. This is reflected in numerous instances of physical and verbal conflict between the peasants and the sehna, mentioned in the Rajasthani sources. Like the covert acts of peasant resistance to the state revenue demand, the manhandling of sehna did not, however, go unpunished. For instance, angered by the sehna's interference, the *raiyati* of pargana Pindayan beat him up and, in turn, were collectively fined Rs.206.8*an.* by the amil.[93] The peasants of Bhadpura village in pargana Mundawar manhandled the sehna—an act penalized by a fine of Rs.23.[94] In pargana Narayana, a fine of Rs.140.4*an.* were imposed on Veeru Patel of Kadavali village and some of his fellow villagers for roughing up the sehna.[95] In the same pargana, when the sehna was beaten up and his *chak* (land-measurement rod) was snatched away by Heera Patel of Sadulpur village and his accomplices, a fine of Rs.51.4*an.* was charged from them by the amil.[96] In pargana Mojpur, Patel Varaiyati of Khohra village was fined for 'misbehaving' with the sehna, and so were the Meo peasants of the same village.[97] In qasba Pindayan of pargana Pindayan, a Brahmin peasant called Bohrala was fined Rs.5.8*an.* for fighting with the sehna.[98] In pargana Harsana, the same fine was imposed on Khajano Meena of Munda village for misdemeanour with the *sehna*.[99]

The fact that acts of making fraudulent claims about crops or cultivated fields and evading land-measurement and crop-assessment, willfully destroying bad crops with the sehna's permission, cutting off standing crops, stealing harvested crops, and resisting the sehna's preventive interventions tooth and nail—were detected and punished by the state on numerous occasions yields several crucial inferences. First, the peasant was not as autonomous an agent of production as Mukhia conceives him to be; rather, he was subject to constant vigilance and various constraints by the state throughout the entire production cycle, right from sowing to final harvesting. Second, thus, the class conflict between the peasant and the state occurred—contrary to what Mukhia argues—very much *within* the production process (i.e. before the produce was distributed between the state and the peasant), just as it did outside the system (when the state sought to appropriate more than its due share of the produce). In fact, the production process itself was the first site of contest between the peasantry and the state, each staking its control over it. And the second site was the distribution of produce upon the completion of the process—a stage where the conflict surfaced prominently. Thus, the peasant's class struggle went on in all stages of the production—from sowing to harvesting—and, of course, beyond it. Third, the peasant's petty acts of deception, lying and fighting with the state officials in order to reduce his revenue burden and 'misappropriate' the state's share of the produce were, in fact, 'weapons of the weak' and 'everyday forms of class struggle',[100] just as petitioning and armed revolts were. It is their weakness as a class before the might of the state that compelled them to use such covert 'weapons' of resistance in their everyday class struggle against the state. Despite the frequent detection and penalization of such acts by the state officials, the peasant was not deterred from committing them, as it was his 'class tendency' and constant endeavour to find ways and means to promote his economic interests best by evading tax payment. Fourth, that the peasants of various castes (Meo, Mahajan, Mali, Meena, Brahmin, and Jat) resorted to tax evasion and disputed with the sehna significantly point to the fact that their conflict with the state rested on a certain awareness of their class interests, cutting across caste divisions.

As argued earlier, the conflict between the peasants and the revenue officials over the assessment of produce even before the payment of revenue could only have been possible if the production, to a great extent, depended on the exertions of the peasant. In other words, the peasant having the greatest stake in the agricultural production would try his best to assert his control over the process and enlarge his own share in the fruits of his labour, i.e. the produce, even at the cost of reducing the state's share and at the risk of clashing with the state officials.

V

While the peasant showed a keen awareness of his customary entitlements and duties vis-à-vis the state—an awareness that underlay his everyday class struggle—this awareness or class consciousness was merged with his caste consciousness, i.e. awareness of his position and those of his fellow peasants in the traditional caste hierarchy.

Attuned to living in a caste-divided social order governed by the
state, he implicitly accepted as customary the differential treatment
of different castes—and identical treatment of castes with the same
or similar social standing—within his community by the state. The
state, too, recognized and reinforced caste differences by charging
differential rates of revenue. For instance, the revenue records such
as *hal bail yaddashtis* and *dastur amals* record the caste identity of the
peasants. Any violation of this customary practice by the state brought
their caste consciousness to the fore. For instance, in 1750, the Meo
peasants of 12 villages of pargana Khohri complained to the amil of the
Amber Raja that they had been charged 50 per cent of their rabi and
kharif harvest as land revenue, while the peasants of Ahir caste paid
40 per cent on the same crops and in the same village; and that such
discrimination between peasant castes was a violation of customary
practices.[101] Interestingly, as a mark of solidarity, the Ahir peasants also
sent their petition to the Amber Raja in favour of the Meos' demand,
requesting that a single *dastur* (crop rate) be adopted for assessing land
revenue demand from both communities. They further argued that if
land revenue were charged at a higher rate from the Meos, it would be
difficult for them to live in the same villages with the Meos who would
blame them for this unequal treatment and might also assault them,
thereby disrupting their brotherhood.[102] The Meo peasants, on their
part, knew that the social status of the Ahirs was equal to theirs and
therefore, both should be charged the same rate of land revenue by the
state. In fact, this caste consciousness among the Meo peasants was so
strong that they never questioned the state's practice of collecting land
revenue from Brahmin, Rajput and Mahajan cultivators at lower rates.
They knew that it was customary for higher castes to be charged land
revenue at lower rates than other peasant castes. On the other hand,
they also recognized that emergency situations demanded reversal of
such customary caste-based discrimination. For instance, in 1712, they
unleashed their anger against the state when the Brahmin cultivators
of five villages of pargana Khohri[103] were provided *taqavi* (agricultural
loan) for buying bullocks and seeds by mahajans on behalf of the amil
during drought, while the Meo peasants were denied this facility since
the amil had refused to act as guarantor for them. The Meos pleaded
with the amil that *taqavi* be extended to all peasant castes during
drought as an emergency measure, and that granting *taqavi* to Brahmin

cultivators alone was a non-customary and unethical practice. When their plea went unheard, they even attacked the Brahmin cultivators of the five villages.[104] Thus, the otherwise caste-conscious Meo peasantry who submitted to customary preferential treatment of higher castes in normal circumstances looked upon such caste-based favouritism by the state officials as unjust in exceptional situations when their survival was at stake. Further, common economic interests—or rather, a common threat to their interests—occasionally united different peasant castes, whereby class consciousness superseded caste consciousness. For instance, small and perpetually needy peasants always depended on *taqavi* from the mahajans living in qasbas, who used to provide it at high interest rates on behalf of the state during the sowing season and expected them to return the principal along with the interest at the time of harvest. In 1704, the peasants of Meena, Lohar and Thorry castes attacked the houses of the mahajans at night in qasba Avery. The latter had taken away their entire sock of grains to recover the money loaned to them, leaving them with nothing to eat. Most of the mahajans fled and presented themselves at the court of the Amber Raja, pleading for the security of their lives and property. The Amber Raja ordered the faujdar of pargana Avery to take action against those peasants who had attacked the mahajans' houses. The amil's report to the diwan of Amber, however, favoured the peasants' case. It stated that while the mahajans had provided the peasants with *taqavi* for seeds and bullocks, the latter suffered the dual pressure to repay their debt and pay their land revenue and were forced to act against the mahajans in desperation.[105]

The peasantry in Mewat comprised self-consciously disparate castes/communities, with different positions in a stratified society and differential access to means of production (and thereby economic status). While there is evidence to suggest a general acceptance, on the part of the peasants (and the state), of the inherited and relatively fixed social status of all castes and the customary economic entitlements of superior castes, there is also evidence to show a disregard of caste differences in exceptional situations that threatened their survival, such as denial of loans in distress or, as discussed previously, imposition of non-customary taxes and unbearable tax burden. Such situations, more common during the period discussed, affected all strata of peasantry and united most of them in recognizing their common interest of survival against odds and countering the source of threat to their survival, whether the mahajans or the Amber state's officials. The state as well did not consider caste differences in punishing rebel peasants for wilful non-payment of revenue. Indeed, the Rajasthani archival sources when mentioning cases of petitions and uprisings by peasants often designate them by the generic term *raiyati* (subjects) and identify them by the names of native villages and parganas. As per the records, the acts of tax evasion were also individually committed by peasants of various castes, indicating that the forms of resistance cut across the caste lines. This suggests that the peasants, while being caste conscious, acted or at least were seen as acting as a class when protecting their common economic interests. In other words, both caste and class consciousness coexisted among the peasants, the former often being subsumed by the latter.

VI

From the foregoing study, it can be surmised that in the late seventeenth and early eighteenth centuries, there raged a political turmoil throughout Mewat. A dominant political entity, i.e the Amber state and an emerging one, i.e. the Jats fiercely competed with each other to acquire the right to collect revenue from the areas under the jurisdiction of mansabdars of the Mughal state. By deriving this right from the Mughal state (or its direct representatives, the mansabdars) through ijara or revenue-farming, they interposed themselves as a new stratum of authority between the mansabdars and the peasants, and constantly contested the legitimacy of each other's claims to agricultural surplus. At the same time, the traditional claims of the Mughal state to land revenue, as also its politico-administrative control, was progressively eroded. On the one hand, this led to the impairment of traditional mechanisms of grievance-redressal for the peasantry who bore the brunt of increased revenue demand due to the imposition of multiple non-customary taxes by the ijaradars, particularly the Amber Raja. On the other hand, the absence of well defined legitimate claims of the state on surplus made it impossible for the peasantry to satisfy the multiple claimants who ruthlessly exploited them.

From the peasant's perspective, the Mughal emperor alone retained the 'legitimate' right to collect land revenue from them on the basis of customary practices. Therefore, saddled with a heavy land revenue demand from the Amber Raja, they often petitioned to the Mughal emperor, seeking his intervention to redress their grievances against the 'illegitimate' levies imposed by the Amber Raja and appealing to *ruh-nyaya* (conscientious justice). They were clearly aware that the Amber Raja used to obtain the ijara of their villages from the imperial mansabdars in lieu of a fixed sum of money (peshkash), but the burden of paying this peshkash was passed down to them in the form of non-customary taxes. The peasants with their faith in an ideal reciprocal relation with the state based on certain customary rights and duties accepted the standard land revenue demand of the state and considered fulfilling it as their duty (*prajadharam*) provided the state was just and caring towards them, i.e. it abided by the ethics of good governance (*rajdharam*). This was a tradition-bound but perceptive conception of an ethical relation between the rulers and the ruled, i.e. the peasant and the state. This traditional conception, combined with an equally traditional but experiential knowledge of their distinct economic interests vis-à-vis the state, became the best expression of their self-consciousness as a distinct class in social, political, economic and ideological terms.

At the same time, the peasants opposed the state's revenue demand if it flouted the customary practices and, in effect, harmed their class interest. Since the exploitative ijara system allowed its beneficiaries like the Amber state and Churaman Jat to demand, levy and coercively collect from peasants non-customary levies, the latter not only found the system, as well as the non-customary levies imposed under it, detrimental to their economic interests, but also perceived it as morally unjust. The system thus eroded the peasants' faith in the state's ability to discharge its *rajdharam* and provoked them to transgress their own *prajadharam* through protests, rebellions and desertion of villages which became, in fact, overt expressions of their class struggle. Such expressions were not limited to conflict over appropriation of surplus but permeated the entire production process. Numerous acts of 'deception' and 'misappropriation' and petty disputes with state officials *within* this process were everyday forms of peasant resistance to what they perceived as unjust control over the process, and thereby expressions of their class struggle.

However, the fuller development of this peasant class consciousness in opposition to the ruling class and the realization of the full potential of this class struggle may appear to have been somewhat stymied by their occasional compromises with the state. But it is to be noted that these compromises were conditioned by their inability to stand up to the might of the state in a sustained manner, by their belief in the ideal of a non-conflictual, harmonious relation with the state, and by a crucial pragmatic economic consideration that they had at stake their right to land use and a certain degree of control over the production process and they would risk losing them in the event of adopting a perpetual adversarial stand vis-à-vis the state. In this sense, the class consciousness of peasantry in late medieval north India was not geared towards making its relation with the state necessarily adversarial, even if the interests of the producing and ruling classes were fundamentally opposed at least theoretically. The class position of the peasants in late medieval north India was evidently much more complex than envisaged by theoretical (Marxist) frameworks on class consciousness and class conflict. It was not exclusive of nor severely impeded by caste consciousness and rather incorporated the latter. When considered vis-à-vis the state/ruling class, this class position, as evident from both folklore and archival records, cannot be reduced to antagonism alone, but is multifaceted. Thus, their opposition to the state's excesses was strong but remained staggered, and the ijara system and their consequent exploitation only became widespread in Mewat during the eighteenth century.

Notes

1. Irfan Habib, 'The Form of Class Struggles during the Mughal Period', in *Essays in Indian History: Towards a Marxist Perception*, London: Anthem Press, 2002, pp. 233–58.
2. Harbans Mukhia, 'Peasant Production and Medieval Indian Society', in *Exploring India's Medieval Centuries: Essays in History, Society, Culture and Technology*, New Delhi: Aakar, 2010, p. 215.
3. Ibid.
4. Ibid., p. 196.
5. R.S. Sharma, 'How Feudal was Indian Feudalism?', *The Journal of Peasant Studies*, vol. 12, nos. 2–3, 1985, p. 36; cited in Mukhia, 'Peasant Production', pp. 196–7. The insertions within brackets are by Mukhia.
6. Mukhia, 'Peasant Production', p. 197.

7. Ibid., pp. 197–8.

8. P.W. Powlett, *Gazetteer of Ulwur*, London: Trübner and Co., 1878, pp. 73–5.

9. Ibid., p. 70.

10. I am grateful to Manoj Sehrawat, son of late Shri Chaudhari Hardhyan Singh, for allowing me to quote these couplets.

11. Narsingh Meo, 'Hasan Khan ki Katha', *Shodh Patrika*, vol. 4, October– December, Udaipur: Rajasthan Vidyapeeth, 1970, pp. 53–62.

12. R.C. Temple, *The Legends of Panjab*, 3 vols., Bombay: Bombay Education Society's Press, 1884.

13. Munshi Ram, 'Mewati Lok Sahitya evam Mewat ka Arthik Vishleshan', in *Shreejan*, ed. Chhangaram Meena, Alwar: Babu Shobharam Rajkiya Mahavidyalaya, 2006, pp. 99–102.

14. Jeevan Singh Manvi, 'Ali Baksh ki Krishanlila evam anya Khyal', in *Shreejan*, ed. Chhangaram Meena, Alwar: Babu Shobharam Rajkiya Mahavidyalaya, 2006, pp. 81–9.

15. Puranchand Sharma, *Pandit Lakhmichand Granthavali*, Chandigarh: Haryana Sahitya Academy, 1996, p. 17.

16. Alexander Cunningham, *Report of a Tour in Eastern Rajputana in 1882–83*, vol. XX, Archaeological Survey of India Reports, 1885; repr., Varanasi: Indological Book House, 1969, pp. 122–4.

17. Meo, 'Hasan Khan ki Katha', pp. 53–62.

18. Shankarlal Yadav, *Haryana Pradesh ka Lok Sahitya*, Allahabad: Hindustani Academy, 1960, p. 430.

19. A north Indian sweet dish prepared by mixing flour and *lassi* (a cold drink made with yoghurt or buttermilk flavoured with sugar, salt, or a mild spice), allowing the mixture to ferment for 8–10 hours and then boiling this fermented mixture. It was, and is, commonly prepared in the peasant households.

20. The patels were socially and economically superior to others in the village community. But, unlike the Rajput *bhomias* (zamindars), they did not possess *garhis* (fortresses) or command armies; they were mainly members of the peasant community and, therefore, used to represent the peasants' grievances before the state authorities from time to time.

21. *Khatut-ahalkarn, Mah Vadi* 6, vs 1740/ce 1683, Jaipur Records, Historical Section, Rajasthan State Archives, Bikaner.

22. *Arzdasht, Fagun Sudi* 3, vs 1740/ce 1683.

23. Ibid.

24. Ibid.

25. *Arzdasht, Asadh Vadi* 5, vs 1744/ce 1685.

26. *Vakil's* report, *Asoj Vadi* 9, vs 1769/ce 1712.

27. *Arzdasht, Miti Asadh Sudi* 3, VS 1769/CE 1712.
28. *Arzdasht, Sawan Sudi* 3, VS 1771/CE 1714.
29. *Chithi* to the amil, pargana Khohri, *Vaishakh Sudi* 9, VS 1785/CE 1728; the amount of *virar* was distributed among the 15 villages on the basis of their area in this manner: Laadaar (Rs.1,560), Shinghawali (Rs.985), Vakushiki (Rs.1,160), Aroda (Rs.765), Nangli (Rs.1,160), Mehrampur (Rs.600), Pali (Rs.565), Rashghana (Rs.665), Naswari (Rs.890), Jarauli (Rs.1,250), Malpur and Bhalodpur (Rs.1,180), Varkhara (Rs.725), Lalwari (Rs.970) and Jaunabarapahar (Rs.540).
30. *Chithi* to the amil, pargana Piragpur, *Asoj Sudi* 7, VS 1786/CE 1729; *Asoj Sudi* 6, VS 1787/CE 1730.
31. Habib, 'The Form of Class Struggles'.
32. *Arzdasht, Sawan Vadi* 14, VS 1783/CE 1726.
33. *Arsatta*, pargana Harsana, VS 1792/CE 1735.
34. *Arsatta*, pargana Mojpur, VS 1792/CE 1735.
35. *Arsatta*, pargana Alwar, VS 1782/CE 1725.
36. *Arsatta*, pargana Sahar, VS 1746/CE 1689.
37. *Mauza* was the administrative term for village in Mughal north India.
38. *Tappa* was the lowest-level administrative unit in north India in the Mughal period.
39. *Arzdasht, Asadh Vadi* 3, VS 1768/CE 1711.
40. *Arzdasht, Miti Mah Sudi* 6, VS 1751/CE 1684.
41. *Arzdasht, Kartik Vadi* 9, VS 1780/CE 1723.
42. *Arzdasht, Chait Sudi* 4, VS 1743/CE 1686.
43. *Arsatta*, pargana Alwar, VS 1782/CE 1725.
44. *Arzdasht, Asadh Vadi* 3, VS 1768/CE 1711.
45. Such peasant protests in Mewat were not absent in the early Mughal period. For instance, in the early fifteenth century, a powerful Meo revolt broke out in the vicinity of Nuh Firozpur Jhirka against the oppressive land revenue administration of the Khanzadas, the ruling elite of Mewat. A large number of Meo peasants were arrested by the Khanzada ruler Ahmad Khan Mewati on account of the non-payment of land revenue, and forced to work for the construction of the fortress at Indore, the capital of Khanzada state (*bandhak* no.13, *granthak* no. 4, Non-archival Records of Alwar State, Rajasthan State Archives, Bikaner). Another Meo peasant revolt took place in some villages of pargana Alwar during the early years of Akbar's reign. The rebel peasants had not paid their revenue for the last few years and harassed and manhandled the revenue officials. Their rebellion was crushed and their villages destroyed by the Mughal army (*bandhak* no. 13, *granthak* no. 1). Yet another powerful Meo revolt took place in the early days of Jahangir's reign. The army of Alaf Khan (Kiyam Khani), the imperial faujdar

of Mewat, destroyed the *gharis* (hill-fortresses) of Meo *bhomias* and arrested many Meo rebels and *bhomias* (Ratan Lal Mishra, *Kiyamkhani Vamsh ka Itihasa evam Samskriti*, 2nd revd edn, Jodhpur: Rajasthani Granthagar, 2002, p. 91). Shah Jahan's reign, too, witnessed a Meo revolt, and a large force under Khimat Parast Khan (Rida Bahadur) murdered numerous rebel Meos and brought a large number of Meo women and children to Agra as prisoners; see H. Beveridge, tr., *The Maathir-ul-Umara*, vol. 1, rev., anno. and compl. Baini Prasad, Patna: Janaki Prakashan, 1979, p. 813. Later, in 1650, Shah Jahan ordered the Amber chief Mirza Raja Jai Singh to wipe out the rebel Meos of Kaman and Pahari parganas in Sahar sarkar and severely punish those jagirdars or zamindars who had tried to protect the rebels in their villages. He also ordered the jagirdars to imprison the rebels of the areas under their jurisdiction. Eventually, the Amber Raja's army captured many Meo rebels in the aforementioned parganas (Mohinder Singh Kharagawat, ed., *Farsi Farmano ke Prakash mein Mughal Kalin Bharat and Rajput Saashak* [Hindi], Bikaner: Rajasthan State Archives, 2010, pp. 122–4).

46. These villages that did not deposit land revenue were Nanaderi, Jawali, Hanauta, Ranauli, Gangwas, Khathmano, Akhau, Kakar, Bhelpur, Nanupur, Bagar, Bijwar, Mamana, Pihavati, Manpur and Lave.

47. *Arzdasht, Kartik Vadi* 14, vs 1766/ce 1709.

48. *Arzdasht, Asadh Vadi* 5, vs 1769/ce 1712.

49. *Arzdasht, Mangsir Vadi* 1, vs 1761/ce 1704; *Chait Vadi* 14, vs 1761/ce 1704; *Vaishakh Sudi* 7, vs 1769/ce 1712.

50. *Arzdasht*s, *Fagun Vadi* 13, vs 1752/ce 1695; *Bhadva Vadi* 6, vs 1752/ce 1695.

51. *Arsatta*, pargana Pahari, vs 1788/ce 1731.

52. *Chithi* to the amil, pargana Khohri, *Bhadva Sudi* 2, vs 1791/ce 1734; *Kartik Sudi* 9, vs 1791/ce 1734; *Chithi* to the amil, pargana Pahari, *Asadh Vadi* 5, vs 1791/ce 1734.

53. Shail Mayaram, *Against History, Against State: Counter Perspective from the Margins*, New Delhi: Oxford University Press, 2004.

54. Suraj Bhan Bhardwaj, 'Migration, Mobility and Memories: Meos in the Process of Peasantisation and Islamisation during the Medieval Period', *Indian Historical Review*, vol. 39, no. 2, 2012, pp. 217–50.

55. Vakil's Report, *Fagun Sudi* 2, vs 1767/ce 1710.

56. Vakil's Report, *Asadh Vadi* 17, vs 1771/ce 1714; *Vakil's* Report, *Jeth Sudi* 11, vs 1771/ce 1714.

57. *Arzdasht, Asadh Sudi* 3, vs 1773/ce 1716.

58. *Arzdasht, Sawan Vadi* 1, vs 1771/ce 1714.

59. akil's report, *Jeth Sudi* 11, vs 1771/CE 1714; *Arsatta*, pargana Khohri, vs 1771/CE 1714.
60. Vakil's report, *Jeth Sudi* 11, vs 1771/CE 1714.
61. Vakil's report, *Jeth Vadi* 8, vs 1771/CE 1714.
62. *Arzdasht, Mangsir Vadi* 10, vs 1774/CE 1714; *Arsatta*, pargana Khohri, vs 1771/CE 1714.
63. Vakil's report, *Taarikh* 19, vs 1769/CE 1712; *Vakil's* report, *Asoj Vadi* 9, vs 1769/CE 1712.
64. *Arzdasht, Asadh Vadi* 7, vs 1769/CE 1712.
65. *Arzdasht, Asadh Sudi* 2, vs 1769/CE 1712.
66. *Arzdasht, Asadh Sudi* 8, vs 1769/CE 1712.
67. *Arsatta*, pargana Khohri, vs 1773/CE 1716.
68. *Arsatta*, pargana Pahari, vs 1773/CE 1716.
69. *Arsatta*, pargana Jalalpur, vs 1773/CE 1716; pargana Mojpur, vs 1774/CE 1717; *Arsatta*, pargana Bharkal, vs 1774/CE 1717.
70. *Arzdasht, Jeth Sudi* 11, vs 1773/CE 1716.
71. Vakil's report, *Asadh Vadi* 5, vs 1768/CE 1711.
72. *Chithi* to the amil, pargana Khohri, *Asadh Vadi* 14, vs 1797/CE 1740.
73. *Chithi* to the amil, pargana Khohri, *Sawan Sudi* 8, vs 1797/CE 1740.
74. Under the *zabti* method, separate cash rates per *bigha* for different crops were prepared for each pargana and for each village within a pargana. Under the *batai-jinsi* system, a simple sharing of the harvested grain took place on the basis of shares agreed upon between the peasants and the state.
75. *Arsatta*, pargana Alwar, vs 1782/CE 1725.
76. Ibid.
77. Ibid.
78. *Arsatta*, pargana Mundawar, vs 1792/CE 1735.
79. *Arsatta*, pargana Narayana, vs 1781/CE 1724.
80. *Arsatta*, pargana Mundawar, vs 1792/CE 1735.
81. *Arsatta*, pargana Narayana, vs 1781/CE 1724.
82. Ibid.
83. Ibid.
84. Ibid.
85. Ibid.
86. *Arsatta*, pargana Mundawar, vs 1722/CE 1665.
87. *Arsatta*, pargana Mundawar, vs 1787/CE 1730.
88. *Arsatta*, pargana Harsana, vs 1787/CE 1730.
89. *Arsatta*, pargana Mojpur, vs 1792/CE 1735.
90. *Arsatta*, pargana Alwar, vs 1782/CE 1725.
91. Ibid.
92. *Arzdasht, Miti Kartik Sudi* 3, vs 1799/CE 1742.

93. *Arsatta*, pargana Pindayan, vs 1792/CE 1732.

94. *Arsatta*, pargana Mundawar, vs 1792/CE 1745.

95. *Arsatta*, pargana Narayana, vs 1781/CE 1724.

96. *Arsatta*, pargana Alwar, vs 1782/CE 1725.

97. *Arsatta*, pargana Mojpur, vs 1787/CE 1730.

98. *Arsatta*, pargana Pindayan, vs 1789/CE 1732.

99. *Arsatta*, pargana Harsana, vs 1787/CE 1730.

100. James C. Scott, *Weapons of the Weak: Everyday Forms of Peasant Resistance*, New Delhi: Oxford University Press, 1990.

101. *Chithi* to the amil, pargana Khohri, *Sawan Sudi* 7, vs 1807/CE 1750; these villages were Verdu, Palko, Alam Shahko, Paliko, Jaishree, Shukairi, Jaishro, Budha Khoh, Bandhako, Vadkari, Parl, etc.

102. *Chithi* to the amil, pargana Khohri, *Sawan Sudi* 9, vs 1807/CE 1750.

103. These villages were Daalawas, Jarautha, Muhal, Naalapur, etc.

104. *Arzdasht, Mangsir Vadi* 6, vs 1769/CE 1712.

105. *Arzdasht, Jeth Sudi* 15, vs 1761/CE 1704.

6

Perceptions of Kingship in Peasant Society

Insights from Folklore in Late Medieval North India

THE IDEA OF kingship in precolonial India has received a good deal of attention from scholars for a long time. Textual sources of varied genres have been conventionally used to reconstruct the conceptions of kingship in ancient and medieval times. Usually, sources of the ancient period used for the purpose are in Sanskrit and present a largely Brahmanical perspective on state and society, while those of the medieval period are Persian court chronicles that ingeniously mould Islamic precepts to construct unique theories of Indo-Islamic kingship for the Sultanate and the Mughal state. Such texts and textual traditions were evidently produced by members of the intellectual and social elite who held certain socio-religious dispensations and were or may have been part of their contemporary power structures. Thus, these sources can be considered, in varying degrees, as having a largely classist and/or statist perspective insofar as the protection of the material interests and social pre-eminence of certain classes and/ or the overarching authority of monarchy is/are privileged by them. Conceptions of kingship in them have been privileged as constituting the dominant precolonial discourse on statecraft and kingship.

In the modern scholarly literature on premodern idea of kingship heavily based on such sources, what has so far eluded—and thus merits—a systematic study is the possibility of locating alternative perceptions/conceptions of kingship. Seeking to fill this vacuum, this chapter argues that such perceptions can be traced in the folk tales and folk songs of precolonial rural society in late medieval north India. Folklore has its obvious problems of chronology, spatial provenance and authorship, which have deterred scholars from using it as a source for history-writing in general and explains their excessive reliance on written records. Nevertheless, folklore can be imaginatively and fruitfully used for understanding what can be considered a subaltern perspective on kingship, among other things—a perspective often emanating from lower sections of the society and hence different from that of the elite. At the same time, considering the fluid and oral nature of folk songs and folk tales, they need to be read with caution with regard to possible changes in content and perspectives in the course of their multiple renditions across time and space.

Beginning with a brief overview of the perceptions of kingship in textual sources, this chapter focuses on the perceptions of kingship in select popular folk tales of north and north-western India (more precisely, eastern Rajasthan, parts of Haryana, western Uttar Pradesh) that were recorded by colonial ethnographers in the late nineteenth century and/or fashioned into musical performative narratives (*sangs*) by rural bards in the late nineteenth and early twentieth centuries and still widely narrated and enacted before rural audiences. The chapter demonstrates that the perceptions of kingship in these stories, while converging and diverging with those in literary sources on several points, constitute a unique discourse on ideal kingship and its ingredients (such as sense of justice, honour and duty, righteousness, honesty, humility, tolerance, forgiveness) prevalent in the politically disempowered and socio-economically under-/non-privileged class/es. This subaltern discourse can be seen as a counterpoint to the dominant elite discourse of ancient Brahmanical normative texts and medieval Indo-Persian court chronicles. For the peasant communities grappling with various forms of inequity and oppression arising out of the state and society through the ages, constructing this discourse and thereby valorizing a simple ethical ideal of kingship was a way of envisioning an alternative socio-political utopia. In times of acute distress such as during the disturbed political conditions following the decline of Mughal imperial authority in the late seventeenth and early eighteenth centuries, engaging in such discourse through remembrance, narration and performance was arguably an inspired way of enduring and even resisting oppression by the political elite. Thus, reconstructing subaltern conceptions of kingship in the peasant society is an important and hitherto unexplored area in the study of medieval Indian history.

In the ancient sources,[1] the *raja* (king) is often seen as a divine/ semi-divine and superhuman figure,[2] but not as one exercising absolute, unbridled authority. Rather, his position, though supreme, is sought to be hemmed by moral, customary and institutional constraints or checks.[3] Further, his duties towards his *praja* (subjects) that constituted *rajadharma* are elaborated and emphasized, his foremost duty being that of protecting his subjects, as also performing acts of public welfare.[4] His deviation from duties, pleasure-seeking and acts of cruelty and oppression are condemned and thought to have fatal outcomes for him; even overthrow and killing of unjust, tyrannical, wayward and evil rulers are justified.[5] Moreover, kingship is occasionally conceived as acquired through the approval and consent of nobles, high functionaries and common people;[6] in some instances, it is even thought to be produced by a sort of social contract between the ruler and the subjects.[7] Corresponding to the idea of *rajadharma* is that of *prajadharma* that chiefly consists of the duty of subjects to pay taxes to the king in respect of the protection given by him,[8] but at the same time the king's power to tax his subjects is sought to be regulated by certain principles to prevent arbitrary taxation and ruthless exploitation.[9] Hence, the relation between the two is envisaged as reciprocal, if not explicitly contractual. This reciprocity lies in their discharge of moral obligations towards each other: the king is to provide protection and efficient grievance-redressal mechanism and promote public welfare, and, in turn, the subjects are to pay him taxes.

Notable among the medieval texts that offer theoretical expositions on kingship is Abul-Fazl's *Ain-i-Akbari*. In this work, kingship is conceived dually, i.e. as originating in divine appointment, and in a social contract between the ruler and his subjects.[10] Divine and contractual nature of a ruler's office, thus, constitute the two pillars in Abul-Fazl's theory of sovereignty.[11] Placing his political patron, Akbar, at the centre of his discussion on the divinity of the sovereign, Abul-Fazl regards him as *farr-i izadi* or 'divine light' and *zil allah* or 'shadow of god', suggesting that he was a representative of god on earth. The divinity of the ruler, emphasized by Fazl, was impressed upon the people through court rituals adopted by Akbar such as *jharokha darshan*, i.e. the practice of giving a glimpse of himself (*darshan*) from a window (*jharokha*) to his admirers every morning—a ritual adapted from the Hindu practice of having a glimpse of the deity. Expounding the idea of social contract between the ruler and his subjects, Abul-Fazl regards taxes as a reward of sovereignty, as an entitlement of the king for treating and protecting his subjects without discrimination on the basis of faith.[12] Abul-Fazl, thus, credits Akbar for creating, through his policy of religious tolerance and non-discrimination, *sulh kul* (lit. 'absolute peace'), i.e. a state of universal peace and social harmony. But at the same time, in Abul-Fazl's view, the king is the protector of the subject's life and honour, and hence no moral limits could be set to the fiscal obligations (i.e. taxes) owed by the latter to the former; the subject should be thankful even if he were made to part with all his possessions by the protector of his life and honour.[13] Overall, in Abul-Fazl's works, it appears that the idea of a ruler's divine origin and absolute power assumes overriding importance in comparison to his contractual relation with the subjects. Both Brahmanical texts and Abul-Fazl's chronicle, belonging to different temporal, political and cultural contexts, emphasize the divine nature of kingship. But while the former tempers royal power with a strong element of obligation and duty, the latter shows greater accent on the absolute paternal authority of the divine emperor Akbar who is envisioned as *insan-i kamil* or the 'complete man', endowed with all desirable qualities or virtues and hence irreproachable and unsurpassable. Thus, while the Brahmanical theory of kingship was general and not modeled on the conduct of any specific ruler, Abul-Fazl's was largely an Akbarid notion of kingship.

Marking a departure from these theories in many ways are folk tales. Folk musical-cum-theatrical performances such as *sang/svang* and *tamasha* played an important role in shaping the peasant's worldview which consisted of, among other things, a clear and simple conception of ideal kingship. This conception was articulated in the form of narratives about the lives of legendary rulers, known for their many virtues, and it was these virtues such as justice, morality, duty, sacrifice, struggle, forbearance and truthfulness that constituted their notion of kingship. It may be reasonably presumed that popular notions of kingship are as old as the very institution of kingship. They have co-existed with elaborate elite theories of kingship and state in religious, semi- and non-religious texts, without gaining visibility in the written records. Thus, although credible information on the history of folk tales in the peasant society of medieval north India is inadequate and fragmentary because of their fluid, oral character, there must have been a well established, long-standing tradition of recounting them in one form or the other since at least the medieval period, considering their survival in the nineteenth century (and even to this day).

In as early as sixteenth century, Narsingh Meo of Kajhota village composed a ballad 'Hasan Khan ki Katha'[14] on Hasan Khan Mewati, a Khanzada ruler of Mewat. This work may be considered the earliest extant example of local perception of historical events in the region preserved through the medium of folk poetry. But it was in the late nineteenth and early twentieth centuries that a large number of folk tales in various parts of north and north-west India were collected and recorded by British officials who donned the mantle of amateur ethnographers and folklorists. Notable among such collections are the three-volume *The Legends of the Panjab* by Capt. R.C. Temple;[15] *The Giant Crab and Other Tales of Old India* by W.H.D. Rouse;[16] *Indian Fairy Tales* by Maive Stokes;[17] *Tales of the Punjab Told by the People* by Flora Annie Steel;[18] and *Romantic Tales from the Punjab with Indian Nights' Entertainment* by Charles Swynnerton.[19] Besides, in the late nineteenth century, Alexander Cunningham had also reported stories of Badgujar Rajput chiefs from the Alwar region of eastern Rajasthan.[20]

These folk tales had been orally preserved and narrated for generations by bards or minstrels (*charans, bhats, mirasis*), wandering mendicants (*jogis, sannyasis*) and Brahmins at least since the medieval period. By the eighteenth century this long tradition of storytelling gradually developed into a rich performative art of *sang/svang* characterized by music, dance and dramatics. Kishanlal Bhat is regarded as the father of the *sang* tradition and placed in the first half of the eighteenth century, more precisely between 1730 and 1750. In the eighteenth century, Saadulla Khan of Aakeda village in the Nuh district of Mewat composed 'Pandun Ko Karo',[21] a Mewati rendition of the Sanskrit epic *Mahabharata*, sung by wandering bards/minstrels (*mirasis*) in the region. By the early nineteenth century, the *sang* art form had further developed so that the number of actors playing different roles increased. In the second half of the century, there emerged two famous exponents of this folk tradition, Ali Baksh and Pandit Deepchand. The former is credited with the composing 'Nal-Daman',[22] a tale of the trials and tribulations of a mythical king Nal and his wife Damayanti, drawn from the *Mahabharata* and popular in the Mewat region. Deepchand is said to have wandered in the villages of Haryana, popularizing his *sangs*, the most notable of which are those on Raja Bhoj and Sarande, Nal-Damayanti, Gopichand Maharaj and Raja Harishchandra.[23] By the early twentieth century several practitioners had played a crucial role in enriching and developing this art form in parts of Haryana, eastern Rajasthan and western Uttar Pradesh. But the credit for taking it to new heights can justifiably be given to Pandit Lakhmichand (CE *c*.1902–48). Prior to his time, performances were staged on open ground by a small number of actors before a standing audience that gathered around them. But Lakhmichand carried out fundamental changes in the performative aspects of *sang* tradition: *sangs* began to be staged on a raised platform, the physical distance between actors and audience increased as the actors performed on the stage while the seated audience watched them from a certain distance, actors and musicians became separate entities, and the success of the show depended as much on the performance of the actors as on the music and lyrics.

In the nineteenth and twentieth centuries, in Haryana, eastern Rajasthan and western Uttar Pradesh, performances based on such folktales attracted thousands of peasants from many villages, near and far. Many of the stories and their protagonists were largely drawn from epic and Puranic legends, but they were reinterpreted or refashioned by the narrators/performers in terms of the peasants' own life experiences and rendered in forms, dialects, idioms and styles familiar and appealing to them. They themselves emerging out of peasant societies, the bards and artistes could hence act as key players and spokesmen in shaping and voicing the peasant worldview. While the historicity of the protagonists remains dubious at best, what is of primary importance is that they are often projected as embodiments of such ideals as justice, integrity, duty, sacrifice, forbearance, compassion and truthfulness, and often pitted against trying or difficult circumstances and/or characters who represent counter-ideals such as injustice, deceit, immorality, greed, lust, hubris and ruthlessness. Through the motif of struggle between the key protagonists and adversarial situations and/or people, these tales unambiguously convey simple binaries of right and wrong, just and unjust, moral and immoral, virtue and sin, sacrifice and greed. These stories when recounted through enlivening musical-cum-theatrical performances before a rural audience helped the peasants perceive an affinity between their everyday struggles, sorrows and miseries and those of the mythical characters and thereby empathize with them.

The stories also gave expression to their struggle against injustice at the hands of the oppressive ruling class. The simple ethical ideas, contained in the stories, came to be imbibed by them as essential components of their culture and value system. Understandably, such stories and performances must have left a deep imprint on the minds of the rural audience, as they still do.

More importantly, for the purpose of this chapter, the ethical content of these stories or songs also shaped the peasant's perception of an ideal ruler and his ideal relation with the state (personified by the ruler). Hence, stories celebrating some rulers for their proverbial justice and benevolence, such as Rama, Vikaramaditya, Mordhvaj, Puranmal and Bhoj, underscore these desirable qualities of a ruler, while other stories of rulers such as Harishchandra, Prahlad, Dhruvbhakt and Nal present them as victims of injustice by the state who emerged victorious through their trials and tribulations. It was through these stories—whether of benevolent, just rulers or dispossessed, suffering ones—that the peasants would have conceptualized the duties of the ruler and the subjects and the relation between them. This made the medieval Indian peasant mentally beholden to his *prajadharam/ prajadharma*, i.e. his moral duty (*dharam*), as a subject (*praja*), to pay a share of his produce as revenue to his ruler (*raja*)—a duty that he had inherited and imbibed from his ancestors. At the same, he held the ruler beholden to its *rajdharam/ rajadharma*, i.e. its duty to govern the subjects 'justly'.[24] In the peasant's worldview, his ideal relation with the ruler was thus based on the reciprocal adherence to their respective customary duties (*rajdharam, prajadharam*). In times of good harvest, the peasant paid the land revenue to the ruler provided it was based on customary rates. However, it was the imposition of non-customary levies, along with crop failures and other natural disasters that roused his ire: he considered such levies unjust, illegitimate and a transgression of *rajdharam*, and resorted to protests or revolts. Thus, historically, a tradition of rebellion/protest against the perceived injustice of the ruling class had always been present in the peasant society and was constantly underpinned by the oral tradition that projected such injustice as a violation of *rajdharam*. Interestingly, stress on the king's moral duty to administer justice and the peasant's to pay customary taxes as well as the oppressed peasants' recourse to rebellions—all echo Dharmashastric prescripts on principles of taxation and justifications for the deposal and killing of tyrant kings, as discussed before. These parallels point to a wider, long-standing perception of kingship shared by the folk tales and Brahmanical normative texts, notwithstanding differences in forms and some ingredients (such as the divinity of the king or the pivotal role of Brahmins stressed in the normative texts but absent in the folk tales).

Against this backdrop of the peasant's worldview articulated through folk tales and folk songs, the chapter will discuss at length certain folk tales that encapsulate the popular perceptions of kingship. As mentioned earlier, Narsingh Meo's sixteenth-century ballad 'Hasan Khan ki Katha' is perhaps the earliest extant specimen of folk poetry[25] that embeds a popular idea of kingship in its account of the historic battles of Panipat (1526) and Khanwa (1527), their key players, viz., Babur; Ibrahim Lodi, the Sultan of Delhi; Rana Sanga, the Rajput ruler of Mewar; and Hasan Khan Mewati, the Khanzada chief of Mewat. Introducing himself as a resident of Kajhauta village in pargana Maujpur of Alwar sarkar, i.e. in the region of Mewat, the bard Narsingh Meo prefaces his narration of the historic battles with a discussion of both ideal and counter-ideal kingship. On the one hand, he praises King Vikaramaditya for his benevolence and justice that made him popular among his subjects and a memorable figure for successive generations. On the other hand, he condemns Ravana, the king of Lanka in the epic *Ramayana*, for his misdeeds and his propensity to cause pain to others.[26] Representing both Ibrahim Lodi and Hasan Khan Mewati as the counter-ideal of kingship, he blames Ibrahim Lodi for his injustice, arrogance and apathy which resulted in his defeat and death at the hands of Babur in the Battle of Panipat (1526),[27] and Hasan Khan Mewati for his foolhardiness which led to his unwarranted involvement in the Battle of Khanwa (1527), and eventually his defeat and death, again, at the hands of Babur. The fateful outcomes of their follies were bloody massacres on the battlefield, extinction of Lodi and Khanzada dynasties and devastation of their kingdoms. In Narsingh Meo's perception, both had failed to discharge their *rajdharam*: Lodi remained indifferent to the threat of Babur's impending invasion despite having a huge army at his command and several chieftains on his side, while Hasan Khan out of sheer hubris and foolishness incurred Babur's enmity by seeking to bring Lodis back to power, despite his son's good counsel and Babur's offer of friendship. One's apathy towards the duty of protecting his kingdom from external invasion and the other's injudicious decision to endanger his kingdom's safety—both constituted acts of injustice to their subjects and hence a violation of *rajdharam*. Thus, two aspects of ideal kingship are discernible in Narsingh Meo's analysis of the battles: one, the king should be just and justice-loving; two, he should protect his subjects (and conversely, not jeopardize their security). While this conception of ideal kingship, used by a rural bard to explain the tragic fate of Ibrahim Lodi and Hasan Khan, is situated in the context of specific historic events in the sixteenth-century north India, it emanated from the peasant society and has a certain degree of universality in reflecting the peasant's perception of state. It could, then, be invoked across time and space in situations where the state or its personification, i.e. the ruler, was seen as committing excesses, particularly in case of fiscal exactions, an area of perennial conflict between the state and the peasant. In such situations, this conception may well have served to inspire, even incite, the peasants' resistance to what they perceived as undue and unjust revenue demands of the state. This explains why this conception is recurrently found woven into folk tales of just and unjust rulers that have been recounted across generations. It is these folk tales that the chapter will turn to in explaining the nuances of the conception of kingship.

The *sang* 'Jyani Chor', composed by Haryanvi bard Pandit Lakhmichand,[28] is centred on the heroic exploits of Jyani Chor, son of a poor Meo peasant Bhura from Chorgarhi village in pargana Tijara in eastern Rajasthan. Bhura was often imprisoned for non-payment of revenue to the state. Jyani's family's dire economic circumstances and his father's mistreatment at the hands of the oppressive state officials forced him to become a bandit in his youth. Hence his name Jyani Chor ('thief' or 'dacoit'). A Robin Hood-like character, Jyani used to rob rich landlords and redistribute the wealth so acquired among the peasants. In the tale, he and his close friend Nar Sultan were on their way to their *dharam-behen* (foster sister) Maravan's home in Narvargarh, when they found, while bathing in a river, a wooden plaque drifting in the waters. Inscribed on the plaque was a plea for help by a woman named Mahakade. Identifying herself as a Hindu Kshatriya[29] woman, Mahakade claimed to be in the captivity of a Muslim ruler, Adali Khan, and entreated any brave Hindu man to rescue her. Jyani Chor took upon himself this daunting task and asked Nar Sultan to continue his journey to Narvargarh. He entered Adali Khan's capital in disguise, but at the same time had the news of his arrival sent to Adali, thereby daring him to catch Jyani. Adali, too, took up the gauntlet and summoned an assembly in his court where he announced that anyone who caught Jyani would be handsomely rewarded. A *sunar* (goldsmith) named Dhammal rose to accept this challenge and assured Adali that he would have Jyani behind bars soon enough. When Jyani came to know of Dhammal's pledge, he decided to teach him a lesson. He reached his home in the guise of his son-in-law whom his daughter had not seen for the last 12 years. Failing to recognize Jyani, Dhammal's daughter was overjoyed at the return of his long-lost husband. So was her mother and Dhammal when he returned in the evening. Thus establishing his identity as Dhammal's son-in-law, Jyani ensconced himself at his house where he was pampered with care and attention, while Dhammal spent days looking hard for Jyani in the city. Finally, one day Jyani tricked his daughter into giving him all her gold jewellery on the pretext of getting them polished and fled. At this Dhammal realized how clever Jyani had duped him and his family, and humbly accepted his defeat before Adali. Next, the city's *daroga* (inspector-in-chief of police) took the charge of apprehending Jyani. The latter, too, set about entrapping him in his net of deception. Guised as a woman, he roamed around the *chauki* (police station), seeking to draw the *daroga's* attention even as he was busy contriving ways to catch Jyani. Expectedly, the *daroga* fell for what he saw as a young woman in blooming health. When Jyani asked him what was keeping him busy, he revealed that he had been entrusted with the task of caging a dangerous and cunning bandit Jyani and showed the cage specially made for him. When asked to demonstrate how he would put such a notorious bandit in the cage, the *daroga* foolishly entered it, and Jyani locked it from outside. As Jyani disclosed his true identity, the *daroga* realized how he had been charmed into incarcerating himself. Adali was infuriated at the *daroga's* humiliation and himself set out on horseback to catch Jyani. Even as the day of frenetic search tuned into an exhausting evening, Jyani Chor was nowhere to be found. Adali came across an old woman whom he asked whether she had seen Jyani. Responding in the affirmative, she said that he had indeed come to her in a tired and worried state, and would later return for an overnight stay at her place, but would flee if he saw Adali. She suggested that he put on her clothes so that Jyani would not recognize him in the old woman's guise. He did so and lay in wait for Jyani through the night. On the other hand, Jyani, who had actually deceived Adali as the old woman, rescued Mahakade from Adali's prison and fled. Adali was outsmarted and left astounded.

That the tale was probably set in the medieval period can be gleaned from the social background of Jyani Chor. Excessive burden of land revenue often forced peasants to desert villages in the Mewat region, as evinced by the Rajasthani archival sources of late seventeenth and early eighteenth centuries.[30] Some may even have taken to banditry in desperation. They can be considered 'social bandits' who lived on the margins of the rural society by robbing and plundering the rich, but remained within the bounds of the moral order of the peasant community. Though regarded by the state as common criminals, they were robbers of a special kind who were hailed by the peasants as heroes, champions, avengers, fighters for justice since they were seen as righting wrongs when they defied the state or its representatives. Social banditry was a widespread phenomenon throughout recorded history in many agricultural societies characterized by the oppression of poor and/or landless peasants by the representatives of state. It embodies a rather primitive and crude form of organized social protest of peasants against such oppression, but the actions of social bandits do not go beyond the restoration of the traditional order which leaves the oppression and exploitation of the weak and poor within certain limits. [31] Driven to banditry by the state's excesses, rising to avenge the injustice committed by the 'evil' ruler and defeating the ruler through sheer force of wit, Jyani Chor conforms to the idea of social bandit and appears to be a folk hero forged by rural bards out of the actual historical incidence of social banditry in medieval north India.

The ruler Adali, the antagonist of Jyani Chor, may be connected to the historical Adil Shah Suri (CE 1555–6) of the Afghan Sur dynasty. His rule was overthrown when the Afghan forces led by his minister and general Hemu were defeated by the Mughal forces led by Bairam Khan in the Second Battle of Panipat (CE 1556). While the tale of Jyani Chor may have originated in the Sur period, the historical context linking the two characters is difficult to determine. First, while the story concerns a Meo bandit, the historical Adil Shah is not known to have ruled the Mewat region directly, and his commander Hemu's attempts to establish his rule there, too, were defeated. Second, the story must have undergone many imperceptible changes in the course of its long oral transmission and multiple renditions till the early twentieth century when it was given its present form by Lakhmichand. However, one change that is discernible in the narrative is the religious color given to the conflict between Jyani Chor and Adali Shah. In the *sang*, the inscription on the wooden plaque found by Jyani and Nar Sultan in the river expresses the anxiety of Mahakade, who identifies herself as a Hindu Kshatriya woman, at the prospect being forcibly married to a Muslim ruler and her earnest plea for rescue addressed to a brave Hindu man. Jyani eloquently expresses his deep anguish not so much at the plight of the woman but at the possibility of Hinduism being destroyed (presumably by the dishonouring of a Hindu woman being forced into marriage with the Muslim ruler). This communal dimension may not have been part of the medieval tale, since there is ample evidence of politically motivated matrimonial alliances between Rajput and other Hindu rulers/chiefs and Muslim ones which did not apparently attract any censure in the contemporary sources. Lakhmichand who rendered this medieval tale into a *sang* is also less likely to have deliberately and consciously introduced this communal tension. Living in the early-twentieth-century north India, he is more likely to have inherited a worldview wherein identities were getting more sharply drawn along communal lines and communities were becoming culturally polarized. Such a cultural worldview that posits relations between communities as irreconcilably antagonistic, when widely held in the society at large and transmitted across generations to individuals, groups and communities, also leaves its imprint in artistic and literary works, as it did in Lakhmichand's rendition of the tale. Thus, the religious colour that the conflict between Jyani Chor and Adali Khan acquired, however briefly, in the story reflects the cultural ethos of the composer's own time period rather than that of the period in which the story originated. However, Lakhmichand seems oblivious to the fact that Jyani, a Meo, belonged to a region where a long process of Islamization since at least sixteenth century had still not given Meos a strong and distinctly Islamic religio-cultural identity even as late as the mid-nineteenth century, leaving them as avid followers of both Muslim and Hindu cultural practices.[32] But it is quite plausible that the story belonged to a period when the Islamic identity of Meos was beginning to be shaped, and hence the fluidity of this inchoate identity perhaps facilitated the projection of

Jyani as a Hindu saviour of a Hindu Rajput woman from the clutches of an oppressive, lustful Muslim ruler.

In the *sang* 'Virat Parva' composed by Pandit Lakhmichand[33] and based on an episode from the epic *Mahabharata*, Pandava brothers after losing in a dice game with their collateral cousins, the Kauravas, were forced to spend 12 years in exile and another year incognito. In the final year, they and their common wife Draupadi took service in the royal household of Virat Nagar under false names. One day the king's evil brother-in-law Kichak lusted after Draupadi who served the queen as a maid under the name Sairandhri. As he tried to force himself upon her, she reprimanded and instructed him in *rajdharam*. She reminded him that he was the ruler (*raja*) and she his subject (*praja*), and spoke at length on the ideal relation between the two. In the perception of his subjects, the king stands only second to god who is the creator and master of all; his right to rule entitles him to this near-divine stature. But the king earns this right through great efforts and struggles and should not take it for granted. He should look upon his subjects as his children just as the latter look up to him as father. He should consider such paternalistic relation with his subjects sacred and inviolable. Every king should rule as did the legendary Rama of the epic *Ramayana*, *ramarajya* being the popular metaphor for an ideal state and Rama being the model for an ideal king in the popular conception of kingship in premodern (north) India (as also contemporary India). This conception enjoins upon the king to adhere to the *rajdharam*: refrain from doing injustice to innocent subjects and punish those who do so. This *sang* makes Kichak and Draupadi the personifications of the ruler and the people, showing how the people could resist when the ruler seeks to violate his *rajdharam* and remind him of his moral duties and obligations.

The *sangs* 'Jyani Chor' and 'Virat Parva' define the ideal of kingship (*rajdharam*) in terms of its antithesis embodied by unethical and unjust rulers (viz., Adali and Kichak) and justify popular resistance to such rulers, whether by way of subterfuge (as in the case of Jyani) or verbal remonstrance (as in the case of Sairandhri). On the other hand, there are *sangs* that define this ideal of kingship in terms of the exemplary conduct of ethical and just rulers, but at the same time emphasize the role of common people as the keepers of royal conscience who admonish such rulers for their faults and/or instruct them on ideal rulership. Both kinds of tales ascribe agency to people as the moral arbiter of the ruler's conduct and, therefore, the source of his legitimacy and authority. In doing so, these tales privilege the popular idea of kingship over the statist one as articulated in texts produced by the ruling elite.

Notable among the tales of just rulers is that of Vikramaditya's justice,[34] which was, and still is, popular in the rural society of north and central India. In this tale, Vikramaditya is shown as a ruler who used to move about the kingdom in disguise in order to find out subjects in distress. The king's nocturnal peregrinations in disguise is a common trope in folk tales that reinforces the popular conception of a 'just' king's commitment to his subjects' welfare through direct involvement in information-gathering. In one such solitary nocturnal trip on horseback, the exhausted King Vikramaditya dozed off while his horse moved into a nearby field and began to eat the standing crops. After a short while, the peasant who had cultivated the field turned up. Seeing the horse eating his crops, he thought that the horseman had deliberately led his horse into the field in order to feed it. He became furious, railed at him and demanded compensation for the damage to his crops. The king proposed to settle the matter with some money, but the peasant refused. Thinking him to be some herdsman or trader, he insisted on taking the case to the royal courthouse and tied both him and his horse to a tree to prevent their escape. Next morning the peasant took them to the courthouse where the judge, upon hearing his plea, decided that the horseman be punished with fifty lashes. But before the punishment could be carried out, a minister present in the courthouse identified the king in disguise and immediately fell at his feet in apology for not accompanying him in his trip. Shocked at finding out that the horseman he was about to punish was none other than King Vikramaditya, the peasant, too, furiously pleaded at his feet for forgiveness. But further shocking everyone, the king solemnly declared that the essence of his justice lay in the inevitable punishment of the guilty and he himself being guilty was not above the law and deserved punishment; he, thus, asked the peasant to whip him and serve the cause of justice.

The ideal of impartial punitive justice as an integral component of the precolonial popular conception of kingship is arguably taken to its peak in this tale: justice while being personal, i.e. stemming from and subject to royal will and dispensation, becomes so impersonal and absolute at the hands of a proverbially just king that he himself, when guilty, is subject to its principle of retribution. In the moral universe of peasants living in a hierarchical society, privileging this sort of retributive justice as a key constituent of ideal kingship democratizes justice in an essentially undemocratic milieu and becomes an ingenious reaction to what were perceived as unjust laws and interventions of the state or ruling class. In doing so, this idea of justice (and by extension kingship) indirectly gives agency and voice to the oppressed underclass of peasants, otherwise denied to them in reality.

Similar in essence to King Vikramaditya's tale are those of Badgujar Rajput chiefs popular in the Alwar region of eastern Rajasthan since the early sultanate period, i.e. the thirteenth century. These stories that laud the legendary justice of Badgujar chiefs were recorded by Alexander Cunningham in the late nineteenth century.[35] In one such story, King Neen had a pond dug for his subjects, but as its water turned red and undrinkable he asked the Brahmin priests for an explanation of this unusual phenomenon. They explained that the water turned red because he had the pond dug by people of different castes, thereby causing an intermixing of castes. They suggested that he bury his son and daughter-in-law alive in the pond in order to purify the water. Accordingly, he performed a grand yajna (sacrifice) and interred his son and daughter-in-law alive within a tomb erected under water. Thereafter, the water miraculously became drinkable again. According to Cunningham, the local people still believed that the spirits of the king's son and his wife roamed around the pond on horseback at night, and that it was their sacrifice that had cleansed the water forever, and hence they still worshipped them. Like Vikramaditya who had himself punished for the sake of justice, King Neen, his son and daughter-in-law made the supreme sacrifice for the welfare of their subjects. In both tales, the conduct of royal personages is modelled on the popular ideal of kingship wherein heightened concern for administering justice and ensuring people's welfare characterize the king's governance.

Somewhat different from the tales of just rulers Vikramaditya and Neen who apparently needed no stimulus or persuasion from their subjects to act justly are the tales of just rulers who occasionally needed a lesson in ethical governance from people. It is in these tales that people are given far greater visibility, voice and agency vis-à-vis the kings, and social hierarchies (of caste, class, gender) are temporarily jettisoned: not only the people score higher over the kings in wit, practical wisdom and worldly experience, but the kings too accept their failings and eventually live up to the popular expectations from an ideal ruler. The first among these tales is the *sang* of Raja Bhoj and Sarande, attributed to Pandit Lakhmichand[36] and immensely popular in the rural society of Haryana. In this tale, Bhoj, the ruler of Ujjain, was a paragon of *rajdharam*. He scouted around the city in disguise with his sidekick, a *bhand* (court jester) named Manva, seeking information about the grievances and miseries of his subjects. One day, Manva *bhand* informed him of a barber who was worried to death over the marriage of his young and beautiful daughter, Sarande. That no suitable boy could be found from within the barber's community for Saranade, who was of marriageable age, gave sleepless nights to the family. As Sarande confided in her friends her parents' worry, one of them told her in jest to marry King Bhoj who was well known for alleviating the miseries of his subjects and would surely end her woes. Besides, he was young and handsome—a reason enough for her to marry him. But Sarande retorted in mock pride that she would not even deign to have her feet washed by him, much less marry him. In other words, she suggested in jest that she did not find even a king suitable for her. As Manva told Bhoj of this friendly banter, the latter mistook Sarande's words of jest for those of insult and summoned the barber to his court where he asked for his daughter's hand in marriage. Even as the barber initially refused the offer on the ground that the king did not belong to his community, his wife's intervention eventually led to Sarande's marriage to the king. However, soon, the king made his motive for marriage clear. He told Sarande that he did not marry her to make her his queen but to avenge his insult. He banished her from the palace and forced her to live a lonely miserable life outside the city walls. But Sarande did not lose courage in the face of this adversity; she assiduously learned to play *been* (flute) and soon became an expert and widely acclaimed flutist. As the renown of her music spread far and wide, she went to the court in disguise for playing flute. Suddenly, in the course of her enthralling performance, she fell on the floor. When asked the reason, she explained that the floor felt burning hot, and asked the king to pour cold water on her feet to cool them off. Captivated by her music, the king fell for her ruse: he got up and unsuspectingly did as asked. At this Sarande broke into peals of laughter and revealed her face. By fulfilling her vow of making the king wash her feet, she outwitted him. But her ingenuity won his admiration, and he happily accepted her back.

The musical rendition of this tale, especially the lively and witty dialogues of King Bhoj and Sarande, in a language and form familiar to peasants have held great appeal for them. This was more so because of its embedded conceptions of kingship and of the sociopolitical relation between the ruler and the ruled. The king who is projected as possessing divine or semi-divine attributes in the ancient and medieval texts that emphasize on supramundane sources of political legitimation is a far cry from the king cast in this folk tale as one who is not superior to his subjects in intellect and wisdom, nor too socially distant from them. Bhoj, a mighty king, is not averse to marrying the daughter of a barber, traditionally ranked quite low in the caste hierarchy, to avenge his perceived dishonour. Moreover, he ends up losing to her in a veritable battle of wits and happily accepts his defeat. The king's proverbial might is no match for a poor low-caste girl's cleverness. If the barber girl Sarande is construed as representing the common people, her diligence in learning music and her intelligence in outsmarting the king suggest the power of people's will and wit that could on occasion even humble a king. The king's close relationship with a jester, belonging, again, to the 'lowly' caste of minstrels, is also quite at odds with the divine conception of kingship. It is the jester, as the king's constant companion and confidante, who serves as a link between the ruler and the ruled by apprising the king of his subjects' conditions and grievances, as well as perceptions about and expectations from him. The jester, therefore, is not merely the king's entertainer but doubles up as his conscience-keeper, representing the people's voice. Here, the jester replaces the high-caste Brahmin priest whose advisory role and legitimizing and corrective powers over the king are so expatiated upon in the Brahmanical texts. Both Sarande's and Manva's relation with the king represent the ways in which people could successfully wield moral power over the king and thereby make his rule 'just' and in consonance with the popular idea of *rajdharam.* Neither the jester's proximity to the king nor the barber girl's symbolic triumph over the king erases or disrupts the actual sociopolitical hierarchies, but they do serve to notionally reduce the distance between the ruler and the ruled by bringing the two closer. In the process, a popular notion of ideal kingship is articulated—a relatively more inclusive and less hierarchical notion that radically departs from the divine conception of kingship wherein the king derives his authority from divinity, is hemmed by a stratified ensemble of socially privileged and politically powerful elite, and remains distanced from the common masses. In the popular notion of kingship, as embedded in this tale, the king is not only powerful, justice-loving and a true follower of *rajdharam*, but is also not above his ordinary subjects in thought and intellect. Moreover, members of lower castes such as minstrel and barber are very much part of the king's political life. Interestingly, such a notion of kingship dispenses with the role of high-born state functionaries intervening between the king and the people. More importantly, internalizing this ethical ideal of kingship through repeated musico-dramatic enactment of such tales made the medieval peasant believe in a customary reciprocal relationship between the ruler and his subjects.

Similar in content and essence to the tale of King Bhoj and Sarande is another *sang*, 'Four Girls and a King', that may have been composed sometime in the late eighteenth century and received its present form at the hands of Pandit Lakhmichand.[37] Like the afore-discussed *sang*, this one too encapsulates the popular idea of kingship. In the tale, like King Bhoj, an unnamed king moved about the city in disguise in order to gather information about his subjects' conditions, troubles and grievances. In one such trip, the king in the tale overheard four girls conversing in a garden. They were discussing what had the best taste in the world. Curious to know more, the king summoned the girls to his court the next day and asked them separately on what they were discussing. The first girl when asked about what she was telling her friends the day before disclosed that she was telling her friends that meat tasted the best. When asked about her caste, she told that she belonged to the *bhand* (minstrel caste). The king countered by saying that the people of her caste did not even touch meat much less eat it and hence it would not be possible for her to know its taste. She admitted that she had never tasted it but assumed that it was the best, since she used to see from her rooftop that in an eatery at the back of her house where meat was served no part of the animal carcass was wasted. After the people had eaten, the leftover bones were devoured by dogs, those discarded by the dogs were carried away by crows, and those still left by the crows crawled with ants. Pleased with her reasoning, the king sent her back with rewards. The second girl when asked the same question said that she thought alcohol tasted the best. But when she claimed to belong to the Brahmin caste, the king questioned how she would know the taste of alcohol if the Brahmins did not consume it. She explained that every evening she watched from her roof people buying and drinking liquor from a liquor shop, and found that the same people who struggled their way back home in a heavily inebriated state would keep coming day after day to consume liquor. This made her conclude that alcohol must taste good enough to draw people every day. Again pleased with her answer, the king rewarded her. The third girl of the *bhat* (bardic caste) said that she thought sexual intercourse to be the most pleasurable act. She admitted that she was too young to experience sexual gratification, but claimed that she could sense it, since she found that her mother who had almost died giving birth to her younger brother was overjoyed at delivering another baby after a few months. This proved wrong her earlier idea that her mother would not risk suffering the pain of childbirth again. She thus reasoned that sexual pleasure must be great enough for people to put their lives at stake. Satisfied with her argument, the king rewarded her as well. Finally, the king summoned the fourth girl and asked her the same questions. The girl belonging to the Jat caste said that lying was the most enjoyable act in the world, and that everyone, including the king, lied. Surprised at her answer, the king asked her to rethink her response, but the girl insisted that she had expressed her opinion, and that she could prove her statement if she got six months' time and a sum of six lakh rupees. The king agreed to her conditions and sent her back with the said sum. After six months, the girl returned and asked the king to accompany her to a new beautiful palace she had built. She claimed that the palace had a beautiful 'spiritual' hall where if a person completely devoted his mind to the thought of god, god would appear in person before him. Upon arriving at the palace, the king sent in his minister to test if her claims were true. The girl told the minister that the god would surely appear to him if he single-mindedly prayed to him, but would not do so to one who was of illegitimate birth. The minister went inside and sat there with his thoughts fixed on god, but after some time looked around and found nobody. He reasoned with himself that if he admitted that he did not see god, he would face the shame and dishonour of being considered a misbegotten child. Hence, after coming out, he lied to the king that he had seen god. When the king asked him about what god said to him, he again lied that god had forbade him to reveal. Not satisfied with his response, the king sent in another minister who, too, thought the same as did the first one when he saw no one inside and lied about seeing god for the fear of public ridicule. Next, the king went inside and had the same dilemma when he saw no god: he thought to himself that if he, unlike his ministers who had claimed to have seen god, admitted that he did not, he would risk not only losing his honour but also facing a revolt by his subjects. He, too, thus ended up lying that he had seen god. When the girl asked him thrice to confirm whether he had seen god, he lied every time and that too unhesitatingly. Finally, as the girl refuted his claim by saying that no one, not even the king, could see god, the king remembered the girl's claim that everyone, including the king, lied. Realizing that the girl had devised an elaborate ploy to make him lie and thereby prove her point, the king admitted lying and so did his ministers. The girl explained that while the poor would lie out of compulsion, the king had no compelling reason to do so, thereby proving that lying was enjoyable in its own way. Impressed at her intelligence and self-confidence, the king asked for her hand in marriage.

In this tale, as in the previous one, a just king in accordance with his *rajdharam* seeks to find out his subjects' woes, aspirations and expectations, and comes across the four girls who 'enlighten' him on some important truths of the sociocultural lives of common people. The girls who represent the common people's voice impress upon the king that meat-eating, drinking, sexual intercourse and lying are not condemnable moral vices but everyday practices in the lives of people, and that kingship is not a sacred, divine institution untouched by such worldly practices. In particular, lying was a means of survival and resistance in the medieval rural society: the peasant would try to 'misappropriate' the share of crop yield payable to the state or its landed intermediaries (zamindars, jagirdars) and, in turn, reduce his own fiscal burden by willfully misinforming the revenue officials about or concealing from them, certain standing crops or the area of land under cultivation of certain crops. Such acts when detected by the state officials were deemed as 'theft of revenue' and punished by way of levying fines, as amply attested in the Rajasthani sources, particularly the *hasil farohi* columns of *arsattas*.[38] Yet the peasants persisted with such acts of deception that actually became 'weapons of the weak', a covert form of peasant's resistance to the state's oppressive revenue demand. In emphasizing the universality of lying, the Jat girl also drove home the fact that for the poor in general, lying was a way of surviving against all odds, and for the peasant in particular, a way of ensuring his subsistence in the face of crushing revenue demands of the state and its landed intermediaries. In this sense, the Jat girl embodying the peasant's voice highlighted his miseries and compulsions before the king who personified the state. Significantly, the fact that the four young girls made the king understand the fundamental existential reality of people's lives suggests that the king was no wiser than his subjects and needed a dose of popular experiential wisdom for 'just' governance. This, in turn, again implies that in popular wisdom ideal kingship and proper discharge of *rajdharam* rested on a close cooperation between the ruler and the ruled. Equally significant is the gendered nature of the class relation between the state and its subjects in the three tales. The personified metaphor for the state is masculine, i.e. a king or a prince, while that for the subjects is feminine, i.e. Draupadi, Sarande and the four girls. In each tale, the wisdom and/or conduct of the dominant is challenged by the subaltern on the grounds of certain common shared socio-ethical values that were supposed to govern and circumscribe the functions of both, but the hierarchical nature of the relationship itself is not questioned. This suggests that class hierarchies, like gender hierarchies, are not considered open to subversion, though the violation of ethical norms of conduct in these hierarchical relationships by the dominant are subject to censure and condemnation.

From the foregoing discussion of the folk tales one can discern certain common features of the peasant's conception of ideal kingship and of the ideal relation between the king and his subjects. First, ideal rulers are just, benevolent and caring towards their subjects; they abide by the rule of law and the principles of justice and altruism. Second, just rulers do not carry a divine or semi-divine stature, nor can claim any social or intellectual superiority over their subjects; rather, they are accessible to and seek access to people. Third, they may occasionally and unwittingly commit acts of injustice or may become oblivious to their fallibility as human beings. At such crucial junctures, they are reminded of their duties by one of their subjects who voices the concerns of the common masses. In such situations, the due performance of *rajdharam* or ethical governance is premised on the reciprocity between the ruler and the ruled, whereby the ruler is receptive to popular wisdom and advice and not averse to acknowledging his faults and making amends. Legitimacy of a ruler is thus derived from his proximity to the people, from his living up to the ideal constructed by them, not from claims to pre-eminence over them. Fourth, rulers who abandon or deviate from their *rajdharam* face remonstrance, rebuke and humiliation at the hands of people. It is the people who adjudge the ethicality of a ruler's conduct or otherwise and respond accordingly. The arbitrary exercise of power by the ruler and/or his officialdom to the detriment of peasants' interests was a strong possibility within the only available political institution in premodern India, i.e. monarchy, and was indeed a harsh reality in many cases, as peasant protests and rebellions throughout the medieval period show. But despite, or probably because of such despotic tendencies of the monarchical setup, the popular idea of benevolent and just kingship throve in the peasant societies, fortifying their resilience, optimism and capacity for resistance.

The preceding discussion of the idea of kinship embedded in the folk tales brings one to the problem of historicizing these stories. In other words, what are the possibilities of locating these stories in specific temporal and spatial contexts. Admittedly, as mentioned before, the provenance of these stories remains uncertain, and can broadly be pinned down to medieval north India. Since they have been part of a long-standing, regionally variegated oral tradition of rural societies in north India and appeared in the recorded history only from late nineteenth century (i.e. in the accounts of colonial ethnographers), they can be justifiably presumed to have existed in the medieval times, or perhaps even earlier. Their survival and popularity owes to their function and relevance in the societies where they have been narrated, sung or enacted. Their function, as discussed before, was to provide the peasant communities a vision of an ideal mythic past when people lived in peace under benevolent and just kings without suffering injustice and oppression. This function of the folk tales assumed greater relevance in hard times when burden of fiscal exactions weighed heavily on them. Conjuring up and collectively invoking and remembering this past through repeated performances infused in them the strength to confront, resist and demand justice from oppressive rulers.

The exaltation of a just and benevolent kingship in the afore-discussed folk tales may well have gained greater currency in the increasingly conflictual relationship between the state and peasantry of north India in the late medieval period. From the Rajasthani archival sources such as *arzdashts*, *arsattas* and *chithis* of the late seventeenth and early eighteenth centuries, it appears that Mughal mansabdars, unable to realize revenue from their jagirs in the wake of uncertainties in collection, were forced to farm out their jagirs to various bidders for revenue collection rights (ijara). In particular, the mansabdars who held jagirs in Mewat resorted to assigning their ijara to the Rajput rulers of Amber and the Jat chieftain Churaman. The latter, in turn, fiercely competed with each other to acquire the right to collect revenue from the areas under the jurisdiction of mansabdars. By deriving this right from the Mughal state (or its direct representatives, the mansabdars) through ijara or revenue-farming, they interposed themselves as a new stratum of authority between the mansabdars and the peasants, imposing numerous non-customary levies on them and constantly contesting the legitimacy of each other's claims to agricultural surplus. At the same time, the traditional claims of the Mughal state to land revenue, as also its politico-administrative control, was progressively eroded. On the one hand, this led to the impairment of traditional mechanisms of grievance-redressal for the peasantry who bore the brunt of increased revenue demand. On the other hand, the absence of well-defined legitimate claims of the state on surplus made it impossible for the peasantry to satisfy the multiple claimants who ruthlessly exploited them.

The peasants with their faith in an ideal reciprocal relation with the state based on certain customary rights and duties accepted the standard land revenue demand of the state and considered fulfilling it as their duty (*prajadharam*) provided the state was just and caring towards them, i.e. it abided by the ethics of good governance (*rajdharam*). At the same time, the peasants opposed the state's revenue demand if it flouted the customary practices and led to their exploitation and immiseration. As is evident from numerous instances of peasant petitions recorded in the Rajasthani sources, the Meo peasants were well aware of the fact that their villages were part of jagirs assigned to imperial mansabdars by the Mughal emperor, not that of the Amber Raja's watan jagir (patrimonial estate), and that the mansabdars had, in turn, assigned the ijara of their villages to the Amber Raja. They viewed the emperor as their highest appellate authority and knew that neither the mansabdars nor the Amber Raja had any legitimate right to respectively transfer revenue-collection rights and collect non-customary taxes. That is why they retained faith in the justice administered by the Mughal state and repeatedly petitioned to the emperor, seeking his intervention against the 'illegitimate' levies imposed and forcibly collected by the Amber Raja. They clearly perceived Amber Raja as a disruptor of their customary relationship with the Mughal state, and the imposition of non-customary taxes by him as a violation of *rajdharam* so exalted in their oral traditions. In other words, the peasants understood the behaviour of the ruling class and expected the state to perform its *rajdharam*, its duty of administering justice to its subjects. But failure to get relief in most cases would have, on the one hand, heavily dented the image of the Mughal rulers and, on the other, provoked rebellions throughout the region.

It was in this context that tales celebrating just rulers and condemning unjust ones assumed greater popularity among the peasants. Such tales articulating the peasant's perception of ideal kingship became the means of eloquently expressing their rejection of and protest against an exploitative state that sharply deviated from the ideal of *rajdharam*. Invoking a mythic idyllic past when rulers were just, caring and self-sacrificing also helped them grapple with a fraught politico-economic situation that led to their increased impoverishment and degradation. The political turmoil of the late medieval period may not have been the only factor lending currency to such folk tales valorizing the conceptions of ideal kingship, since such inspirational tales would have been deployed time and again in all situations of state repression that provoked peasant rebellions, but the intensity of exploitation and the frequency of peasant complaints and uprisings in this period certainly would have added considerable vigour and life to these tales. Hence, the recurrent contestations between the state and the peasantry in the medieval period made these tales an enduring integral part of the peasant culture.

The medieval context of these tales perhaps also explains why they do not exalt historical rulers, much less the Muslim rulers. While the long-known and widely-circulated epico-Puranic stories of Hindu rulers may well have provided the template for the folk tales, the oppressive revenue system of medieval states in north India often headed by Muslim rulers may not have been conducive to idealizing any historical ruler. As far as it is evident, the burden of taxes in medieval India was not necessarily heavier than that in early India, nor were the Muslim rulers any more oppressive than their Hindu counterparts in early India. But the choice of glorifying Hindu rulers of dubious historicity and situating them in a remote mythic past was a conscious one, for doing so would help to ideologically contest and undermine the legitimacy of any actual ruler/state when the peasants perceived him/it as oppressive to the extent of breaching the idealized customary relationship between the ruler and his subjects. That the rulers of these folk tales such as Vikramaditya or Bhoj were archetypes of ideal rulers and not compared to, or even comparable to, any actual historical ruler facilitated the construction of the desired conception of kingship in the peasant communities. On the other hand, since the Mughal emperors, as also many of their officials holding jagirs/mansabs, in large parts of medieval north India were *incidentally* Muslim and the revenue demands of Mughal mansabdars/jagirdars and, later, ijaradars were becoming increasingly onerous for the peasantry particularly in the late medieval period with bleak prospects of justice or relief from exploitation, the peasant communities had no reason to extol the Mughal emperors as exemplary kings in their folk tales (not even Akbar, projected as a tolerant and just emperor by Abul-Fazl and other chroniclers, found space in them).[39] At the same time, Muslim rulers are not vilified in these tales either (except in the story of Adali and Jyani Chor whose communal overtones are arguably the handiwork of Lakhmichand in early twentieth century). This suggests that the folk conception of kingship, while explicitly laudatory of mythical Hindu rulers, was not an overt, summary rejection of Muslim rulers on grounds of religious affiliation.[40]

Another notable feature of the conception of kingship in these tales is its contrast with that in Rajasthan. This is linked to the differences in the behaviour of the ruling class vis-à-vis the people and to the presence or absence of political patronage to bards in different areas. In Rajasthan, which witnessed the evolution of Rajput states from the early medieval period, the people's attitude towards the Rajput rulers in general has been one of respect and honour even to this day. A sizeable class of bards (*charans, bhats*) and Brahmins, receiving patronage for generations from these rulers, has over a long time inculcated in mass's obedience to and respect for the ruling elite through their songs, tales and genealogical records that valorize Rajput dynasties and rulers.

The Rajput rulers, on their part, have registered their presence and participation on numerous public occasions, particularly festive and ritual ones. Their visibility and accessibility has helped sustain their power and influence as well as a notion of benevolent kingship in the public mind.[41] Such an exalted image of kingship cannot be seen in Mewat, Haryana, western Uttar Pradesh or parts of Punjab. In these areas, no oral tradition of glorifying real dynasties or rulers took roots, as there were no long-established dynasties, like those of the Rajputs, to patronize a class of bards and/or priests who could compose eulogistic tales and genealogies. On the other hand, as discussed before, these areas witnessed recurrent rural unrest, particularly so in the wake of the breakdown of Mughal administrative machinery, the rise of competing claimants to power, territory and revenue, and the intensification of exploitation of peasantry in the late medieval period. In this context, the notion of kingship articulated through a long-developing tradition of *sang* could only be shaped by the peasant society's perception of an ideal ruler, i.e., one who is righteous, justice-loving and caring. In other words, this notion encapsulated the peasant's vision of a non-oppressive and just political system, and did not cater to the ruling elite's need for political legitimacy and power.

The conception of kingship in the folklore of rural societies does not constitute an elaborate, systematic and coherent theory such as those found in the ancient Brahmanical texts or medieval court chronicles. Yet, it has several ingredients of such a theory: the position, qualities and duties of a king; the relation between the king and his subjects; the customary and moral checks on the king's power; and the avenues of addressing the problem of monarchical despotism. In this sense, the discourse on kingship in the folk tales, if closely seen in their socio-political and geographical contexts, reveals not a mere wishful longing for some unattainable political utopia of a mythical past, but an embedded, heightened political consciousness of an otherwise unlettered, powerless peasantry grappling with the harsh political reality of their times (growing revenue demand, abuse of power by revenue officials, landed intermediaries and armies of state, collapse of grievance-redressal mechanisms, depredations of contenders for politico-economic control of territories). It was this consciousness that helped to shape a conception of kingship that was composed of sharp binaries of rulers who are little more than symbols of justice and injustice, benevolence and malevolence, morality and immorality. And it is this ethically charged conception that acted as a mode of protest against oppression by real kings and posed a challenge to their legitimacy. This conception, born of the peasant's life-experiences and worldview and autonomous of any political patronage or control by the ruling elite, was, therefore, a driving force for struggle, resistance and survival in the peasant's lives—more powerful than the alternative folk conceptions in other areas (such as northern and western Rajasthan) that extolled the ruling dynasties, legitimized their political authority and cultivated deference and obedience to it.

Notes

1. These are Vedic ritual texts, epic poetry (e.g. *Mahabharata* and *Ramayana*), prescriptive treatises on socio-religious norms (e.g. *Dharmasutras* and *Dharmashastras*), *Purana*s, and treatises on statecraft (e.g. *Arthashastra*, *Shukranitisara*, *Rajanitiprakasha*, *Kamandakiya nitisara*). Relevant portions of these texts have been collated and compiled by P.V. Kane in volume 3 of his monumental five-volume *History of Dharmaśāstra*, Poona: Bhandarkar Oriental Research Institute, 1973.

2. For instance, several texts such as *Manusmriti*, *Naradasmiriti*, *Markandeya*, *Agni* and *Bhagavata Purana*s, *Arthashastra*, *Rajanitiprakasha*, etc., tend to project the king (*raja*) as associated with various deities (as made from or having in his person their parts, as their human incarnation or as performing their functions on earth). Even outside the realm of Brahmanical texts, this tendency of glorification of the king's office can be seen in the attempts of court panegyrists and poets to trace the descent of various dynasties to the sun, moon or, later, fire; in the practice of addressing kings as *deva* ('god') in the Sanskrit dramas, in the use of epithets *devanampiya/devanampriya* ('beloved of the gods') and *devaputra* ('son of god') for the Mauryan emperor Ashoka and the Kushana rulers, respectively; see P.V. Kane, *History of Dharmaśāstra*, vol. 3, 2nd edn, Poona: Bhandarkar Oriental Research Institute, 1973, pp. 23–4.

3. The ancient texts address various exhortations to the king in order to exercise a restraining and corrective influence. These exhortations repeatedly emphasize the observance of *dharma*, a broad, multi-interpretable, sacred and inviolable sociopolitical ideal or principle that encompasses norms, laws, duties and obligations for individuals and social groups. Besides impressing upon the king the importance of performing his *dharma*, these exhortations also enjoin the king to seek counsel of ministers, the *purohita* (royal priest) and learned

Brahmins, and respect the dictates of *Shastra*s; they even prophesize and justify the ruination, destruction or deposal of whimsical, cruel, tyrannical, misguided and incompetent kings. The *Ramayana*'s account of Rama abandoning his wife Sita despite knowing her to be chaste because the people suspected her chastity after her long stay in Ravana's captivity suggests that the pressure of public opinion also could force the king to take certain decisions against his will. Thus, the texts bind the royal power with many checks and limitations; see ibid, pp. 96–8.

4. For instance, the *Shantiparvan* of the *Mahabharata* and *Manusmriti* extol protection as the highest *dharma* of the king. The protection, according to Brihaspati cited in *Rajanitiprakasha*, consists in punishing internal aggression (such as by thieves, robbers and trespassers) and meeting external aggression. The *Gautama Dharmasutra* assigns to the king the special responsibility to award just punishment and protect the *varnas* and *ashramas* according to the Shastric rules and bring them back to the path of their proper duties if they swerve from it; see ibid., p. 56. Kamandaka's *Nitisara* clarifies that the subjects need protection from the king's officers, favourites and enemies, as also from thieves and even the greed of the king himself; see ibid., pp. 58–9. The *Manusmriti* enjoins upon the king, when protecting his subjects against invasion, not to run away from battle and promises heaven as a reward for kings who die fighting in battles; see ibid., p. 57. Besides protection, public welfare constituted another major set of duties. The *Arthashastra* calls upon the king to support the helpless and aged people; the cripple, blind and diseased; lunatics, widows, orphans and pregnant women; and the victims of calamities by providing them medicines, food, lodging and clothing according to their requirements. The *Rajanitiprakasha* prescribes relief of unemployed men of various castes as the king's duty. Medhatithi, a commentator on the *Manusmriti*, advises that the king support his subjects in famine by distributing food from his treasury; see ibid., p. 59. Indeed, equating the people's welfare with the king's welfare, the *Arthashastra* states: 'In the happiness of the subjects lies the happiness of the king, in their welfare lies his welfare; . . . what is pleasing to the subject s constitutes his good'; see ibid., p. 61. In a similar vein, the *Santiparvan* and *Nitiprakashika* declare that the king, like a pregnant woman, should not do what is pleasing to him, but what would conduce to the good of the people. Privileging secular acts of welfare over religious ones, the *Shantiparvan* dismisses the utility of *tapas* (austerities) and *yajña* (sacrifice) for a king who looks after his subjects well; see ibid., pp. 61–2. Linked to the idea of welfare-oriented kingship is that of paternalistic kingship: texts such as *Arthashastra*, *Yajnavalkyasmriti* and *Shantiparvan* advise the king to act as a father to his subjects, while the *Ramayana* highly praises Rama for doing so. This idea is also reflected in an

edict of the Mauryan emperor Ashoka where he calls all men his children; see ibid., pp. 62–3.

5. For instance, the *Shukranitisara* considers a king who oppresses his subjects and causes the loss of *dharma* as made up of the parts of demons (*rakshasas*). The *Manusmirti* states at one place that a king who harasses his subjects loses his life, family and members, and at another that the *danda* (the royal sceptre symbolizing the king's punitive authority) when wielded by a voluptuous and unjust king recoils on its head and destroys him together with his relations. Further, there are instances of and prescripts for killing and deposing tyrannical kings in the ancient literature. The *Santiparvan* and *Bhagvata Purana* mention the story of King Vena killed by the Brahmins because he was jealous of the gods, wanted sacrificial offerings to be made to himself and violated *dharma*. The *Arthashastra*, when dealing with the evil results of the lack of discipline in kings, points to hot-tempered kings falling victim to popular fury or the fury of ministers. The *Shatapatha Brahamana* refers to the expulsion of Dushtaritu Paumsayana. The *Anushasanaparvan* of the *Mahabharata* sanctions the killing of a cruel king by the people, while the *Santiparvan, Manusmriti, Yajnavalkyasmriti* and *Shukranitisara* permit deposing such a king; see ibid., pp. 25–7, 97.

6. For instance, the *Ayodhya-kanda* of the *Ramayana* refers to king Dasharatha summoning an assembly of vassal kings, citizens and rural inhabitants to seek their approval for his choice of crown prince, viz., his eldest son Rama. The *Adiparvan* of the *Mahabharata* mentions the unanimous selection of Parikshita as king by the citizens of the capital at the death of his father, Janamejaya. There is also some inscriptional evidence for the popular election of historical kings, such as the Shaka Kshatrapa Rudradaman in Saurashtra and the Pala ruler Gopala in Bengal. Further, the Chinese Buddhist pilgrim Hiouen Thsang refers to Harshavardhana being made a king by an assembly of ministers summoned by the chief minister Bhandin after the death of Rajyavardhana. The *Rajatarangini* narrates the story of a poor man Yashaskara being chosen as king by the Brahmins; see ibid., pp. 29–31.

7. For instance, in the legend of Manu Vaivasvata narrated in the *Arthashastra*, he was made a king by the people who agreed to assign one-sixth of their produce as the royal share in respect of the protection accorded by him; see ibid., p. 31. However, this does not suggest that the king was projected as a democrat in social terms; rather he was exhorted to defend the hierarchal four-fold caste system, confer and protect various privileges due to the Brahmins and rule in concord with them and in accordance with their advice; see ibid., p. 25.

8. The texts cite several reasons for the people to pay taxes. The *Gautama Dharmasutra* states that they should do so because the king protects them;

see ibid., p. 189. Protection being the rationale for taxation, the *Manusmriti* condemns to hell a king who levies them without affording protection; see ibid., p. 191. The *Shantiparvan, Manusmriti, Baudhayana Dharmasutra, Naradasmriti* and *Arthashastra* consider taxes as the *vetana* (wages) of the king, the result of a contract between the people and the first human king, Manu. The *Katyayanasmriti* justifies the king's entitlement to one-sixth of the produce of land on the ground that he is the real owner of the earth, while those residing on the land have only a qualified ownership; see ibid., p. 189. The *Shantiparvan* and *Shukranitisara*, while enumerating three principal and perennial sources of royal income, viz., land revenue, tolls and custom duties, and fines levied on wrongdoers and defeated litigants, implicitly regard peasants, traders, manual workers and artisans as the principal tax-payers; see ibid., pp. 190–1.

9. The *Dharmashastras* or *Smritis*, prescribe several principles for taxation. First, they ordain that the king could not levy taxes at his pleasure or sweet will, but only at rates fixed by the *Smritis* or varying according to the value of the taxed commodity or the situation (whether normal or perilous/calamitous). The *Dharmasutras* of Gautama and Vishnu and the *Manusmriti* sanction the king's entitlement to one-sixth of the produce in normal times, while the *Arthashastra, Manusmriti, Shantiparvan* and *Shukranitisara* prescribe one-third as the royal share in times of distress. Even while recommending heavy taxation, the texts advise the king to temper this extreme step in various ways: the *Arthashastra*, for instance, requires that the king beg/request people for heavy taxes, not impose such taxes more than once in the same distress, nor do so on inferior lands; the *Shantiparvan* gives a specimen of a long address to be given by the king to the people wherein heavy taxation is demanded and justified on the ground of countering enemy invasion, which, if successful, would lead to the loss of their lives and property. Second, the texts prescribe that the taxes be imposed in such a way that they are felt to be light and not excessive by those taxed. Explaining this principle through analogy in a poetical language, the *Udyogaparvan* of the *Mahabharata* states that just as a bee draws honey from flowers without injuring them, so too should a king take wealth from men without harming them. Describing this principle somewhat differently but with as much flourish, the Buddhist text *Dhammapada* states that the king should act like a gardener who prepares garlands without harming trees or their leaves and not act like one who prepares coals from trees (i.e. by burning them). The *Manusmriti* advises the king not to tax the subjects heavily out of greed, and thereby cut off the roots (of prosperity, contentment, etc.) of the people, nor to levy no taxes at all and thereby cut off his own roots (i.e. reduce himself to bankruptcy). Third, as the *Shantiparvan* recommends, the taxes, if and when raised, should be increased

gradually; see ibid., pp. 184–6. Further, the texts complement the principles of taxation with those of expenditure, suggesting that the royal income be earned, preserved and spent judiciously. For instance, the *Manasollasa* advises the king to spend three-fourths of the yearly revenue and save one-fourth, while the *Shukranitisara* prescribes that the king save one-sixth of his total income and spend half of it on the upkeep of army, one-twelfth each on charity, ministers, inferior officials and his private expenses, and also that king have as much stock of grain as required for three years' consumption in his kingdom; see ibid., pp. 187–8.

10. Iqtadar Alam Khan, 'Akbar's Personality and Traits and World Outlook: A Critical Appraisal', in *Akbar and His India*, ed. Irfan Habib, New Delhi: Oxford University Press, 1997, p. 90.

11. Irfan Habib, *Bharatiya Itihas me Madhyakaal*, tr. and ed. Ramesh Rawat, Delhi: Granthshilpi, 1999, pp. 162–3.

12. Ibid., pp. 162–3.

13. Abul-Fazl, *Ain-i-Akbari*, vol. 1, 3rd edn, Calcutta: Royal Asiatic Society, 1977, p. 291; Irfan Habib, *The Agrarian System of Mughal India 1556–1707*, 2nd rev. ed., New Delhi: Oxford University Press, 1999, p. 230.

14. Narsingh Meo, 'Hasan Khan ki Katha', *Shodh Patrika*, vol. 4, October–December, Udaipur: Rajasthan Vidyapeeth, 1970.

15. R.C. Temple, *The Legends of the Panjab*, 3 vols., Bombay: Bombay Education Society, 1884.

16. W.H.D. Rouse, *The Giant Crab and Other Tales of Old India*, London: David Nutt, 1897.

17. Maive Stokes, *Indian Fairy Tales*, Calcutta, 1879; repr. London: Ellis & White, 1880.

18. Flora Annie Steel, *Tales of the Punjab Told by the People*, London: Macmillan & Co. Ltd., 1917.

19. Charles Swynnerton, *Romantic Tales from the Punjab with Indian Nights' Entertainment*, London: Archibald Constable, 1908.

20. Alexander Cunningham, *Report of a Tour in Eastern Rajputana in 1882–83*, vol. XX, Archaeological Survey of India Reports, 1885; repr. Varanasi: Indological Book House, 1969, pp. 122–4.

21. Munshi Ram, 'Mewati Lok Sahitya evam Mewat ka Arthik Vishleshan', in *Shreejan*, ed. Chhangaram Meena, Alwar: Babu Shobharam Rajkiya Mahavidyalaya, 2006, pp. 99–102.

22. Jeevan Singh Manvi, 'Ali Baksh ki Krishanlila evam anya Khyal', in *Shreejan*, ed. Chhangaram Meena, Alwar: Babu Shobharam Rajkiya Mahavidyalaya, 2006, pp. 81–9.

23. Puranchand Sharma, *Pandit Lakhmichand Granthavali*, Chandigarh: Haryana Sahitya Academy, 1996, p. 17.

24. *Rajadharam* and *prajadharam* are the colloquial variants of the Sanskrit terms *rajadharma* and *prajadharma*, respectively. Hereafter, these colloquial forms are used in the chapter as they are in the folk tales.

25. This work was found transcribed in *gutka* no. 213, kept in the Digambar Jain temple of Neminath Swami in Tonk district, Rajasthan. The year of composition is *posh vadi* 14, vs 1639/ce 1582. Its untranslated original version was published in Devanagari script by Mahavir Prasad Sharma in October–December issue of *Shodh Patrika* (Sahitya Sansthan, Rajasthan Vidyapith, Udaipur) in 1970. The work is in verse and has a mix of words from old Mewati dialect and Persian. For a transcription of the entire work in Roman script and a summary of its content, see Suraj Bhan Bhardwaj, *Contestations and Accommodations: Mewat and Meos in Mughal India*, New Delhi: Oxford University Press, pp. 242–55.

26. More specifically, Narsingh Meo blames Ravana for making many enemies with his misdemeanour and undue interference in others' affairs. He abducted Sita and did not even heed his wife Mandodari's good counsel. He thus incurred the enmity of Rama (Sita's husband). As a result, Rama's army (of monkeys) wreaked havoc on his prosperous city of Lanka. The consequences of his misdeeds destroyed his wealth and well-being.

27. According to Narsingh Meo, Ibrahim Lodi, in the heat of youth, had his opponents killed or buried alive in the walls of his fort and thus had made many enemies in his 'home'. Further, while Babur was marching from Kabul to attack Hindustan, he was busy playing dice (*chaupar*) in his palace all the time. Hasan Khan rejected Babur's offer of 100 parganas in and around Bayana and his own granddaughter in marriage to Nahar Khan, Hasan Khan's son, and, instead, was bent upon fighting Babur for no reason except that he wanted to put Muhammad Lodi, the dim-witted minor son of Ibrahim Lodi, on the throne of Delhi.

28. Puranchand Sharma, *Pandit Lakhmichand Granthavali*, Chandigarh: Haryana Sahitya Academy, 1996, pp. 44–73.

29. Kshatriya is the warrior caste and second to the priestly caste of Brahmins in traditional Hindu caste hierarchy.

30. See Chapter 5 of this volume.

31. E.J. Hobsbawm, *Primitive Rebels: Studies in Archaic Forms of Social Movement in the Nineteenth and Twentieth Centuries*, Manchester: Manchester University Press, 1959; E.J. Hobsbawm, *Bandits*, London: Weidenfeld & Nicolson, 1969; Anton Blok, 'The Peasant and the Brigand: Social Banditry Reconsidered', *Comparative Studies in Society and Economy*, vol. 14, no. 4, 1972, pp. 494–503.

32. See Chapter 3 of this volume.

33. Sharma, *Pandit Lakhmichand Granthavali*, pp. 267–312.

34. This story was narrated to me in 1988 by Mr Banwari Lal, son of Bakhtawar Mal, Dhareru village, district Bhiwani, Haryana.

35. Cunningam, *Report of a Tour in Eastern Rajputana in 1882–83*, pp. 122–4.

36. Sharma, *Pandit Lakhmichand Granthavali*, pp. 170–90.

37. A.K. Ramanujam, ed. and coll., *Bharat ki Lokkathaye*, tr. Kailash Kabir, Delhi: NBT, 2001, pp. 93–7.

38. See Chapter 5 of this volume.

39. However, Akbar and his favourite companion Birbal have been the subject of many anonymously composed popular humorous stories and jokes that had been circulating in north India since at least the early eighteenth century. These stories that often end in Birbal outwitting Akbar can be read in contrary ways: as signifying 'Hindu' subversion of 'Muslim' power, or as signifying a form of apotheosis of Akbar. Indeed, the stories have a subversive aim in establishing a clever Brahmin jester's victory over a mighty Muslim emperor in the battle of wits, but, through the agency of humour, they seek to humanize implicitly, even glorify Akbar who inspired in the masses awe and reverence, *not* to direct some suppressed communal antagonism towards him and dehumanize him into a demon. By integrating Akbar into the popular culture of north India, the stories enormously add to his stature as a humane ruler and, hence, are as much a visible and valuable indicator of his impact on Indian history as his forts, chronicles written by his court historians and paintings painted by his artists are; see C.M. Naim, 'Popular Jokes and Popular History: The Case of Akbar, Birbal and Mulla Do-Piyaza', *Economic and Political Weekly*, vol. 30, no. 24, 1995, pp. 1456–64. At the same time, it must be noted that these amusing stories cannot be seen as commentaries on contemporary political situation, while the folk tales, as discussed in the chapter, have a decidedly political subtext.

40. It is quite possible that the folk tales celebrating the just rule of mythical Hindu kings helped buttress the colonial historians' interpretation of medieval period as that of Muslim tyranny and their depiction of Muslim rulers as oppressive and anti-Hindu, in contrast to their projection of British rule as based on the rule of law and justice.

41. Marzia Balzani in her historico-anthropological study of the survival of kingship in the modern city of Jodhpur in northern Rajasthan shows how a form of kingship persists in this area though legally kings do not exist; see Marzia Balzani, *Modern Indian Kingship: Tradition, Legitimacy and Power in Jodhpur*, Oxford: James Currey, 2003. Through a set of ritual practices and appeals to a fluid notion of tradition, the royal power and the notion of divine/semi-divine kingship is legitimized and consolidated and the Rathore rulers continue to command deference from people.

Bibliography

Primary Sources

Rajasthani[1]

I. **Archival Records**, Jaipur Records, Historical Section and
Daftar Diwan Huzuri, Rajasthan State Archives, Bikaner.

Arsattas, Mujmil, Jaipur Records, Historical Section

Pargana Khohri: vs 1721/ce 1664; vs 1723/ce 1666; vs 1769/ce 1712;
vs 1770/ce 1713; vs 1773/ce 1716; vs 1783/ce 1726; vs 1784/ce 1727;
vs 1785/ce 1728; vs 1790/ce 1733; vs 1798/ce 1741; vs 1800/ce 1743;
vs 1801/ce 1744; and vs 1804/ce 1747.

Pargana Pahari: vs 1773/ce 1716; vs 1781/ce 1724; vs 1788/ce 1731;
vs 1790/ce 1733; vs 1791/ce 1734; vs 1792/ce 1735; vs 1794/ce 1737;
vs 1796/ce 1739; vs 1798/ce 1741; vs 1799/ce 1742; vs 1800/ce 1743;
vs 1802/ce 1745; vs 1803/ce 1746; and vs 1804/ce 1747.

Pargana Gaji ka Thana: vs 1787/ce 1730; vs 1788/ce 1731; vs 1791/
ce 1734; vs 1792/ce 1735; vs 1794/ce 1737; vs 1797/ce 1740; vs 1798/
ce 1741; vs 1799/ce 1742; vs 1800/ce 1743; vs 1804/ce 1747; vs 1805/
ce 1748; and vs 1807/ce 1750.

Pargana Jalalpur: vs 1723/ce 1666; vs 1746/ce 1689; vs 1748/ce 1791;
vs 1766/ce 1709; vs 1768/ce 1711; vs 1770/ce 1713; vs 1773/ce 1716;
vs 1775/ce 1718; vs 1777/ce 1720; vs 1780/ce 1723; vs 1792/ce 1735;
vs 1794/ce 1737; and vs 1796/ce 1739.

Pargana Wazirpur: vs 1769/ce 1712; vs 1771/ce 1714; vs 1773/ce 1716;
vs 1774/ce 1717; vs 1777/ce 1720; vs 1779/ce 1722; vs 1782/ce 1725;
vs 1802/ce 1745; vs 1803/ce 1746; vs 1804/ce 1747; vs 1805/ce 1748;
and vs 1806/ce 1749.

Pargana Piragpur: vs 1785/ce 1728; vs 1787/ce 1730; vs 1789/ce 1732;
vs 1791/ce 1734; vs 1792/ce 1735; vs 1793/ce 1736; vs 1794/ce 1737;
vs 1797/ce 1740; and vs 1798/ce 1741.

---

[1] All these documents are dated in the Vikrami Samvat (vs) which is ahead of
the Common Era (ce) by 57 years. I have converted the years of Vikarmi Samvat
into the years of Common Era.

Pargana Atela Bhabra: vs 1721/ce 1664; vs 1768/ce 1711; vs 1769/ce 1712; vs 1785/ce 1728; vs 1787/ce 1730; vs 1788/ce 1731; vs 1790/ce 1733; vs 1791/ce 1734; vs 1793/ce 1736; vs 1794/ce 1737; vs 1797/ce 1740; vs 1798/ce 1741; and vs 1799/ce 1742.

Pargana Mojpur: vs 1747/ce 1690; vs 1770/ce 1713; vs 1777/ce 1720; vs 1779/ce 1722; vs 1787/ce 1730; vs 1789/ce 1732; vs 1792/ce 1735; and vs 1806/ce 1749.

Pargana Pindiyan: vs 1772/ce 1715; vs 1777/ce 1720; vs 1774/ce 1717; vs 1779/ce 1722; vs 1786/ce 1729; vs 1787/ce 1730; vs 1789/ce 1732; vs 1792/ce 1735; and vs 1806/ce 1749.

Pargana Harsana: vs 1722/ce 1665; vs 1774/ce 1717; vs 1770/ce 1713; vs 1778/ce 1721; vs 1779/ce 1722; vs 1787/ce 1730; vs 1789/ce 1732; vs 1792/ce 1735; and vs 1806/ce 1749.

Pargana Mandawar: vs 1722/ce 1665; vs 1770/ce 1713; vs 1787/ce 1730; vs 1789/ce 1732; vs 1792/ce 1735; and vs 1806/ce 1749.

Pargana Sahar: vs 1746/ce 1689; vs 1747/ce 1690; and vs 1749/ce 1692.

Pargana Bharkol: vs 1774/ce 1717; vs 1778/ce 1722; vs 1783/ce 1726; vs 1786/ce 1729; vs 1787/ce 1730; vs 1789/ce 1732; vs 1800/ce 1743; and vs 1806/ce 1749.

Pargana Naharkhoh: vs 1774/ce 1717; vs 1778/ce 1722; vs 1774/ce 1717; vs 1783/ce 1726; vs 1786/ce 1729; vs 1787/ce 1730; vs 1789/ce 1732; vs 1800/ce 1743; and vs 1806/ce 1749.

Pargana Todathek: vs 1774/ce 1717; vs 1778/ce 1721; vs 1779/ce 1722; vs 1783/ce 1726; vs 1786/ce 1729; vs 1787/ce 1730; vs 1789/ce 1732; vs 1800/ce 1743; and vs 1806/ce 1749.

Pargana Hasanpur: vs 1722/ce 1665; and vs 1747/ce 1690.

Pargana Kotla: vs 1722/ce 1665; vs 1770/ce 1713; and vs 1773/ce 1716.

Pargana Alwar: vs 1768/ce 1711.

Amber Records, vs 1721/ce 1664–vs 1776/ce 1719.

Arzdashts, ce 1675–1749, Jaipur Records, Historical Section.

Chithis, Jaipur Records, Daftar Diwan Huzuri. Parganas Khohri, ce 1725–57; Pahari, ce 1727–35; Jalalpur, ce 1728–9; Atela Bhabra, ce 1712–34; Piragpur, ce 1725–49; Gaji ka Thana, ce 1754–68; Alwar, ce 1726–32; Bharkol, ce 1729; Bairatha, ce 1727–9; Sonkhar, ce 1726; Jaitpura, ce 1728–34; Pawta, ce 1730–8; Chatsu, ce 1738–46; Averi, ce 1727–32; Hindaun, ce 1722–57; Narnol, ce 1746; Bahatri, ce 1746; Banawar, ce 1737.

Dastur amals, Jaipur Records, Historical Section. Parganas Khohri, ah 1049/ce 1639/40; Atela Bhabra, vs 1767/ce 1710; Sonkhar Sonkhari, vs 1773/ce 1716; Mojpur, vs 1770/ce 1713; Narnol, vs 1803/ce 1746.

Dehai-Ferhashtis, Jaipur Records, Historical Section. Pargana Khohri, CE 1710–50.

Jamabandis, Jaipur Records, Historical Section. Parganas Khohri, CE 1665–1747; Pindayan, CE 1666–1729; Jalalpur, CE 1691–1714; Bawal, CE 1665–6; Kotla, CE 1665; Baroda Rana, CE 1665; Chalkaliyana, CE 1666; Mojpur, CE 1729; Harsana, CE 1729.

Hal Bail Yaddashtis, Jaipur Records, Historical Section. Parganas Chalkaliyana, VS 1721/CE 1664; Kotla, VS 1723/CE 1666; Pindayan, VS 1783/CE 1726; Pahari, VS 1784/CE 1727; Mauzabad, VS 1723/CE 1666.

Vakil Reports, Jaipur Records, Historical Section, CE 1693–1715.

Khatoot Ahalkarans, Mah Vadi 6, VS 1740/CE 1683; *Asadh Sudi* 4, VS 1780/ CE 1723; *Mah Vadi* 4, VS 1775/CE 1718.

Dastur Komwar, Tozi Dastur Komwar, bundle no. 3, VS 1774–90.

Farmans, tr. Shujawat Khan Naksbandi (Hindi), vol. 1, Rajasthan State Archives, Bikaner, 2010.

II. Non Archival Records of Alwar State, Rajasthan State Archives, Bikaner

Bandhak no. 3, *Granthank* nos. 66, 81; *Bandhak* no. 4, *Granthank* nos. 43, 83; *Bandhak* no. 5, *Granthank* no. 89; *Bandhak* no. 6, *Granthank* nos. 71, 83; *Bandhak* no. 11, *Granthank* no. 112; *Bandhak* no. 12, *Granthank* nos. 10, 13, 89; *Bandhak* no. 13, *Granthank* no. 1; *Bandhak* no. 66, *Granthank* nos. 3, 7; *Bandhak* no. 67, *Granthank* nos. 4, 6; *Bandhak* no. 68, *Granthank* nos. 4, 5; *Bandhak* no.71, *Granthank* nos. 6, 7, 12.

III. Jagga Records, *Pothi* nos. 1 and 2 in personal possession of Jagdish Jagga, son of Shri Ghasi Ram Jagga, village Khuteta Kalan, tehsil Ramgarh, District Alwar, Rajasthan.

Persian

Abdullah, 'Tarikh-i-Daudi', in *The History of India as Told by Its Own Historians*, vol. 4, ed. H.M. Elliot and John Dowson, Allahabad: Kitab Mahal, 1975.

Abul-Fazl, *The Ain-i-Akbari*, vol. 1, tr. H. Blochmann, 3rd edn, Calcutta: Royal Asiatic Society, 1977.

Abul-Fazl, *The Ain-i-Akbari*, vol. 2, tr. H. Blochmann, corr. and ann. Sir Jadunath Sarkar, 3rd edn, Calcutta: Royal Asiatic Society, 1978.

Abul-Fazl, *The Akbarnama*, vol. 2, tr. H. Beveridge, 1902–39; repr., Delhi: Low Price Publications, 1993.

Abul-Fazl, *The Akbarnama*, vol. 3, tr. H. Beveridge, 1902–39; repr., Delhi: Low Price Publications, 1993.

Afif, Siraj, 'Tarikh-i-Firozshahi', in *The History of India as Told by Its Own Historians*, vol. 3, ed. H.M. Elliot and John Dowson, Delhi: Low Price Publications, 2001.

Ahmad, Khwajah Nizamuddin, *Tabaqat-i-Akbari*, 3 vols., ed. and tr. B. De and M. Hidayat Hossain, Calcutta: Bibliotheca Indica, 1913–35.

Arif Qandhari, Muhammad, *Tarikh-i-Akbari*, tr. Tasneem Ahmad, Delhi: Pragati, 1993.

Babur, *Baburnama*, vol. 2, tr. A.S. Beveridge, 1921; repr., New Delhi: Low Price Publications, 1995.

———, 'Tuzuk-i-Baburi', in *The History of India as Told by Its Own Historians*, vol. 4, ed. H.M. Elliot and John Dowson, Allahabad: Kitab Mahal, 1975.

Barani, Ziauddin, *Tarikh-i-Firoz Shahi*, in *The History of India as Told by Its Own Historians*, vol. 3, ed. H.M. Elliot and John Dowson, Delhi: Low Price Publications, 1990.

Beveridge, H., tr., *The Maathir-ul-Umara*, vol. 1, rev. ann. and com. by Baini Prasad, Patna: Janaki Prakashan, 1979.

Chisti, Abdur Rahman, 'Mirat-i-Masudi', in *The History of India as Told by Its Own Historians*, vol. 2, ed. H.M. Elliot and John Dowson, Delhi: Low Price Publications, 2001.

Hashim Khafi Khan, Muhammad, *Muntakhab-al Lubab*, vol. 1, tr. Anees Jahan Syed as *Aurangzeb in Muntakhab-al Lubab*, Bombay: Somaiya, 1977.

Juzjani, Minhaj Siraj, *Tabaqat-i-Nasiri*, tr. H.G. Raverty, 1881; repr., Delhi: Oriental Books Reprint Corp., 1970.

———, 'Tabakat-i-Nasiri', in *The History of India as Told by Its Own Historians*, vol. 2, ed. H.M. Elliot and John Dowson, Delhi: Low Price Publications, 1990.

Khan, Inayat, *The Shahjahannama*, tr. A.R. Fuller, ed. and comp. W.E. Begley and Z.A. Desai, New Delhi: Oxford University Press, 1990.

Khan, Khafi, 'Muntakhab-ul-Lubab', in *The History of India as Told by Its Own Historians*, vol. 7, ed. H.M. Elliot and John Dowson, Delhi: Low Price Publications, 1993.

Khan, Saqi Mustad, *Maasir-i-Alamgiri*, tr. Jadunath Sarkar, 2nd edn, Delhi: Munsiram Manoharlal, 1986.

Khan, Zain, *Tabaqat-i-Baburi*, tr. S. Hasan Askari, Delhi: Idarah-i Adabiyat-i Delli, 1982.

Khusrau, Amir, 'Khazaina-i-Futuh and the Kiranu-i-Sadain (The Poem of Amir Khusrau)', in *The History of India as Told by Its Own Historians*, vol. 3, ed. H.M. Elliot and John Dowson, Delhi: Low Price Publications, 2001.

Mustaqi, Shaikh Rizqullah, *Waqiat-e-Mustaqi*, tr. and ed. I.H. Siddiqui, Delhi: Northern Book Centre, 1993.

Naimutulla, 'Tarikh-i-Khan-Jahan Lodi', in *The History of India as Told by Its Own Historians*, vol. 5, ed. H.M. Elliot and John Dowson, Delhi: Low Price Publications, 1990.

Sirhindi, Yahya bin Ahmad bin 'Abdullah', *The Tarikh-i-Mubarak Shahi*, tr. H. Beveridge, Delhi: Low Price Publications, 1990.

Timur, 'Malfuzat-i-Timuri', in *The History of India as Told by Its Own Historians*, vol. 3, ed. H.M. Elliot and John Dowson, Delhi: Low Price Publications, 2001.

Tughlaq, Firozshah, 'Futuhat-i-Firozshahi', in *The History of India as Told by Its Own Historians*, vol. 3, ed. H.M. Elliot and John Dowson, Delhi: Low Price Publications, 2001.

Yadgar, Ahmad, 'Tarikh-i-Salatin-i-Afghana', in *The History of India as Told by Its Own Historians*, vol. 5, ed. H.M. Elliot and John Dowson, Delhi: Low Price Publications, 1990.

Urdu

Makhdum, Sheikh Muhammad, *Arzang-i-Tijara*, Agra: Agra Akhbar, AH 1290/CE 1873, translated into Hindi by Anil Joshi, Alwar, 1989.

Shakur, Abdul, *Tarikh Mev Chatri*, 1919; repr., Nuh, Gurgaon: Chaudhuri Yasin Mev High School, 1974.

Hindi

Narsingh Meo, 'Hasan Khan ki Katha', *Shodh Patrika*, vol. 4, October–December, Udaipur: Rajasthan Vidyapeeth, 1970, pp. 53–62.

European Travelogues

Bernier, Francois, *Travels in the Mogul Empire, AD 1656–68*, tr. and ed. Archibald Constable, repr., Delhi: Munshiram Manoharlal, 1983.

Pelseart, Francisco, *Jahangir: India: The Remonstratre of Franscisco Pelsaert*, tr. W.H. Moreland and P. Geyl, Cambridge: W. Heffere, 1925.

Colonial Reports

Channing, F.C., *Land Revenue Settlement of the Gurgaon District*, Lahore: Central Jail Press, 1882.

Cunningham, Alexander, *Report of a Tour in Eastern Rajputana in 1882–83*, vol. XX, Archaeological Survey of India Reports, 1885; repr., Varanasi: Indological Book House, 1969.

Fraser, A., *Statistical Report of Zillah Gurgaon*, Lahore: n.p., 1846.

Ibbetson, D., *Panjab Castes: Being a Reprint of the Chapter on "The Races, Castes and Tribes of the People" in the Report on the Census of the Panjab Published in 1883*, Lahore: Superintendent, Government Printing, 1916.

Powlett, Major P.W., *Gazetteer of Ulwur*, London: Trübner & Co., 1878.

Watson, J. Forbes and John William Kaye, eds., *The People of India*, vol. 4, London: W.H. Allen & Co. for the India Museum, 1869.

Secondary Sources

Vernacular

Habib, Irfan, *Bharatiya Itihas me Madhyakaal*, tr. and ed. Ramesh Rawat, Delhi: Granthshilpi, 1999, pp. 162–3.

Kharagawat, Mohinder Singh, ed., *Farsi Farmano ke Prakash mein Mughal Kalin Bharat and Rajput Saashak*, Bikaner: Rajasthan State Archives, 2010.

Lal, Shri Govind, 'Haroti ki Krishi Kahavate', *Manu Bharati*, *varsha* 13, *anka* 3, 1965, pp. 41–58.

Lalus, Sita Ram, ed., *Rajasthani-Hindi Sankshipt Shabdakosh*, vol. 2, Jodhpur: Rajasthan Oriental Research Institute, 1988.

Manvi, Jeevan Singh, 'Ali Baksh ki Krishanlila evam anya Khyal', in *Shreejan*, ed. Chhangaram Meena, Alwar: Babu Shobharam Rajkiya Mahavidyalaya, 2006, pp. 81–9.

Mishra, Ratan Lal, *Kiyamkhani Vamsh ka Itihasa evam Samskriti*, 2nd revd edn, Jodhpur: Rajasthani Granthagar, 2002.

Ram, Munshi, 'Mewati Lok Sahitya evam Mewat ka Arthik Vishleshan', in *Shreejan*, ed. Chhangaram Meena, Alwar: Babu Shobharam Rajkiya Mahavidyalaya, 2006, pp. 99–102.

Ramanujam, A.K., ed. and coll., *Bharat ki Lokkathaye*, tr. Kailash Kabir, Delhi: NBT, 2001, pp. 93–7.

Saraswat Rawat, *Mina Ithihas* (Hindi), Jaipur: Jhunthlal Nandala, vs 2025.

Sharma, Puranchand, *Pandit Lakhmichand Granthavali*, Chandigarh: Haryana Sahitya Academy, 1996.

Yadav, Shankarlal, *Haryana Pradesh ka Lok Sahitya*, Hindustani Academy, Allahabad, 1960.

English

Aggarwal, Pratap C., *Caste, Religion and Power: An Indian Case Study*, Delhi: SRC, 1971.

Alam, Muzaffar, *Crisis of the Empire in Mughal North India: Awadh and the Punjab, 1707–48*, New Delhi: Oxford University Press, 1986.

Ali, Athar, 'Ethnic Character of the Army during the Delhi Sultanate (13th–14th Centuries)', in *Medieval India 2: Essays in Medieval Indian History and Culture*, ed. Shahbuddin Iraqi, Delhi: Manohar, 2008, pp. 165–72.

———, *The Mughal Nobility under Aurangzeb*, Bombay: Asia Publishing House, 1966.

Ali, Hashim Amir, *The Meos of Mewat*, New Delhi: Oxford University Press, 1970.

Aziz, Abdul, 'Measurement of Agricultural Productivity, A Case Study of Mewat', unpublished PhD thesis, North Eastern Hill University, Shillong, 1981.

Balzani, Marzia, *Modern Indian Kingship: Tradition, Legitimacy and Power in Jodhpur*, Oxford: James Currey, 2003.

Banga, Indu, *Agrarian System of the Sikhs: Late Eighteenth and Early Nineteenth Century*, Delhi: Manohar, 1978.

Bayly, C.A., *Rulers, Townsmen and Bazaars: North Indian Society in the Age of British Expansion, 1770–1870*, Cambridge: Cambridge University Press, 1983.

Bhadani, B.L., 'The Mughal Highway and Post Stations in Marwar', *Proceedings of the Indian History Congress*, Delhi, 1990, pp. 141–55.

Bhardwaj, Suraj Bhan, 'Conflict over Social Surplus: Challenges of *Ijara* (Revenue Farming) in 18th-Century-CE North India: A Case Study of Mewat', in *Revisiting the History of Medieval Rajasthan: Essays for Professor Dilbagh Singh*, ed. Suraj Bhan Bhardwaj et al., Delhi: Primus, 2017, pp. 45–52.

———, 'Peasant-State Relation in Late Medieval North India (Mewat): A Study in Class Consciousness and Class Conflict', *Medieval History Journal*, 2017, vol. 20, no. 1, pp. 148–91.

———, 'Agrarian Revolts: A Study of the Changing Relations between the Peasantry and Zamindars and the State in Eastern Rajasthan During the Late 17th and Early 18th Century', in *Historical Documents and History: Re-evaluations*, ed. Anuradha Mathur, Jodhpur: Rajasthani Granthagar, 2016, pp. 75–81.

———, *Contestations and Accommodations: Mewat and Meos in Mughal India*, New Delhi: Oxford University Press, 2016.

———, 'Migration, Mobility and Memories: Meos in the Processes of Peasantisation and Islamisation in the Medieval Period', *Indian Historical Review*, 2012, vol. 39, no. 2, pp. 217–50; reprinted in *Migrations in Medieval and Early Colonial India*, ed. Vijaya Ramaswamy, New Delhi: Routledge, 2016, pp. 87–126.

———, '*Qasbas* in Mewat in the Medieval Period: A Study of the Interface between the Township and the Countryside', in *Cities in Medieval*

India, ed. Yogesh Sharma and Pius Malekandathil, Delhi: Primus, 2014, pp. 319–38.

———, 'Socio-economic Conditions in the Mewat Region, c.1650–1750', unpublished PhD thesis, Centre for Historical Studies, Jawaharlal Nehru University, Delhi, 1990.

Bhargava, Meena, ed., *The Decline of the Mughal Empire*, New Delhi: Oxford University Press, 2014.

Bingley, A.H., *History of Caste and Culture of Jats and Gujars*, 1899; repr., Delhi: Ess Ess, 1978.

Blok, Anton, 'The Peasant and the Brigand: Social Banditry Reconsidered', *Comparative Studies in Society and Economy*, vol. 14, no. 4, 1972, pp. 494–503.

Chandra, Satish, *Medieval India: Society, the Jagirdari Crisis and the Village*, New Delhi: Macmillan, 1982.

———, 'Mughal Relations with the Rajput States of Rajasthan', in *Essays on Medieval Indian History*, New Delhi: Oxford University Press, 2003, pp. 357–407.

———, 'Some Aspects of Indian Village Society in Northern India during the 18th Century: The Position and Role of *Khud-kasht* and *Pahi-kasht*', *Indian Historical Review*, vol. 1, 1974, pp. 51–64.

———, *Parties and Politics at the Mughal Court, 1707–40*, Aligarh: Aligarh Muslim University Press, 1959.

Chandra, Satish and Dilbagh Singh, 'Structure and Stratification in the Village Society in Eastern Rajasthan', *Proceedings of the Indian History Congress*, vol. 33, 1972, pp. 196–203.

Das Gupta, Ashin, 'Trade and Politics in 18th century India', in *Islam and the Trade of Asia: A Colloquium*, ed. D.S. Richards, Pennsylvania: University of Pennsylvania Press, 1970.

Dwivedi, G.C., *The Jats: Their Role in the Mughal Empire*, Delhi: Arnold, 1989.

Fukuzawa, H., *The Medieval Deccan: Peasants, Social Systems and States, Sixteenth to Eighteenth Centuries*, New Delhi: Oxford University Press, 1991.

Gopal, Lallanji and V.C. Srivastava, eds., *History of Agriculture in India (up to c.1200 AD)*, vol. V, pt. I, History of Science, Philosophy and Culture in Indian Civilization, ed. D.P. Chattopadhyaya, Delhi: Concept, 2008.

Grover, B.R., *Mughal Land Revenue Apparatus*, vol. 5 of *Collected Works of Professor B.R. Grover*, ed. Amrita Grover et al., Delhi: Low Price Publications, 2010.

———, *Land and Taxation System during the Mughal Age*, vol. 4 of *Collected Works of Professor B.R. Grover*, ed. Amrita Grover et al., Delhi: Low Price Publications, 2009.

————, *Landed Hierarchy and Village Community during the Mughal Age*, vol. 1 of *Collected Works of Professor B.R. Grover*, ed. Amrita Grover et al., Delhi: Low Price Publications, 2005.

————, 'Nature of Land Rights in Mughal Indian History', *Indian Economic and Social History Review*, vol. 1, no. 1, 1963, pp. 1–23.

Gulati, G.D., *Mewat: Folklore, Memory, History*, Delhi: Dev, 2013.

Gupta, S.P., *The Agrarian System of Eastern Rajasthan (c.1650–1750)*, Delhi: Manohar, 1986.

Gupta, S.P. and Shireen Moosvi, 'Bhomi in the Territories of Amber c.1650–1750', *Proceedings of the Indian History Congress*, vol. 32, part I, 1970, pp. 353–9.

————, 'Ijara System in Eastern Rajasthan', *Medieval India: A Miscellany*, vol. 2, Aligarh: Centre of Advanced Study, Department of History, Aligarh Muslim University, 1972, pp. 263–8.

Habib, Irfan, *The Agrarian System of Mughal India, 1556–1707*, 2nd revd edn, New Delhi: Oxford University Press, 1999.

————, 'Caste System in Indian History', in Irfan Habib, *Essays in Indian History: Towards a Marxist Perception*, London: Anthem Press, 2002, pp. 161–79.

————, 'The Eighteenth Century in Indian Economic History', in *The Eighteenth Century in India*, ed. Seema Alvi, New Delhi: Oxford University Press, 2002, pp. 55–82.

————, 'Postal Communications in Mughal India', *Proceedings of the Indian History Congress*, vol. 46, 1985, pp. 236–52.

————, *An Atlas of the Mughal Empire*, New Delhi: Oxford University Press, 1982.

————, 'Potentialities of Capitalist Development in the Economy of Mughal India', *Enquiry*, n.s., vol. 3, no. 3, Winter, 1971, pp. 1–56.

————, 'The Social Distribution of Landed Property in the Pre-British India: A Historical Survey', *Enquiry*, no. 12, 1965, pp. 21–75.

————, 'The Form of Class Struggles during the Mughal Period', in Irfan Habib, *Essays in Indian History: Towards a Marxist Perception*, London: Anthem Press, 2002, pp. 233–58.

Habib, M. and K.A. Nizami, *The Delhi Sultanat, AD 1206–1526*, vol. 5 of *A Comprehensive History of India*, Delhi: People's Publishing House, 1970.

Habibullah, A.B.M., *The Foundation of Muslim Rule in India*, Allahabad: Central Book Depot, 1961.

Hasan, S. Nurul, 'Further Light on Zamindars under the Mughals: A Case Study of (Mirza) Raja Jai Singh under Shah Jahan', *Proceedings Indian History Congress*, vol. 39, pt. I, 1978, pp. 497–502.

————, *Thoughts on Agrarian Relations in Mughal India*, New Delhi: People's Publishing House, 1973.

————, 'Zamindars under the Mughals', in *Land Control and Social Structure in Indian History*, ed. R.E. Frykenberg, Madison: University of Wisconsin Press, 1969, pp. 17–32.

Hasan, S. Nurul and S.P. Gupta, 'Prices of Foodgrains in the Territories of Amber (c.1650–1750)', *Proceedings of the Indian History Congress*, vol. 29, pt. I, 1967, pp. 345–68.

Hasan, S. Nurul, K.N. Hasan and S.P. Gupta, 'The Pattern of Agricultural Production in the Territories of Amber (c.1650–1750)', *Proceedings of the Indian History Congress*, vol. 28, 1966, pp. 244–64.

Hobsbawm, E.J., *Bandits*, London: Weidenfield & Nicolson, 1969.

————, *Primitive Rebels: Studies in Archaic Forms of Social Movement in the Nineteenth and Twentieth Centuries*, Manchester: Manchester University Press, 1959.

Husain, A.M., *Tughluq Dynasty*, Calcutta: Thacker Spink, 1963.

Kane, P.V., *History of Dharmaśāstra*, Poona: Bhandarkar Oriental Research Institute, 1973.

Khan, A.R., *Chieftains in the Mughal Empire during the Reign of Akbar*, Shimla: Indian Institute of Advanced Study, 1977.

Khan, Iqtidar Alam, 'The Nobility under Akbar and the Development of His Religious Policy, 1560–1580', *Journal of the Royal Asiatic Society of Great Britain and Ireland*, 1968, pp. 29–36.

————, 'Akbar's Personality and Traits and World Outlook: A Critical Appraisal', in *Akbar and His India*, ed. Irfan Habib, New Delhi: Oxford University Press, 1999, pp. 79–96.

Kulkarni, A.R., 'The Indian Village with Special Reference to Medieval Deccan (Maratha Country): General Presidential Address', *Proceedings of the Indian History Congress*, vol. 52, 1991, pp. 1–62.

Kumar, Dharma and Meghnad Desai, eds., *The Cambridge Economic History of India, vol. 2: c.1757–c.1970*, Cambridge: Cambridge University Press, 1982.

Lal, Kishori Saran, *History of the Khaljis, AD 1290–1320*, Delhi: Asia Publishing House, 1967.

Ludden, David, *An Agrarian History of South Asia*, Cambridge: Cambridge University Press, 1999.

Malcolm, Major-General Sir John, *The Political History of India from 1784 to 1823*, vol. 2, London: John Murray, 1826.

Mayaram, Shail, *Against History, Against State: Counterperspectives from the Margins*, Delhi: Permanent Black, 2004.

————, *Resisting Regimes: Myth, Memory and the Shaping of a Muslim Identity*, New Delhi: Oxford University Press, 1997.

Mishra, Pratibha, *Soil Productivity and Crop Potentials: A Case Study (District Alwar-Rajasthan)*, Delhi: Concept, 1984.

Moosvi, Shireen, *Economy of the Mughal Empire c.1595: A Statistical Study*, New Delhi: Oxford University Press, 1987.

Moreland, W.H., *Agrarian System of Moslem India*, Cambridge: W. Heffer & Sons, 1929.

Mukhia, Harbans, 'Presidential Address: Was There Feudalism in Indian History?', *Proceedings of the Indian History Congress*, vol. 40, 1979, pp. 229–80.

————, 'Illegal Extortions from Peasants, Artisans and Menials in Eastern Rajasthan during the Eighteenth Century', *Indian Economic and Social History Review*, vol. 14, no. 2, 1977, pp. 231–45.

————, 'Peasant Production and Medieval Indian Society', in *Exploring India's Medieval Centuries: Essays in History, Society, Culture and Technology*, Delhi: Aakar, 2010, pp. 188–223.

Naim, C.M., 'Popular Jokes and Popular History: The Case of Akbar, Birbal and Mulla Do-Piyaza', *Economic and Political Weekly*, vol. 30, no. 24, 1995, pp. 1456–64.

Pande, Ram, 'Raja Bishan Singh's Campaign against the Jats (1688–93)', *Proceedings of the Indian History Congress*, vol. 29, pt. I, 1967, pp. 173–6.

Rana, R.P., *From Rebels to Rulers: The Rise of Jat Power in Medieval India, c.1665–1735*, Delhi: Manohar, 2006.

————, 'Agrarian Revolts in Northern India during the late 17th and early 18th Century', *Indian Economic and Social History Review*, vol. 18, nos. 3–4, 1981, pp. 287–325.

Rao, M.S.A., 'Rewari Kingdom and the Mughal Empire', in *Realm and Region in Traditional India*, ed. Richard G. Fox, Delhi: Vikas, 1977, pp. 79–89.

Raychaudhuri, Tapan and Irfan Habib, eds., *The Cambridge Economic History of India, vol. 1: c.1200–c.1750*, Cambridge: Cambridge University Press, 1982.

Rizvi, S.A.A., *A History of Sufism in India*, vol. 2, Delhi: Munshiram Manoharlal, 1983.

Rizvi, S.H.M., *Mina: The Ruling Tribe of Rajasthan: Socio-Biological Appraisal*, Delhi: B.R. Publishing Corporation, 1987.

Rouse, W.H.D., *The Giant Crab and Other Tales of Old India*, London: David Nutt, 1897.

Sahai, Nandita Prasad, *Politics of Patronage and Protest: The State, Society and Artisans in Early Modern Rajasthan*, New Delhi: Oxford University Press, 2006.

Scott, James C., *Weapons of the Weak: Everyday Forms of Peasant Resistance*, New Delhi: Oxford University Press, 1990.

Sharma, G.D., 'Indigenous Banking and the State in the Eastern Rajasthan during the Seventeenth Century', *Proceedings of the Indian History Congress*, vol. 40, 1979, pp. 432–41.

Sharma, R.S., 'How Feudal was Indian Feudalism?', *The Journal of Peasant Studies*, vol. 12, nos. 2–3, 1985, pp. 19–43.

Siddiqi, N.A., 'Land Revenue Demand under the Mughals', *Indian Economic and Social History Review*, vol. 2, no. 4, 1964, pp. 373–80.

Singh, Chetan, *Region and Empire: Panjab in the Seventeenth Century*, New Delhi: Oxford University Press, 1991.

Singh, Dilbagh, *The State, Landlords and Peasants: Rajasthan in the 18th Century*, Delhi: Manohar, 1990.

———, 'Tenants, Sharecroppers and Agricultural Labourers during the Eighteenth Century Eastern Rajasthan', *Studies in History*, vol. 1, no. 1, 1977, pp 31–43.

———, 'Caste and Structure of Village Society in Eastern Rajasthan during the Eighteenth Century', *Indian History Review*, vol. 2, no. 2, 1976, pp. 299–311.

———, 'Local and Land Revenue Administration of the State of Jaipur (c.1750–1800)', unpublished PhD thesis, Centre for Historical Studies, Jawaharlal Nehru University, 1975.

———, 'Rural Indebtedness in Eastern Rajasthan during the 18th Century', *Proceedings of the Indian History Congress*, Pali, 1974, pp. 83–9.

———, 'The Role of the Mahajans in the Rural Economy in Eastern Rajasthan during the 18th century', *Social Scientist*, vol. 2, no. 10, 1974, pp. 20–31.

———, 'Position of the Patel in Eastern Rajasthan during the Eighteenth Century', *Proceedings of the Indian History Congress*, vol. 32, 1970, pp. 360–6.

Sinha, Nandini, 'Reconstructing Identity and Situating Themselves in History: A Preliminary Note on the Meenas of Jaipur Locality', *Indian Historical Review*, vol. 27, no. 1, 2000, pp. 29–43.

Sinha, Surjit, 'State Formation and Rajput Myth in Tribal Central India', *Man in India*, vol. 42, no. 1, April–June 1962, pp. 35–80.

Skaria, Ajay, *Hybrid Histories: Forests, Frontiers and Wilderness in Western India*, New Delhi: Oxford University Press, 1999.

Spate, O.H.K., *India and Pakistan: A General and Regional Geography*, London: Metheun, 1957.

Steel, Flora Annie, *Tales of the Punjab Told by the People*, London: Macmillan & Co., 1917.

Stokes, Maive, *Indian Fairy Tales*, Calcutta, 1879, repr., London: Ellis & White, 1880.

Swynnerton, Charles, *Romantic Tales from the Punjab with Indian Nights' Entertainment*, London: Archibald Constable, 1908.

Temple, R.C., *The Legends of Punjab*, 3 vols., Bombay: Bombay Education Society, 1884.

Thapar, Romila, *From Lineage to State: Social Formations of the Mid-first Millennium BC in the Ganga Valley*, New Delhi: Oxford University Press, 1990.

———, *Cultural Transaction and Early India: Tradition and Patronage*, New Delhi: Oxford University Press, 1987.

Tod, James, *Annals and Antiquities of Rajasthan*, vol. 2, London: G. Routledge & Sons, 1914.

Umar, Muhammad, *Muslim Society in Northern India during the Eighteenth Century*, Delhi: Munshiram Manoharlal, 1998.

Wink, André, 'Maratha Revenue Farming', *Modern Asian Studies*, vol. 17, no. 4, 1983, pp. 591–628.

Index

www.ingramcontent.com/pod-product-compliance
Lightning Source LLC
Chambersburg PA
CBHW030941150426
42812CB00064B/3090/J